BURNING ZEAL

BURNING ZEAL

The Rhetoric of Martyrdom
and the Protestant Community
in Reformation France,
1520–1570

Nikki Shepardson

Lehigh
University
Press

Bethlehem: Lehigh University Press

Associated University Presses
2010 Eastpark Boulevard
Cranbury, NJ 08512

The paper used in this publication meets the requirements of the American National Standard for Permanence of Paper for Printed Library Materials Z39.48–1984.

Library of Congress Cataloging-in-Publication Data

Shepardson, Nickki, 1969-
    Burning zeal : the rhetoric of martyrdom and the Protestant community in Reformation France, 1520/1570/Nicki Shepardson.
        p. cm.
    Includes bibliographical references and index.
    ISBN-13: 987-0-934223-87-4 (alk. paper)
    ISBN-10: 0-934223-87-4(alk. paper)
1. Reformation—France. 2. Martyrdom—Christianity. 3. France—Church history. I. Title.

BR370.S54 2007
273'.60944—dc22
                                            2006017304

For Bill

Contents

Acknowledgments

Iт is a pleasure to acknowledge those who aided and abetted my pursuit of these sixteenth-century martyrs. I would like to express first my deepest gratitude to Donald R. Kelley for his encouragement, counsel, and patient support on matters both scholarly and personal. Countless hours of conversation with him provided the foundation for this work and to him I owe my greatest intellectual debt.

During my research in Paris I relied on the kindness and support of many people. The librarians at the Bibliothèque de la Société de l'Histoire Protestantisme Française were exceedingly generous with their knowledge and enthusiastically assisted me in my research. Also I would like to acknowledge the help of the staff at the Bibliothèque Nationale. Philippe de Zwinglestein and John Iverson were amazing benefactors, graciously opening their homes and lives to me, providing me with a haven and the best introduction to Paris that one could ever hope for.

Over the years I have enjoyed an intellectual exchange with numerous scholars that helped shape this book. A year at the Rutgers Center for Historical Analysis introduced me to many new ideas and approaches to studying religious history. From my time at Rutgers, I would like to thank Mary Blanchard, Barbara Cutter, Amy Forbes, Robin Ladrach, Jennifer Milligan, Judith P. Zinsser, and the much-missed Becca Gershenson for their intellectual camaraderie. Phyllis Mack and the late J. H. M. Salmon carefully read and made suggestions on an earlier version of the manuscript. Additionally I owe debts of gratitude to Elizabeth Castelli, Tom Freeman, Brad Gregory, Jacob Meskin, Andrew Pettegree, Gordon Schochet, Bonnie Smith, the late Traian Stoianovich, Alfred Soman, Christie Sample Wilson, and D. R. Woolf for suggestions and guidance that came at various stages of this project. My colleagues in the History Department at

Rider provided an intellectually stimulating and supportive atmosphere which helped in the completion of this work.

At Lehigh University Press and the Associated University Presses, Judi Mayer was tremendously helpful with shepherding the project through the publication process. The reader for Lehigh University Press, Annette Finley-Croswhite, made many insightful suggestions that have certainly made this a much better book.

My family, both immediate and extended, has been a source of motivation and support. My siblings stimulated a longtime interest in martyrdom in ways that only youngest sisters and brothers understand. Nikos Pharasles has been a fountain of knowledge regarding the classical world, and his lifelong dedication to historical inquiry has been an inspiration. I would also like to thank Carol Gallo, Mary-Ann Shea, and Heather Mergentime for their cheerful encouragement and unstinting willingness to help out in a pinch. But I am most grateful to William Connell, my gentlest critic, three-thousand year man, and irreplaceable partner, without whom this project would never have come to fruition. And to my daughters Zoë and Livia, who consistently remind me that joy and excitement are essential components of learning.

One debt that I will never be able to repay is that which I owe to my parents, Robert and Lilyan Shepardson. Though he died long before this was written, my father's influence and inspiration may be found on every page. My mother, more than any martyrly examplar found in this work, has shown me the meaning of sacrifice, dedication, and faith.

While I consider this book to be a "communal" effort, any and all errors are my own.

BURNING ZEAL

1

The Rebirth of the
Rhetoric of Martyrdom

HISTORY WOULD KNOW LITTLE ABOUT THE FRENCH NOBLEMAN Anne Du Bourg had it not been for his stand in the spring of 1558 in the Parlement of Paris. There, during an official visit by King Henri II, Du Bourg made his Calvinist sympathies known, and in so doing began a journey that led to his execution on December 23, 1559. As a result of his sacrifice, accounts of Du Bourg's trial and death were included in contemporary martyrology, a literary genre that was reborn out of the conflicts of the Reformation in France and throughout Europe.

During the sixteenth century there were many other persons who, through their deaths, became weapons in the Reform movement's struggle for survival in the face of persecution by both state and church. The experiences of Du Bourg and others have survived in collections of narratives about people who "carried [their] afflictions with an indescribable joy."[1] It was their commitment to and confession of the Protestant faith that led them down the path to martyrdom. The accounts of those who gave "proper" witness for their faith with their lives became some of the most powerful tools of the French Reformation. As one Protestant propagandist put it, "the death of one was the renewal of life for a hundred others."[2]

From the 1530s until the Saint Bartholomew's Day Massacre in 1572, martyrdom and suffering shaped and in important respects defined the struggle of the French Reform movement. The persecution brought about a resurgence of the tradition of Christian martyrdom and a renaissance in the writing of polemical martyrology. A specific rhetoric concerning martyrdom, recovered from the early history of the church, was used to resist persecution and to legitimate the existence of the faith, to strengthen the movement from within, and to recruit new followers. The rhetoric of martyrdom harnessed the conviction, constancy, and sacrifice of the martyr, and applied these traits to the experiences and worldview of the entire Calvinist community. This rhetoric is found not only in works that specifically recount the stories of those who died for their faith, but also in the sermons, histories, religious treatises, and political pamphlets penned by sixteenth-century Protestants. This book studies the rhetoric of martyrdom that developed around exemplary individuals like Anne Du Bourg and colored the discussions of broader issues that confronted the Calvinist community in France and its leaders.

EVOLUTION OF A TRADITION

The title "martyr" is subjective. One movement's martyr is usually another's criminal, suicide, heretic, or infidel. Whereas the latter terms are pejorative, the former is deemed praiseworthy. Whether martyr or suicide, the individual who has been identified as such has chosen a "voluntary death." The interpretation of that individual's posthumous identity, however, is contested ground. Since September 11, 2001, and the horrific terrorist attacks on New York and Washington, D.C., there is a profound urgency to further our understanding of this process of creating martyrs. We are witnessing a new wave of violent martyrdom on a global scale. In response, we must learn to look beyond labeling individuals "fanatics" and continuing the modern Western dismissal of them as "irrational" to examine how martyrdom functions as a weapon in the larger context of community, identity building, and the struggle against persecution, whether real or perceived.

The Western concept of the "noble death" evolved from Hellenistic philosophy and Judaic tradition.[3] In the Greco-Roman world, Plato and the Stoics developed more or less positive views of voluntary death. To be sure, Plato's acceptance of voluntary death had specific limits. He identified four circumstances that would allow for such an act. In the *Phaedo,* Plato discussed the necessity of "divine compulsion" as an acceptable reason for suicide. In the *Laws,* however, he located the justifications in the realm of man and society: on the order of the polis, after unbearable misfortune, or following intolerable and extreme humiliation.[4] The early Stoics appear to have followed Plato's approach, but some later Stoics, especially Seneca, advocated an individual's ultimate right to choose death as a sign of his or her freedom.[5] In his "On Providence," Seneca unfavorably compared the suicide pact of Petreius and Juba, having decided to fight each other to the death rather than beg for Caesar's unlikely pardon, to the controlled and voluntary suicide of Cato.[6] For Seneca suicide was a matter of honor, dignity, and the proving one's ultimate mettle. It should be emphasized that these approaches dealt primarily with the right of an individual to choose death over life in circumstances that were deemed extraordinary. Voluntary death was not thought to take place within a larger eschatological context or to have a didactic and inspirational purpose.

A complete doctrine of martyrdom comprising many of the features we now associate with the phenomenon was first developed by the Jews of Palestine in the mid-second century BCE at the time of the Maccabee uprising.[7] In this revolt, Jews attempted to resist hellenization and cultural homogenization by the Seleucid king Antiochus. Out of this conflict arose the stories of Eleazar and of the sacrificing mother of seven pious sons found in 2 Maccabees. Eleazar, a devout Jewish scribe, refused to eat the flesh of a pig that had been ritually sacrificed in the honor of the king's birthday. His refusal, intended to uphold Judaic Law, led to his torture and death. The mother and her seven sons steadfastly and one by one met the same fate when they too refused to break God's Law.[8] Historians have held that 1 Maccabees is the most historically accurate of the four Maccabeean texts, and the veracity of the other books, including 2 Maccabees, has been questioned. Nevertheless, the incorporation of these stories, and the accompanying editorializing, established them as prototypical and paved the way for later martyrological narratives. In Maccabees we see the coming together of the major ingredients of Christian martyrdom. Within Judaism during this period, martyrdom functioned as a form of heroic resistance against idolatry imposed by gentiles, as a manifestation of nationalism (in the sense that Jews were united as a nation through their religious law) in a hostile environment, and as a symptom of a larger eschatological struggle that pitted God against the "evil one." God would avenge and reward those who embraced martyrdom, while those who disdained martyrdom would be shamed and punished for their faithlessness.[9] The purposes of relating the stories of those who were put to death in this struggle were to make an internal statement to the faithful, to provide a heroic model of faith, and to make an eschatological statement indicating that the suffering of the Jews would be rewarded.

The early Christians built upon the model of the Maccabees, though they refined martyrdom in a number of important ways. They removed the nationalistic character of Judaic martyrdom and replaced it with a universalizing interpretation. To the early Christians, a martyr did not die for the sake of a messiah attached strictly to one nation, but for the savior of all humankind. Thus early Christian martyrdom was not nationalistic, but missionary. The act of martyrdom (or its representation) was a statement intended not only to reinforce the faithful, but also to undermine persecutors and even to convert nonbelievers. In the early church, the Greek verb *marturein,* meaning to bear witness or to testify, defined the martyr's act and came into usage in its sacrificial sense sometime in the mid-second century.[10] A Christian martyr voluntarily "witnessed" or "testified" for Christ with the spilling of his or her blood.

The ante-Nicean Fathers wrote passionately on martyrdom, exhorting persecuted Christians to carry their crosses in the name of Christ. Persecution, according to Tertullian, who wrote in the late second century, was willed by God, a test for Christians to endure and succeed in.[11] For those who would take up the cross and become imitators of Christ, the reward was heaven.[12] But obtaining this reward had its price. The martyr was exhorted to voluntarily abandon the material world of the flesh, including children, spouses, and parents to follow Christ.[13] The flesh must endure the torments of prison and pain of torture, though the spirit could roam free. Tertullian and others separated the body from the spirit, and as one suffered the other rejoiced.[14] The rhetoric employed by these writers revolved around the importance of sacrifice, the centrality of suffering, and the rewards to be gained by remaining firm in their faith and rejecting idolatry regardless of persecution.

A key image in the writings of both Tertullian and Origen was that of the soldier or athlete. For Origen, writing in the early third century, martyrdom was a "contest" and even a battle. The martyr was a "noble athlete" or a "champion" in an eschatological struggle.[15] The martyr's experience in prison was equated with a type of boot camp in preparation for the final battle of actual martyrdom. Tertullian describes the martyr as a soldier in God's army, fortified by the Holy Spirit.[16] This martial imagery reinforced not only the struggle, but community as well. All who were baptized were Christian soldiers engaged in both the eschatological and worldly battles in Christ's name.

The first Christian texts that identified martyrs as such functioned as calendars commemorating the deaths of early Christian champions.[17] In their earliest forms these calendars were for the most part local collections. Not until Eusebius's *Ecclesiastical History* (early fourth century) was martyrdom treated from a broader geographical and historical perspective that combined the political and the religious contexts. This work identified the martyrs and their acts as the driving force behind the early Christian movement, and as the primary weapon against the persecution and idolatry. Eusebius helped to define the interpretation of martyrdom and persecution as part of God's larger plan for his chosen ones, or faithful, further expressing the earlier concept of persecution as sent by God. He also continued some of the specific themes and textual images expressed by Origen, Tertullian, and other ante-Nicean Fathers regarding martyrdom. For example, Eusebius consciously described the martyrs as imitators of Christ.[18] They were "athletes of God," "athletes of religion," and "champions." He retained the earlier martial imagery and language of struggle. Through the lens of Eusebius's history-cum-martyrology, the martyr embodied the faith and defended orthodoxy against dissension from within and persecution from without.

The martyrs in Eusebius's *History* invert authority through their mandate from God. The weak become the strong, and the persecutors falter in the face of the "righteous." It is here that the martyr's primary power is located. This type of inversion is particularly found in the accounts describing women and children. Eusebius's "weak" martyrs shame and humiliate their persecutors through their constancy. Female martyrs such as Mercuria (an old woman), Dionysia (a mother who chose martyrdom over her children), and Blandina (a frail, small servant) spectacularly inverted the might of their persecutors.[19]

Early Christians and those of late antiquity used the history and memory of persecution and suffering to create a framework from which to build their community and identity. Their rewriting of martyrological narratives was not solely for commemorative purposes, but served to shape their culture and even interpretations of power and legitimacy.[20] Christian writers of this period, due to the church's own successful martyrological campaign, were all too aware of the power of martyrdom and recognized that it could, in turn, be used against them. In the struggle against heresy, most notably against the Donatists, the creation of "heretical" martyrs became a great concern. For example, Augustine in 412 CE argued expressly for this reason against the death penalty for Donatist heretics.[21] Augustine's "just war" doctrine, however, was to become the basis for Christian-on-Christian persecution.[22] And later, in 421, he did advocate the execution of a Donatist bishop to prevent him from continuing to lead his congregants in their "errors."[23]

It is during late antiquity and the early Middle Ages that the genre of hagiography begins to take precedence over martyrology as the dominant form of sacred life-writing.[24] There are some crucial differences between the two genres that highlight a larger change in the religious context of medieval Europe. The subjects of martyrology are limited to those who witness Christ with their blood: it is their sacrifice that qualifies them as worthy of recognition. Hagiographical writing encompasses edifying texts pertaining to the lives of the saints regardless of the causes of their deaths.[25] Medieval Hagiography served new devotional purposes, as veneration of saints and miracles became widespread in Christendom from about the sixth century. Interest in religious biography extended beyond the sainted to include the lives of celebrated clergymen or particularly pious laypersons, a genre described today as "sacred biography."[26] Obviously there is some overlap between these genres since martyrology is a form of hagiography and sacred biography, but the latter two should not be confused or conflated with martyrology, which imposed a specific qualification on its subjects.

The shift from martyrology to hagiography was in part a result of the legal recognition of Christianity from the time of Constantine the Great in the fourth century. As the Church became institutionalized, it became apparent in the early Middle Ages that opportunities for martyrdom were few and far between, save for missionary work in hostile territories. For the devout Christian in this new context, the pious *lives* of the saints (including those of the martyrs) and the miracles they performed offered more useful models for behavior than the martyrs' *deaths*. Writers on the lives of martyrs such as Bede in the eighth century and Usard in the ninth had the luxury of writing when the Church was ascendant and consolidated. Hence, their representation of martyrdom and martyrs differed from that of Eusebius and the other early martyrologists. These later writers used martyrs not as polemical weapons, but as examples of piety. Whereas Euse-

bius's martyrs challenged authority and hierarchy, the later martyrologies and commentaries reframed and reinterpreted martyrdom
emphasizing correct doctrine and pious behavior while downplaying
the more troublesome aspects of righteousness. The sanctity of the
martyr and his miraculous attributes became the focal points of their
accounts, rather than the martyr's inversion of authority. Jacobus de
Voragine's influential *Legenda sanctorum* (thirteenth century) followed the same blueprint, which continued to prevail through the
later Middle Ages.

Canon Law at this time generated distinctions that more precisely
defined the term "martyr." This resulted in specific requirements
that had to be met to merit this title: the martyr had to face both the
threat and reality of death; the death must have been inflicted by a
third party; and the cause of death had to be attributed to the martyr's belief in Christianity.[27] At the heart of all three of these requirements was the martyr's voluntary acceptance of this death. Given the
choice between life and abjuration or death and fidelity, the martyr
knowingly chose the latter. Evidence of the martyr's verbal confession of the faith, supported by witness testimony, provided proof of
the martyr's constancy and the reasons for death.

While the immediacy of martyrdom as an issue and the frequency
of its occurrence continued to diminish throughout the later Middle
Ages, interest in the martyrological narratives did not. Some Renaissance writers even offered new models, constructing accounts that
were reminiscent of the pagan ideal of the noble death. According
to Alison Knowles Frazier, fifteenth-century authors cast martyrdom
as a form of *devotio*, a "ceremony of self-sacrifice" in which a military
man "atoned for civic failings and promised victory in times of crisis
by dying in some spectacular way." This indicates, she continues, an
interest in the "military aspect of martyrdom" rather than in a death
more passively endured.[28] But some humanists also dared to question the social utility of martyrdom. And although the church encouraged a revised style of martyrology along humanistic lines, this
proved problematic. Questions difficult to resolve arose as the eager
humanist pursuit of "authentic" texts clashed with medieval "legends" and with martyrological texts that could not be verified. Thus
the new martyrology of the Renaissance proved stillborn.[29]

Martyrdom and martyrology became more immediate for many
Europeans and certainly more frequent in the sixteenth century
when large-scale religious persecution was revived in response to the

Protestant Reformation. Reaction to Protestantism varied from state to state, and indeed at times it would prove difficult for many to determine who was a Protestant. While most European states had nascent humanist reform movements already afoot by the 1520s, the introduction of Lutheran criticisms of the Catholic Church posed a greater challenge due to their broader reach and less conciliatory approach. The works of Luther and other reformers spread quickly due to the advent of the printing press, and their ideas disseminated rapidly among the popular classes. Reverberations of the reformers' protests were felt most keenly in the Low Countries, the German states, England, Scotland, Scandinavia, and France.

Exactly what was the perceived threat posed by this new form of Christianity? Briefly, European monarchies were resolutely Catholic, though for many their relationship with Rome might not have been the friendliest. Coronations were decidedly Catholic events, replete with religious symbolism and evocations. Royal authority had its foundations within the realm of the divine as articulated by Catholicism. Additionally, life within the cities, towns, and countryside was defined by the rhythms of church feast days, holy holidays, baptisms, and funerals. Communities defined themselves by parish and displayed solidarity through church-related events such as processions. Protestantism, with its challenges to Catholic hierarchy, practices, and traditions, threatened to undercut the accepted understanding of authority and community. Many states reacted to this perceived menace as if it were a cancer in need of excision.

This resulted in a "renaissance" for both martyrs and martyrological narratives. No fewer than seven major Protestant martyrologies were produced throughout Europe, many in multiple editions and translations.[30] These works drew especially on premedieval models, and the martyrs once again became weapons in an eschatological struggle. These Protestant texts abandoned the medieval emphasis on miracles. Interestingly, however, the requirements laid down in Canon Law concerning the death of the martyr continued to provide the basis for the identification of Protestant martyrs. In light of the multiplicity of claims to the name "Christian," the Protestant martyrologists built upon these marks, and emphasized the need for the confession of "correct" doctrine. Nevertheless, the Protestant writers, in many cases, could not avoid incorporating aspects of the medieval models, especially when it came to reinterpreting the potentially disruptive actions of the martyrs.

The introduction of Protestantism in France in the 1520s laid the seeds of conflict that would trouble the emerging state until the later half of the seventeenth century. Protestantism's very existence in France threatened the foundation of the emerging nation state: "one faith, one law, one king." As religion and politics were so deeply interwoven and nearly inseparable during this period, a disturbance in one area would create a ripple effect in the other. The first references to martyrdom as such in France emerged during the late 1520s.[31] Polemicists of the Reform wasted little time considering that the French state had just begun the sporadic persecution of Protestants in the mid-1520s. But this early stage of the French Reformation was not defined by persecution. It would not be until midcentury that the most important applications of the rhetoric of martyrdom took shape. Prior to this, especially during the 1520s and 1530s, reform-minded humanists could be found and protected in the courts of the royal family. Jacques Lefèvre d'Étaples and Guillaume Briçonnet enjoyed the patronage of the king's sister, Marguerite d'Angoulême. King François I himself protected others such as Clement Marot and Louis de Berquin, humanists and early writers of the French reform.[32] However, this tolerance by the king was severely challenged in 1534 after the *affaire des placards*. In the aftermath of the plastering of Paris (among other places) with broadsheets decrying the Mass, François I then began a policy of repression, though with a period of relaxation under the Edict of Coucy (1535).

By 1540 Protestantism's roots had sunk deeper into French soil. In response, the crown and institutions of law (both canonical and secular) pushed the policy of repression and persecution into high gear. With the Edict of Fontainebleau (1540) François I declared the "Lutheran heresy," "high treason against God and mankind, popular sedition, and the disturbance of our state and public tranquility"—a crime punishable by torture, forfeiture of goods, public humiliation and restitution, and/or death.[33] This edict explicitly stated the crown's intention to "extirpate" the "heresy," greatly increasing the threat to the Huguenots, as the French Protestants came to be known. The second generation of Huguenots were bolder, more audacious and outspoken than the previous generation. The state responded with a full barrage of anti-heresy legislation and the creation of a special chamber in 1547 within the Parisian Parlement, ominously called the Chambre Ardente (the "Burning Room"), dedicated to the prosecution of heretics.[34]

In the next fifteen years, the rising persecution in France generated two large martyrologies, Jean Crespin's *Livre des Martyrs* (1554)
and Antoine de la Roche Chandieu's *Histoires des pérsecutions, et martyrs de l'Église de Paris, depuis l'An 1557, jusques au temps du Roy Charles
neufviesme* (1563). Of the two, only Crespin's martyrology underwent
extensive growth in multiple subsequent editions. Crespin's *Livre des
Martyrs*, or as it is called in the 1570 edition, *Histoire des vrays tesmoins*,
has much more depth, breadth, and significance, in terms of both its
content and popularity, than does Chandieu's. The *Histoire des vrays
tesmoins*, then, will be the primary text relied on below in discussing
many of the issues that deal directly with the compilations of martyrological accounts.

Just as the genre of martyrology was reborn in the sixteenth century, so too was the rhetoric of martyrdom. This rhetoric employed
many of the same textual images used by the ante-Nicean Fathers
Origen and Tertullian, such as the martyr as champion or warrior of
God, and the martyr as an imitator of Christ and inheritor of his suffering.[35] Their language of sacrifice and anti-materialism, resonated
with sixteenth-century Huguenots. Origen especially reminded his
readers that every earthly tie—including bonds of property and family—must be hated and rejected in favor of upholding God's truth.
This sacrifice, as described by both church fathers, would be rewarded a hundredfold in the kingdom of God. Once cited by Origen and Tertullian as a clarion call for martyrdom, Matthew 10:37–
39 (RSV), "He who loves father or mother more than me is not worthy of me; and he who loves son or daughter more than me is not
worthy of me; and he who does not take his cross and follow me is
not worthy of me. He who finds his life will lose it, and he who loses
his life for my sake will find it," found champions once again among
the Protestant reformers and martyrologists. The reformers redis-
covered and employed once again this rhetoric of sacrifice in the
Calvinist struggle against persecution.

The language and imagery of martyrdom, however, was not confined to the martyrologies. Along with the compilations of Chandieu and Crespin, numerous pamphlets were produced from both
theological and political perspectives utilizing the rhetoric of martyrdom. While many of these works do not directly refer to the martyrs themselves, the language and symbolism found in these pamphlets nevertheless celebrated the same values embodied by the
martyrs: sacrifice, suffering, constancy, responsibility to both God

and the community of the faithful, and the primacy of the soul over the body. The rhetoric served to console and unite the faithful, while as the same time defining their world view vis-à-vis persecution. We see it in the attempt to create a new community, bound by faith and common suffering. We see it expressed in a gendered perspective regarding a prescribed role of women in the larger struggle of the Reform movement. We see that it lay at the heart of the Reformed reconceptualization of the history of the Church, just as the martyrology functioned to organize and shape communal memory. And we see it in the resistance theories forwarded by the Reform that favored a more passive approach, allowing the movement to subvert terrestrial law while still claiming loyalty to the state. Most importantly, the language of sacrifice and responsibility to uphold the Gospel over all earthly concerns, both of which were embodied in the examples of the martyrs, were at the crux of the message disseminated to the faithful in France by reformers such as Calvin and Viret.

THE STUDY

In light of the significant role of the imagery and rhetoric of martyrdom in the ideology of the Reform, it becomes clear that much of the historiography of the French Reformation has overlooked or underestimated the function of the rhetoric of martyrdom.[36] Historians for the most part have focused on such questions as who were the individual martyrs and what were the exact circumstances of their deaths. Others have looked at broader issues such as the intellectual traditions from which they emerged, the social and political context that shaped their experiences, or even the popular belief systems to which they belonged. And many valuable studies continue to examine these issues and produce significant contributions to our knowledge of the martyrs' experiences and the history of the production of the martyrological texts.

One of the most significant recent works on martyrdom, Brad Gregory's *Salvation at Stake*, rectifies a major gap in the field. Gregory's exhaustive study compares Catholic, Protestant, and Anabaptist martyrs and martyrologies, identifying the links or breakages between the different denominational approaches.[37] Gregory's argument emphasizes how the willingness of martyrs to die was in large part an affair of individual conscience, a religious choice reflecting the martyr's desire to do God's will and ensure his or her salvation. This conclusion then provides some coherence to the phenomenon during the period. Essentially Gregory is reinfusing martyrdom with belief, contrary to the approaches taken by postmodern literary scholars. Indeed, his goal is to contextualize martyrdom within the broader religiosity of early modern Europe. At the core of his argument is the centrality of the absolute belief and spirituality of the martyrs and their fellow believers regardless of their religious confession. While I agree that many recent studies have neglected this fundamental aspect, this argument underestimates the pivotal community-building and -defining aspects of martyrdom and martyrology. In other words, the rhetoric employed by the reformers, martyrologists, and indeed the martyrs themselves in their own letters, reveal just how central community was to all involved.

Additionally, Gregory's attack on postmodernist interpretations of martyrdom and martyrology is too dismissive and strident. Postmodernist literary criticism sheds new light on how the genre of martyrology functioned and indeed poses new questions about the creation and construction of the martyr. Arguably a martyr is created and identified through a textual reconstruction. But this type of narrative is laden with more than just a recounting of the individual. Postmodernist close readings of the narratives explore issues of representation and symbolism that transform the individual into a venerated ideal. Gregory is correct, however, to identify the limiting nature of this methodology as it typically does not acknowledge or examine the belief that fueled persecution and martyrdom nor does it look beyond the text to tradition or historical context. Thus, this study attempts to reconcile the two perspectives.

Gregory is writing in direct response to approaches taken by postmodernists such as Catherine Randall Coats and Frank Lestrignant. Randall and Lestrignant examine the French martyrologies from a literary perspective, and they succeed in providing provocative interpretations.[38] Yet, their studies do have profound limitations, most visible in the separation of texts and rhetoric from their historical context.[39] For example, Coats's thought-provoking study, "Reconstituting the Textual Body in Jean Crespin's *Histoire des martyrs* (1564)," argues that Crespin's martyrology attempts to resuscitate the martyrs through their own words. She correctly reveals as a conceit Crespin's claim that he is solely an editor. Crespin, she argues, was consciously constructing his own conception of Christian martyrdom, rather than simply relying on medieval models of hagiography, through his particular assemblage of material and presentation of the accounts. While I agree thus far with Coats, I would argue that Crespin was purposely following the Eusebian model of polemical martyrology. In other words, he was not creating something unique or different; rather, he was establishing a new layer on the continuum he established by linking his martyrs with the early Christian "champions."[40] Additionally, by focusing on the "textual body" this approach misses the central tenet of martyrdom and thus Crespin's message: the martyr's act as witness, with the sacrifice his body and blood. I would argue that the act, not the body, is at the heart of the accounts and the soul of the martyrology. For instance, we find a plethora of martyrological accounts in Crespin that contain only an acknowledgment of the martyr's name, death, and locale. The absence of more information is probably due to Crespin's lack of sources, but their inclusion notwithstanding highlights the act of martyrdom, not the individuals themselves who suffered it or their "textual reconstitution."

David El Kenz's invaluable work, *Les bûchers du roi*, successfully combines close textual readings and historical context. And while his work and this study share a common approach, differences exist in terms of the roles and breadth of the rhetoric of martyrdom studied, especially with regard to the case Anne Du Bourg. El Kenz argues that martyrdom ceases to function effectively as a weapon after the death of Du Bourg in 1559. A question must be raised, then: If martyrdom "ceases to be effective," why, after Du Bourg's death, were at least three more editions of Crespin's *Livre des Martyrs* (the most comprehensive produced in 1570) and the martyrology of Antoine de la Roche Chandieu published after Du Bourg's death in the 1560s? Additionally, why did polemical pamphlets continue to advocate this more passive form of resistance even as the Wars of Religion began in France? Many religious pamphlets produced from the late 1550s through the 1560s utilized a strong rhetoric of martyrdom to console and exhort, as well as encourage, the faithful. While El Kenz argues that the acts of the martyrs would be superseded (though not completely replaced) by active warfare on the part of the Reform movement, the argument put forth in this work is that in light of the open conflict, the rhetoric of martyrdom, rather than abating, shifted from a more passive approach to an active form.[41] For the most part, the Reform movement still represented itself, up until the St. Bartholomew's Day Massacre in 1572, as comprised of loyal subjects of the king who were wrongly persecuted due to the influence of the ultramontane house of Guise. The acts of the martyrs, in many ways, counterbalanced and complemented the overt resistance of the warring Huguenots, providing even further legitimacy to civil insurrection.

This study then fully examines the rhetoric developed by French Protestants, and more specifically, how it functioned to shape and define their identity in light of the chaos that swirled around them as France was torn apart by persecution and open warfare. The book focuses specifically on the fifty-year span from 1520 and 1570 when the rhetoric of martyrdom flourished in the Reform movement's struggle against persecution. The beginning of this period is defined by the first recorded execution in France in 1523 of an identified "Protestant." From this point onward until the St. Bartholomew's Day Massacre in 1572, the rhetoric of martyrdom played a central role in how the Reformed faithful understood the world around them and their place within it. It gave meaning to their suffering as well as legitimacy to their struggle against their persecutors. Within the rhetoric of martyrdom, the faithful could be both victims and victors, loyal subjects to the misled king and rebels against tyranny. In the larger political context, this period encompasses the decades in which the Reform movement advocated a moderate approach to resistance, an approach embodied by the at times contradictory nature of martyrdom. The end point of the study is the St. Bartholomew's Day Massacre of 1572. After this event, the rhetoric changed dramatically. No longer would a moderate approach be effective against a crown that massacred its subjects. The enormity of the event could no longer be balanced by the sacrificial language of martyrdom and interpretation of the persecution. From that point on, survival trumped sacrifice.

Each of the following chapters of this book focuses on an aspect of the functioning of the rhetoric of martyrdom in the context of the French Reformation. The chapters treat martyrdom's rhetoric on a scale that increases progressively, beginning with a two-part examination of the transformation of an individual into a martyr, proceeding to a specific segment of the Reformed community (women), then analyzing the role of the rhetoric of martyrdom in the Reformed community as a whole first through the Nicodemite controversy and finally by examining the creation of a new identity and communal memory. This multi-leveled approach illustrates the pervasiveness of the rhetoric of martyrdom, and how it functioned in a myriad of ways to support and defend the Reform movement.

Chapters 2 and 3 address the case of Anne Du Bourg, a *conseiller-clerc* in the Parlement of Paris. The aim is to show how an individual was transformed into a symbol in sixteenth-century France. Du Bourg's case necessarily involves negotiating a path among the multiple stories that were told concerning his case. There were stories told by the state, by the martyrologists, by contemporary historians (both Protestant and Catholic), and by various anonymous Protestant polemicists. Additionally, there are the accounts given by modern historians who use Du Bourg to understand other issues, such as the beginning of the Wars of Religion, the religious and intellectual leanings of the legal professionals of the period, or various shifts in the French legal system in the repression of heresy. As is argued below, most of these modern accounts have accepted and furthered a rather sanitized version of Du Bourg's martyrdom. Chapter 2 is thus an attempt to sort through these narratives, and it both complicates and revises our understanding of Du Bourg and his experience. While the absolute bottom line (the "real Du Bourg") will always remain elusive, I have reconstructed the account through a comparison and analysis of all the available sources, sources that need to be read with an understanding of the context in which Du Bourg's case developed. This, therefore, is something of a control study as it shows the complexities that precede the labeling of a "martyr."

Chapter 3 shows what happened to Du Bourg's reputation after his death—how he became a martyr. This is an important part of Du Bourg's story as he only became significant to the Reform movement through his role as a martyr. By analyzing the rhetoric of the authors who told his story, we see how these writers shaped the representation of Du Bourg's experience according to the changing needs of the Reform movement. The martyr was not just an individual: he represented and embodied the ideology of the Reform. The retelling of the martyr's act was a process in which the individual was transformed into something greater than himself. The martyr became an archetype defined and shaped both by the traditions of the church and by the particular needs of the movement that claimed the martyr. The transformation was brought about by manipulating the language and textual images that were used to construct the martyr's story. Chapter 3 thus examines how martyrological tradition and editorial manipulation produced multiple versions of the story of Anne Du Bourg that could be used as propaganda as circumstances varied.

A principal question for the Reformed martyrologists was the relation of the martyr to established authority. When a martyr, or the posthumous representation of a martyr, appeared to challenge authority and hierarchy, this presented no real problem for the Reform movement so long as the movement's chief concern remained the struggle against persecution. But the movement needed to maintain social order. One area in which this was especially evident was in the role of the sexes, as discussed in chapter 4. The martyr's perceived mandate from God allowed him or her to defy the authority of the persecutor, essentially obliterating social deference and the traditional limitations imposed by assigned social or gender roles. Thus the martyr was celebrated as someone who inverted the traditional categories of victor and vanquished, power and weakness, and legitimate authority and obedience. But the martyr proved problematic when there was a concern to maintain the gendered social order. Chapter 4 examines, then, how the rhetoric of martyrdom upheld the gender roles prescribed within the ideology of the Reform, while still celebrating the individual female martyr's ability to challenge authority.

An inherent tension existed between Calvin's thought regarding the role of the "godly" woman, and his need for women's (especially noblewomen's) active participation within the Reform's struggle in France. According to Calvin, a woman's sphere of activity was limited to the household. Since God created woman as inherently weak and inferior to man, she should be obedient, subservient, and passive. The female martyrs, however, especially through their activities outside of the household, challenged the gendered social order. Since these martyrs were presented as examples for common women to follow, the question needs to be asked: How were these martyrs reconciled with the gendered ideology of the Reform? The first section of the chapter addresses the difference between martyrdom and martyrology, showing how the two functioned in separate, and indeed almost mutually exclusive rhetorical spheres. This provides a methodological framework from which the problem can be further examined. The second section looks to the rhetoric of martyrdom as it was applied to women, and here we find the answer to the question: through language, imagery, and changes in emphasis, the independent female martyr was reconciled with her "godly" counterpart in the martyrological narrative.

Chapter 5 broadens the analysis of the rhetoric of martyrdom as it looks at the definition and defense of a "new" community based on the language and imagery of sacrifice and suffering. At the heart of this community were the martyrs. Although absent because now dead, they were its rallying call, its heroes, and the embodiment of its faith. Through the rhetoric of martyrdom, they were used to bind the community together, to rewrite and reinterpret its history, and to construct a type of communal memory. This community, however, needed to be defended from within and without. The anti-Nicodemite discourses, as manifestation of the rhetoric of martyrdom, provided such a defense. Calvin and Viret, two of the most prolific writers on the subject, attempted to infuse a type of social consciousness into the decisions facing those who were suffering persecution. They defined the individual's responsibility to avoid idolatry not only through his or her duty to God, but also to the community.

This book aims to enrich and complicate our understanding of the sixteenth-century martyr and his or her context. While martyrdom was a matter of an individual's choice at a particular moment in time, the representation of this choice, and its repercussions on the community of the faithful, involved many more issues than those that surrounded the individual during a final moment of crisis, commitment, and death. Through its study of the rhetoric of martyrdom, this book explores a profound gulf that exists between the highly personal choice to relinquish one's life in the service of one's God and faith, and the uses that others, claiming to serve the same God and faith, may make of that choice.

2

The Trial and Death
of Anne Du Bourg

WRITING FOUR DECADES AFTER AN ESPECIALLY MEMORABLE EXECUTION
of an important French Protestant, Florimond de Raemond reminisced:

> I remember how, when Anne Du Bourg, councillor in the Parlement
> of Paris, was burned, all Paris was astonished by the constancy of that
> man. We melted in tears in our colleges when we returned from the
> execution, and we pled his case after his death, blaming those unjust
> judges who had justly condemned him. His preaching on the gallows
> and on the bonfire did more harm than one hundred ministers
> would have known how to do.[1]

Raemond wrote this passage as a staunch defender of the Catholic
faith after having spent a period in his youth as a Calvinist. This passage is taken from his polemical *History of the Birth, Progress, and Decline of Heresy in This Century*. Raemond's words, especially the phrase
"unjust judges who . . . justly condemned him," reveal a deep affection and admiration for Du Bourg that persisted years after Raemond's reconversion to Catholicism. What made Du Bourg such an
important figure for the Calvinist Raemond and his fellow students
at the time? And why did he continue to hold the Catholic Raemond's attention decades later?

Anne Du Bourg was one of the most celebrated martyrs of the
French Reformation. At least six contemporary pamphlets told his
story, the two major French martyrologies celebrated his "sacrifice,"
and many other treatises and histories written by both Catholics and
Protestants at the time referred to his case as a major event and de-

scribed the profound impact of his execution on the collective psyche of Paris. However, unlike the Englishman Thomas More, who shared a background and fate similar to that of our French martyr, Du Bourg's legend has faded and remains familiar for the most part only to historians. Even among historians of the French Reformation, in many of the recent studies dealing with the prosecution and persecution of French Protestants, Du Bourg merits only a few pages of superficial treatment. The last truly comprehensive study of Du Bourg was written by Matthieu Lelièvre in the latter part of the nineteenth century.

So why not continue to consign Du Bourg to a minor role in the history of the French Reformation? The story of Anne Du Bourg is important for a myriad of reasons, not the least of which is the insight his case provides into the complexities of martyrdom, its rhetoric, and its transformative power. This chapter, then, reconstructs Du Bourg's story taking into account his faith, his various missteps, and his identities as a magistrate, man, and martyr.

Why Du Bourg—aside from the status and notoriety given to him by his contemporaries? The trial and execution of Du Bourg is intense and complicated material. Both state (Catholic) and Protestant narratives are dramatic, full of passion, contradiction, fear, exaltation, betrayal, loyalty, and debate. Du Bourg's multiple appeals before his execution; his "ambiguous" confession preceding his final, unequivocal one; two escape attempts; and his need for a "mere" woman to demonstrate to him the resolve of a true martyr; all suggest doubt as to whether he was truly a willing martyr. The hagiographic works produced after his death would have us believe that he embraced martyrdom enthusiastically, even as he was exhausting all avenues of appeal and assisting in plots for his escape. Yet, his final confession and address to the Parlement, the last statements he made, and his refusal at the gibbet to recant or compromise justify the image of the steadfast martyr. In other words, his case exposes the complexities of martyrdom. The most uncompromising aspect of his martyrdom—the conscious and willing embrace of death over recantation—is not as clear-cut as it seems. The most difficult, indeed impossible, factor to ascertain is whether the individual unequivocally embraced his fate. A historian never can know what was truly in the heart of the subject after pen and paper are taken away.

Approaches to Du Bourg

Many historians have addressed different aspects of Du Bourg's life, but they used parts of his story to prove a particular point or explore a particular issue that his case illustrates. The only comprehensive study of Anne Du Bourg is a series of three articles by Matthieu Lelièvre that approach Du Bourg from a decidedly confessional perspective.[2] In these essays, we find a Du Bourg who was, for the most part, a willing martyr and a dignified man of the law who, before his death, justifiably chastised his fellow judges for debasing their magistracies. Lelièvre's Du Bourg was not a rebel, but a man of faith who attempted to work within the system to enlighten his colleagues and king. When this approach failed, Du Bourg embraced his fate unquestioningly. In Lelièvre's confessional treatment we never forget that Du Bourg was a martyr for his cause. Du Bourg, then, appears less problematic and rather two-dimensional. Yet although some recent scholars shun or ignore Lelièvre's work—possibly owing to suspicion of this overtly confessional approach—his essays cover a wide range of sources and provide useful insights into both the relevant documents and Du Bourg's own experience.[3] Ironically, both Lelièvre essays and the ways in which some historians have used (or ignored) them remind us that the identity of a martyr is always in question, that the sincerity of the martyr's faith remains contested ground long after his or her death.

More recent studies that examine Du Bourg's case in some detail, such as those of William Monter, Nancy Roelker, and Donald Kelley, discuss Du Bourg in light of his legal experience and institutional role as a judge, rather than treat him in the way in which he proved most useful to the Reform—as a symbol and a martyr.[4] Only David El Kenz extensively discusses Du Bourg within the framework of martyrdom and martyrology. In his study of the culture of French Calvinist martyrdom, David El Kenz turns Lelièvre's relatively hagiographical Du Bourg on his head, describing a seditious rebel who advocated regicide. El Kenz justifies Du Bourg's execution and proves that in the end he really was guilty of lèse-majesté. In placing this execution in the larger context of martyrdom as a weapon, El Kenz concludes that Du Bourg's death marks a crucial stage in the Reform movement when "the martyr no longer seems effective enough to offset the desire for the death of the sovereign."[5] This conclusion, however, overlooks the ways in which martyrdom and the rhetoric of martyrdom continued to portray Huguenot loyalty to the king even as they took up arms against him. Except for Du Bourg's *Oraison,* talk of regicide or explicit discussion of divided sovereignty was anathema in the Huguenot movement until 1572.[6]

The chapter that follows constructs a narrative that recounts Du Bourg's confrontation in the Parlement, trial, and execution, and explains his possible motivations. To do so, the study relies on Protestant pamphlets, state documents, and Catholic histories. The narrative reconstructed below provides a comparative model for the "martyrological" Du Bourg discussed in the following chapter. This latter chapter then examines how the complex individual Du Bourg was transformed posthumously into a venerated stereotype and weapon for the Reform movement. In other words, chapter 2 tells the story of a man, while chapter 3 analyzes rhetoric used in the creation of a martyr.

Prologue: Paris
in the 1550s

Persecution of Protestants in France was relatively light until the 1540s. In this earlier period, especially during the 1520s, King François I had worked to create a glittering court populated by intellectuals, and indeed to do so meant tolerating some less than orthodox views from reform-minded humanists. But François I took this a step further, even defending and sheltering crypto-Protestants. For example, in 1523 humanist Louis Berquin had been found to possess Lutheran writings and defenses of Luther written in his own hand. The books were condemned and ordered to be burned; however, the king asked that the judgment be nullified. The Parlement of Paris, the highest and most prestigious of the sovereign courts of France, ignored the king and summoned Berquin to appear before the judges to defend his views. Once again, the king interceded on his behalf. The Parlement again called for his arrest and trial, but for a third time, the king rescued him by sending "royal officers" to liberate him.[7] Unfortunately for Berquin, the king was taken hostage in 1525 during the Italian Wars and sent to Madrid. It was during this time that Parlement took advantage of his absence and had Berquin arrested again. With the king's return, the humanist was released in 1526. Berquin could not leave well enough alone and attempted to clear his name in 1529. This resulted in his final arrest and execution, without intercession by the king, that same year.[8]

Berquin's case highlights the lack of a unified, coherent policy toward the treatment of Protestants during the 1520s. However, with the *affaire des placards* of 1534, any patience the king may have had was temporarily exhausted. On the night of October 4, 1534, posters were plastered all over Paris, even on the king's bedchamber door, proclaiming "The true articles against the horrible, gross, and insupportable abuse of the popish mass."[9] The immediate result was the burning at the stake of nine men, although hundreds had originally been rounded up. Interestingly, a period of leniency followed the immediate aftermath of the *affaire*. This has been attributed to the urging of the new pope, Paul III, and it is recognizable in the more moderate tone of the Edict of Coucy of 1535.[10]

In 1540, however, after the "previously ineffective" efforts (i.e., the Edict of Coucy) to eradicate the heresy and to stem the growing numbers of Protestants, François I promulgated the Edict of Fontainebleau, which took a hard line against the Protestants, outlining the procedures to be taken in their prosecution, naming the courts in which their cases would be tried, and most significantly identifying heresy as a crime both secular and religious.[11] While this edict is important, the decade of the 1540s is defined even more significantly by the death of François I and the assumption of the throne by Henri II. Henri shared very little of his father's interest in the arts or culture, and his reign, starting in 1547 marks the beginning of the high point in the persecution of French Calvinists.

In the 1550s France was at a turning point. It was a period of intensified religious hatreds and the emboldening of the Reform movement, especially in Paris. This decade witnessed an increased toleration by, and even the conversion of, a good number of prominent Parisian notables to Protestantism. They came from key families in the economic, governmental, and legal arenas within the city. The Reformed Church of Paris had just been formed in 1555, establishing a following and assembling mostly in secret, but nevertheless with an increasing boldness.[12] By 1560, the new church's activities had ceased "to be clandestine and nocturnal, becoming public, in plain day. It was manifestly a provocation in the eyes of the authorities."[13] Most notably, in the spring of 1558, a number of Protestants began gathering in the public space of Pré aux Clercs to sing psalms, though such assemblies were illegal.[14] It began as a few students who had gathered, "not thinking at all to incite the others to do the same."[15] Over the course of the next few days, the numbers grew dramatically, over six thousand according to one historian and four thousand to another, and included such high born persons as François d'Andelot and Antoine de Bourbon.[16] The illegality of the assembly was compounded by the fact that the gentlemen at the assembly were carrying arms, openly flouting the interdiction of the edict of Compiègne.[17] The impunity with which they were publicly worshipping à la mode de Genève, without any intervention by the authorities, infuriated the surrounding Catholic population, local priests, the bishop of Paris and the "Sorbonnistes," and eventually the king himself, although the Parlement resisted carrying out the punishment for sedition.[18] This resulted in numerous confrontations in the quarter, and increased tensions between the king and the Parlement.

This new generation of Huguenots was certainly more aggressive and audacious than their predecessors. One observer, Claude Haton, writing of the year 1557, described the belligerence of this generation: "The heretics of France, who are called Lutherans, make great work to increase their number and win some princes or great lords, to sustain and defend them in everything and everywhere before all men and against all men."[19] Jean Crespin, in 1554, had just published the first edition of his Livre des Martyrs, cataloging not only the general persecution of Protestants in Europe but also individual accounts of those who had been put to death for their faith. Crespin's martyrology was augmented and reissued twice more in this decade (1555 and 1556), testifying to the importance of martyrdom during this period. The rebirth of the martyr as a role model for the community and as a propagandist weapon against persecution was underway.

On the Catholic side, popular hostility and opposition increased proportionately with these shifts in the Reform movement. After the establishment of the Reformed Church of Paris, active persecution of Protestants resumed after a lull in the 1540s. One vivid example of this hostility is the *affaire de la Rue Saint-Jacques* in 1557. On September 4 of that year three or four hundred Protestants had secretly gathered at a private house on Rue Saint-Jacques, behind the Sorbonne, near the Collège du Pléssis, to worship together. They were discovered by some student priests who noticed the arrival of an unusual number of people. The students notified the local watch and soon the house was surrounded by a Catholic crowd, barring escape. The crowd lit fires along the street near the house so that none of its occupants could escape unnoticed. Some of the gentlemen in attendance at the house managed to fight their way out, leaving a group of about one hundred and thirty people inside, mostly women. By the time the watch had arrived, the crowd had gotten bigger and the scene more explosive. As the newly taken prisoners were led to jail, the mob had lined the streets, hurling both insults and excrement at the captives, and tearing their clothes and beating them with no regard for their sex, status, or age.[20] This confrontation between Protestants and local Catholics resulted not only in popular violence, but also in the state executing seven Protestants for heresy, six men and one noblewoman. The *affaire* was not an isolated incident, though the magnitude of the event captured the attention of both Catholic and Protestant writers. The initiative taken by the crowd before the watch arrived, and their extreme hostility even after the captives were taken into custody, illustrates the depth of the perceived offense of the Protestants.

Within the legal and judicial realms, the tension between the increased toleration and presence of Protestantism, and the hostility of the more ultramontane (or pro-papal and what would later be called Tridentine Catholic) faction at both court and in the Parlement of Paris rose during this decade. These tensions were compounded by "turf wars" over issues of jurisdiction between the Parlement, the Church, and ecclesiastical judges over heresy proceedings. Jurisdiction, up until the Edict of Chateaubriand in 1551, was fluid and often changed.[21] This edict established the absolute sovereignty of the parlements in genernal in trials concerning *cas privilegié* (cases involving public unrest) without appeal.[22] The ecclesiastical courts then held jurisdiction over cases of *délit commun* (misdemeanors) and the trials of clergy accused of heresy.[23] With the Edict of Compiègne in July of 1557, Henri II, dissatisfied with the failure of secular and ecclesiastical judges to implement his edicts, assigned prosecution of heresy to the Inquisition, led by the Cardinal de Guise.[24] The edict also mandated the death penalty for those who adhered to or advanced Protestant beliefs in just about any way. One historian describes this act as "a declaration of war by the king against his Protestant subjects. It is therefore not surprising that they prepared to defend themselves."[25] The edict was met with resistance in the Parlement, which viewed this act as an infringement upon their rights and upon Gallican liberties. The Parlement of this period was in turmoil as it was ideologically divided into three factions, struggling over the issue of heresy and its prosecution: the constitutionalists, who favored a form of Gallican (or uniquely French) Catholicism and resisted the imposition of the Inquisition; the ultramontanes; and a third faction with Protestant sympathies.[26] This conflicted atmosphere of court and city would become the crucible in which Du Bourg's fate took shape.

Anne Du Bourg
and the Mercuriale

By the spring of 1558 divisions within the Parlement of Paris over the matter of the prosecution of Protestants had become painfully apparent. In the aftermath of the assemblies of Pré aux Clercs, dissension within the court had surfaced as the Tournelle, the criminal chamber of the court, continued to impose lenient punishments on the Protestants convicted of heresy. Traditionally, unrepentant heretics would receive a death sentence, but the Tournelle had instead chosen banishment in the case of four men accused of being "Lutherans and contrary to the Roman Church: that this was a scandal to the people and to the subjects of the King."[27] On the other side of the divide, the Grand'Chambre, the older of the two chambers, had no difficulty implementing the king's Edict of Compiègne (1557) demanding capital punishment for heresy. The Mercuriale, or meeting of all the chambers of the Parlement, demanded by the royal prosecutors in light of this exceptional sentence revealed the differences of opinion in vivid form.

During the first session of the Mercuriale, the most senior judges were asked their opinion first on the matter. Four or five agreed with the Edict of Compiègne and confirmed the death sentence for the "Lutherans persevering in this, and who must as such be judged."[28] At the following session, President Du Ferrier advocated assembling a council that would rid the church of "the errors and heresies that multiply."[29] It was at the third session, however, that blatant Protestant sympathies were made known. Antoine Fumée, speaking freely and supposedly protected by the tradition of secrecy within the gathering of the Parlement, produced a laundry list of all the abuses and errors of the Catholic Church. He advised calling a general council that would determine what should be considered heresy. In the meantime, he recommended the suspension of the persecution and capital punishment of those accused of holding Protestant beliefs— a view shared by others at the Mercuriale.[30]

Rumors that his sovereign court was infected with the Protestant heresy quickly reached the ears of King Henri II.[31] The king, now aware of and frustrated by Protestant sympathies in the court, attended the last session of the extended Mercuriale on June 10, essentially holding a *lit de justice,* a formal royal assemby with the king enthroned in the parlement and reserved for "highest matters of state."[32] At this assembly, all the members were to speak their opinions in the royal presence, and were recorded by the greffier. The two most outspoken, Anne Du Bourg and Louis Du Faur, speaking freely and without fear, not only advocated calling a council and suspending prosecution of those espousing Protestantism, but also openly defended these beliefs.[33] Du Bourg stated, "Is it not the case that what makes them look like seditious men, is that they have discovered the favor of the light of Scripture, and that they have discovered and revealed the turpitude of Roman power, which slopes toward its ruin, and demand a salutary reformation?[34] The king, probably as much in shock as in fury, quickly withdrew from the court and after consultation with the cardinal of Lorraine, the princes of Montpensier and La Roche-sur-Yon, and the Connétable, ordered the arrest of Du Bourg (toward whom he had a special enmity) and Du Four in an attempt to make an example of them. According to one source, the king was so enraged that he declared that he would see Du Bourg burn before his own two eyes.[35] Du Bourg's crime vis-à-vis the king was a double insult. Not only was he a member of the king's sovereign court speaking completely contrarily to what the king saw as his sacred duty—upholding the sanctity of the Catholic faith—but he was also a *conseiller-clerc,* a magistrate who had taken religious orders, who was espousing heretical views in the king's presence. In doing so, Du Bourg was not attacking Rome and papal authority in order to defend or benefit the state (i.e., defending Gallican liberties in the face of encroaching papal political interference); instead, he was indirectly (though unmistakably) challenging the king's own policies and royal edicts as registered in the Parisian Parlement.

Not satisfied with imprisoning two of the most overtly sympathetic if not completely Protestant judges, the king demanded that Antoine Fumée, Arnauld Du Ferrier, Nicole Du Val, Claude Viole,

Ustache De La Port, and Paul De Foix be taken into custody as well for their more moderate stance. They were paraded down the grand boulevards to the Bastille in plain daylight "so as to be a spectacle for the people" and were held incommunicado, without paper, ink, or books.[36]

Of this group, only Du Bourg saw the stake.

THE INTERROGATION

The next phase was Du Bourg's interrogation, which proved to be more difficult for his captors than expected. The interrogation was to begin on June 19, conducted by President De Saint-André, Jean-Jacques De Mesmes (Maître des Requêtes), magistrates Louis Gayant and Robert Bouette, Eustache du Bellay (the bishop of Paris), and the inquisitor Antoine de Mouchy (also known as Democares).[37] Du Bourg, a jurist more than familiar with the rights and privileges associated with the Parlement, protested their involvement, refusing to answer their questions and calling for his "Natural judge, which was the court of the Parlement . . . following the ancient custom that they said had always been observed."[38] In light of this refusal, the king issued two letters patent, forcing Du Bourg and the other prisoners to answer questions, "on pain of being declared, arraigned, and convicted in the cases in which they were charged, and also of rebellion against the king."[39] When faced with this accusation of sedition, Du Bourg relented, begging the pardon of the king, and his interrogation began on June 20, lasting two days. This extraordinary procedure was to be the basis of Du Bourg's appeals at a later date.[40]

It appears that Du Bourg's interrogators had three main goals: first, to ascertain his precise beliefs, and in doing so, determine the depth of his heresy; second, to uncover the identities of his co-religionists and the details of their assemblies; and third, to see how these views affected his interpretation of the authority of the state and church in terms of his own obedience and, in general, the prosecution of heresy. Regarding the first goal, Du Bourg was questioned in detail on his views of the laws, tenets, and traditions of the Catholic Church (e.g., seven sacraments, transubstantiation, purgatory, intercession of the saints, councils, ecclesiastical obedience, and hierarchy), to which he responded with solid Reformed doctrine. In sum, he held to the Calvinist doctrine of the primacy of the Gospel as the only basis of faith and practice.

In an effort to reach their second goal, the interrogators questioned Du Bourg in depth about his involvement with illicit assemblies and his avoidance of the Mass. He refused to name his co-religionists, stating that he would neither offend God nor jeopardize others. More precisely, he declined to identify the houses in which the assemblies were held, the time of day of the services, or number of those in attendance. The only information he provided regarding his co-religionists was that he never attended the assemblies with any counselor or president of the Parlement, and he willingly conceded that he did not attend Easter Mass this year, nor had he received communion, nor made a confession to a priest since the previous Easter.

With regard to questions about the state's and church's authority, Du Bourg was very careful with his answers. He tread a fine line, using rhetoric and his understanding of the law to avoid a direct challenge to the authority of the state or church. When dealing with questions about theology, Du Bourg cited chapter and verse from the Bible and gave rather straightforward answers, having faith in the correctness of his beliefs; but when the questions moved away from belief and into practice or legality, Du Bourg became evasive. Replying to a statement by his interrogators that what he had said during the *lit de justice* greatly scandalized the king and was contrary to his profession, his sacred orders, and God's commandments, Du Bourg refused to address that issue and instead replied that "he thought he had said nothing against the order he had professed, and the commandments of God and the Church, which he would not want to do."[41]

Additionally, he openly conceded that "one must obey the Ministers of the Church, the Curés and others, who have charge of our souls, in what they command that conforms with the word of God."[42] Hence, Du Bourg went to some length to express his loyalty to the throne and his obedience to the authorities, both secular and ecclesiastical. More precisely, he never challenged the right of the state to prosecute heresy and instead insisted that it must do so. However, those who prosecute heresy must know what it is–thus his insistence on a council.[43]

When backed into a corner, however, regarding his ambiguous answers and what eventually turned out to be an outright lie, Du Bourg was forced to address the political and legal ramifications of his situation. On the previous day, June 20, Du Bourg had admitted he did not attend Easter services that year and had not taken communion since the previous Easter. On the next day, Du Bourg's interrogators pointedly read him the transcript of that question and his answer. Since they did so, Du Bourg must have realized that he had been caught in a lie, and his attendance at an illicit assembly to celebrate Easter that year and sharing in communion had been reported in some way. The reasons for Du Bourg thinking he had been caught or the means by which his interrogators had discovered his untruthfulness were not recorded. Nevertheless, Du Bourg then confessed to have lied about his having received communion and conceded that he had answered untruthfully. He immediately begged forgiveness from God—but not his interrogators—for denying such a "grand benefice." Nevertheless the damage was done and there would be no evading what was to follow.

The probable reason for his first denial was that Du Bourg wanted to avoid any line of questioning that involved naming his co-religionists. By denying he had taken communion, he downplayed his involvement at the assembly, possibly hoping to appear more passively involved. In doing so, he perhaps could avoid more rigorous questioning. The previous day, when he lied, his interrogators had asked only one question about other Protestants, but phrased it in a way that gave Du Bourg room to maneuver. They asked him "to name those who are of his opinion that he had declared above, who do not revere the Sacred Mass . . . and the other Sacraments." Du Bourg's evasive reply was "that he could not judge the conscience of others."[44] The question was a dead end without further evidence of his involvement. His interrogators then moved on, abandoning for that day the pursuit of his co-religionists; but on the next day, almost all of their questions (after Du Bourg admitted to being caught in the lie) dealt exclusively with that issue. His admission of the lie had opened the door.

After he refused to answer, or gave vague responses to, numerous questions about the assemblies and the people involved, Du Bourg's interrogators urged him to tell the truth as he promised he would. Again, Du Bourg attempted to evade addressing the direct conflict between his position as a magistrate bound to uphold the law and the requirements of his faith. He instead claimed to be speaking the truth and that "he is in accord with the Civil Laws, and that it is laudable for each to redeem his blood by such ways of which he thinks for himself."[45] But instead of addressing the particular truth his in-

terrogators were looking for, he spoke of the greater truth that he
was imprisoned for. Not to be distracted, his interrogators pushed
harder, reminding him that as a magistrate of the king and thus con-
strained by the law, he must answer their questions truthfully and
fully or be accused of *lèse-majesté*. Du Bourg, for the third time in
this phase of the interrogation, answered evasively. He claimed that
God was not pleased that he had been arraigned on a charge of *lèse-
majesté* against Him (*lèse-majesté divine*), and that "of course he offended and offends God's majesty from time to time, but that he believes that His Majesty will have mercy on his soul through the merit
of the precious blood of His Son."[46]

This episode illustrates Du Bourg's attempts to stay within the law
and to avoid direct confrontation over issues of authority. Whereas
his religious beliefs were unambiguous, he purposely sidestepped
the political and legal issues. This could be due to his stated belief in
the possibility and importance of a council to determine grounds for
the condemnation of a heretic. If Du Bourg believed that this council could or would be convened, it makes sense then that he would
strenuously avoid making any statements that would brand him seditious or rebellious against the state. In this way, he could maintain
his reputation and identity as a magistrate. Du Bourg alluded to his
perception that a council would be convened: "If it pleased the king,
through his beneficent grace, for the charity that he bears towards
his subjects, he has the means to assemble a Council to root out the
heresies of today: and to determine by this without any doubt who
can remain in the Religion, and who among the ignorant: hence
what his Majesty himself promised in the first article of the Treaty of
Peace."[47] Thus, Du Bourg remained careful and cautious when dealing with issues outside of doctrine.

Outside the interrogation room, the effects of Du Bourg's arrest
and imprisonment began to ripple throughout Paris. The hunt for
and persecution of Protestants in Paris was stepped up on the orders
of the cardinal of Lorraine, President Saint-André, and Antoine de
Mouchy in order to intimidate the Protestants in the countryside.
Most notably there were at least twelve executions of Protestants in
Paris between June and December.[48] For example, caught up in the
search was an unnamed lawyer and his family who had held religious
services at their home. Two spies, formerly Protestants themselves,
for the Cardinal and his cohorts had stayed with them and reported
back to the authorities that they had witnessed at this home "a very

great concourse of people of both sexes . . . and that after the candles were put out, each had satisfied his desires . . . that one among them had had criminal intercourse with the daughter of the lawyer, and had even satisfied his passion up to three times."[49] Contemporary historian Jacques-Auguste de Thou, a Catholic who recorded this event, wrote with disdain that these were outright lies and the accusers scoundrels, but that "the lie easily found credence in the minds of the people and augmented the hatred towards the Protestants."[50]

Du Bourg's friends and supporters were the least immune to harassment. After Du Bourg's interrogation, upon threat of deprivation of their goods and estates, his brothers were forced out of Paris where they had come to lobby for his release.[51] This threat and the apparent intimidation of his friends and supporters were not without cause. The reasons for these actions are not given, though in all likelihood they were designed to put pressure on Du Bourg to recant either by isolating him from his support network, or by playing on his sympathy for them. Either way, these acts, done at this particular time after Du Bourg had made his beliefs clear yet while there was still some hope in the minds of his captors of reconversion, are evidence that his case held great importance to the state. His reconversion would deal a blow to the Reform faction, and would be a much greater prize than his execution; hence, sincere efforts would be placed on obtaining a recantation. While for the Reform movement, Du Bourg's exoneration (which they knew would be unlikely) or martyrdom would be a potent weapon for their cause. As a magistrate of the Parlement held for either "upholding the Gospel" or espousing heresy, Du Bourg's case would provide much grist for the Reform propaganda mill, and would cause much concern on the part of his captors. This would be especially evident later on when Du Bourg would waver in his commitment to the cause and produce an "ambiguous" confession.

LEGAL STRATEGY:
THE APPEALS AND DEGRADATION

The result of the interrogation was a condemnation of Du Bourg by Du Bellay as a heretic, the sentence of degradation of his Orders, and the transfer of his person to the secular authorities. Du Bourg unsuccessfully appealed this sentence to both the ecclesiastical courts as well as to Parlement. While still a cleric, at the level of the diaconate, Du Bourg appealed Du Bellay's ruling to the Parlement on July 7, then to the archbishop of Sens. Following that refusal, he turned again to the Parlement on August 2 only to be rejected at the end of the month. Again, he turned to the ecclesiastical system, this time in September to the archbishop of Lyon, who refused to overturn the sentence. His last appeal was to the Parlement, and their denial (on November 18) paved the way for the degradation and execution.[52]

While other historians have listed the grounds for Du Bourg's appeals, his demands for counsel and the recusation of a number of "hostile" judges, there has been a distinct lack of attention paid to Du Bourg's legal strategy itself. Interestingly enough, Du Bourg's defense opens a window onto his state of mind—revealing not an eager, willing martyr; but a man of the law using every means at his disposal to obtain a favorable outcome. Protestant sources claimed that Du Bourg was merely trying not precipitously to bring about his own death before his time and not to forget anything that might serve to justify him. Additionally, Crespin stated that Du Bourg himself wrote to the faithful, reassuring them that he was not attempting to win more time or prolong his life by subterfuge.[53] Yet, his appeals reveal a strategy that went beyond the law—one that involved playing on the identity and factionalism of the Court itself.

Most revealing is Du Bourg's appeal *comme d'abus*, an appeal protesting a flaw in the legal procedure that if found correct, would require a new trial.[54] This appeal he set before the Parlement in the beginning of August. Just as Du Bourg did at the beginning of his interrogation, he again demanded to be heard by all the assembled chambers of the Parlement. Dumesnil had dismissed Du Bourg's request on the grounds that although it was his privilege to be heard by all the chambers, "it was not customary."[55] It appeared as if Du Bourg at no point in his *procès*, or trial, would receive this privilege.

His insistence on being heard by all the chambers—first during the *procès* and then during the appeal—was not just the desire for the proper form nor to simply uphold his privilege, but instead it was an essential part of his legal strategy. Du Bourg in all likelihood had hoped that he would be able to draw on the support of his friends and more moderate members of the court to counter the zeal of the ultramontane faction. According to the report of June 13 by the English ambassador Nicholas Throckmorton, the majority of those who spoke at the fateful Mercuriale favored the calling of a general council and opposed the death sentence for the Protestants.[56] Thus, it would make sense that Du Bourg would insist on this privilege, rather than be heard only by a cabal headed by the ultramontanes. Du Bourg strenuously objected to being heard only by the Grand'Chambre, which, as stated above, was heavily weighted toward assigning the death penalty for heresy.[57]

Du Bourg, on August 3, sent a petition to the court outlining the grounds for recusations and counsel. Although he opened it with the formulaic "I very humbly plead in protest," the document was in no way humble or diffident. He listed two main grounds for appeal, one based on the order, form, and procedure of the judgment against him, and the other based on the substance and principle. The first ground involved the disregarding of his privileges as a magistrate of the court considering that he was not heard originally by all the assembled chambers. The second ground manipulated both the legal limitations on ecclesiastical authority and the identity of the Parlement. Du Bourg claimed that "If said Sentence were executed, the consequence would be to deprive him of his position as Counselor Cleric, which he could not hold without the said Orders. Here is an overture to the Bishop of Paris or other Judges of the Church, to have, as a consequence of the said degradation, the power to deprive a Counselor Cleric of his said position of Counselor, which is a true usurpation of jurisdiction."[58] In other words, by stripping him of his orders (which was within their jurisdiction), the ecclesiastical judges were overstepping their bounds regarding the consequences of this sentence: once degraded, he could no longer serve as conseiller-clerc and would thus be deprived of his position in Parlement, a penalty outside of their authority.[59]

By decrying these two abuses, Du Bourg was playing to the spirit and traditions of the Parlement—not the law—as to its identity as a sovereign court.[60] In doing so, he could draw on the court's solidarity as a body (though not as an ideologically unified one) and the need to defend its privileges as such. Du Bourg's identification of the second abuse was in direct accord with tensions described above between the secular (royal) courts and ecclesiastical courts over jurisdiction. This was an issue that penetrated to the heart of the Parlement's sovereignty.[61] Most importantly, in his petition, Du Bourg

reminded the judges about the defense of their privileges. He ominously states, regarding the letters patent from the king, about the
privilege of being heard by all the chambers, that

> His Majesty did not intend by these [letters patent] to derogate from
> the said privilege; and when the derogatory clause is there, (which it
> is not) the said Court has been accustomed to deliberate on such let-
> ters with all the Chambers assembled, and to make remonstrances to
> see them reviewed according to the importance of the cases, before
> dealing a blow that would break such privileges, which are of as
> much consequence as the one that is presently being considered,
> *which touches all of you, my said Lords, and of which you yourselves are the
> defenders.*[62]

In other words, "if my privileges can be violated so easily, so could
yours; thus, by defending mine, you defend yours as a sovereign
body."

After he listed the grounds for appeal, Du Bourg included several
requests, among which were demands for the recusation of a number of judges from presiding over his appeal (Le Maistre, François
Saint-André, Minard, Louis Gayant, Bouette, and De Dormans), and
for advocates and counselors to plead the appeal itself. Du Bourg's
demand for the recusations were based on the ostensible fact that
these presidents and magistrates were involved in various aspects of
his *procès*—either as interrogators or witnesses—or in his sentenc-
ing, thus they were already biased against him. In reality, there were
much deeper grounds for his resistance to some of these judges.
Saint André and Gayant had presided over or been part of the
Chambre Ardente, the temporary chamber of the Parlement lasting
from 1548 to 1550 and set up solely to prosecute Protestants. Thus,
their lack of sympathy for the Reform and its faithful was well established.[63] Le Maistre and Minard were known to have betrayed the tradition of Parlement and informed against the moderates to the king
at the Mercuriale, hence their inability to act in accordance with the
laws and tradition of the Court were well known—aside from their
hard-line ultramontane stance. Thus, Du Bourg sought to have these
members recuse themselves for not only the reasons listed in the petition, but also probably for grounds that went beyond.

Du Bourg's legal strategy involved more than simply following
legal procedures. He attempted to appeal to the Court's identity
and its animosity toward the ecclesiastical courts. He also sought to

"stack the deck," so to speak, by demanding that his case be heard by all of the chambers. These maneuvers reveal a man less than willing to seek out martyrdom. But in the end, they failed: both grounds were found invalid and no abuse was identified. The Parlement's third rejection of him in November closed the door on that part of his legal strategy, and on November 21, Du Bourg was stripped of his clerical status at the Bastille in a solemn ceremony by the bishop of Treguyer.[64]

According to the *procès verbal*, or transcript, of the ceremony, the bishop was assisted by Nicolas de Saint-Ouen (a theologian and abbé of Montebourg) and Eustache du Bellay (the Bishop of Paris). Also at the ceremony were Jacques Quetier and Phillipes Bryault (church canons), Jean Aleaume (a theologian), Antoine de Mouchy (the inquisitor and one of Du Bourg's interrogators), Jehan Moreau, Noel Bruslart, Jean Haton, and Geoffroy Le Maistre. After the officials read the judgment against him and noted his failed appeals, Du Bourg declared that he had wanted to leave his orders for some time, that he had only taken them to obtain his position in Parlement. The ceremony proceeded at that point. Du Bourg was dressed in the vestments of his order—the black robe and surplice. In his hands were the Gospels and sacred books, a chalice, the flagons of oil, wine, water, and tapers. All these vestments and ornaments symbolizing the orders he had taken were then solemnly removed, and the bishop of Treguyer then spoke the final words revoking his orders. The bishop's aides then presented Du Bourg with the clothes and cap of a layman, which he refused to take, and instead insisted on being dressed in the robes of a magistrate of the court—a *robe de chambre*, in violet.[65]

This one act, that of demanding his *robe de chambre*, showed Du Bourg at his finest and highest minded—not as a man of religion, but a man of the law. He insisted on maintaining this identity even as he was stripped of the very orders that enabled him to continue as such. The act was symbolic, denying the church the ability to divest him of his identity as a magistrate. It also illustrates Du Bourg's continued emphasis on the fact that he was being persecuted (and prosecuted) for nothing more than his beliefs. This was reiterated throughout the ceremony such as when he denied that his orders ever meant anything to him, and that they were the means to the end he desired—his position in Parlement. Even in *procès verbal*—the state version of the event—this was made clear. Other sources built on his refusal to consider the sacredness of the ceremony and his orders: the author of the *Vraye histoire* wrote, "by this means the mark of the beast, which was spoken of in the Apocalypse, was removed from him: and he bore no longer the stain of the Anti-Christ of Rome."[66] Most importantly this ceremony paved the way for his execution as he was no longer sheltered by his clerical status.

Vacillation and Determination: The Final Days

During the final appeal to Parlement in December, Du Bourg apparently wavered from his original confession made during his interrogation. Du Bourg's friends in Parlement, especially his attorney Marillac (whom he requested in August), counseled him "to soften his judges with tempered responses and by this avoid a harsh sentence."[67] Following their advice on December 13, Du Bourg "abjured all the heretical and erroneous propositions he had held, and did so in the presence of the judges."[68] This caused a ripple of fear through the ranks of the newly established Reformed Church of Paris, and they quickly responded to the possible loss of a potential martyr. Augustin Marlorat, the pastor of the church, sent him at least one letter urging him to recant this confession: "He is obligated then to reject the cowardly counsel of his friends, who would like to persuade him to spare his life, to the prejudice of his reputation and eternal salvation, and to prepare himself with great courage, and a pure conscience, to sustain the fight."[69] Marlorat's message was that God was more powerful than man, that rewards in heaven for witnessing God's truth were greater than a longer life on Earth, and that he would gain these rewards "after having left men with this great lesson."[70] He encouraged Du Bourg to embrace martyrdom as it would be God's will and his duty. In another account of the letter found in Chandieu's martyrology, the message is more blunt: "That the news of his constancy was not only all over France, but in all Christendom, and that it had strengthened many of the weak and roused others to make inquiries into their salvation. That the eyes of all were upon him . . . [I]f out of fear he makes a choice contrary to his first confession, he would be the cause of a tremendous ruin [to the movement]."[71] For a young and previously obscure judge (he was thirty-seven or thirty-eight at the time), the pressure on Du Bourg must have been unbearable. His life and trial became a battlefield on which three forces fought: his friends in Parlement, who endeavored to save his life; the Catholic Church and his judges, who did not want to create a martyr but sought his return to the fold for religious and political reasons; and the Reform movement, which hoped in the end to celebrate him as a martyr. Marlorat's words eventually hit home, and in span of a few days (December 19) Du Bourg issued a final confession in writing restating the beliefs he expounded during his interrogation.[72]

This new confession, together with the assassination of President Minard, assured that Du Bourg would be convicted and sentenced to die.[73] On December 18, Minard, one of the judges Du Bourg attempted to have recused from his trial and who was also accused by Protestants of having informed the king of the presence of "Lutherans" in his court, was returning to the Palais. When he neared his house, an unknown assassin shot him dead on the street. Rumors flew through Paris associating Du Bourg with the plot, supposedly motivated by his hatred of the man who had been so instrumental in his downfall.[74] From this moment on, there was no question as to the outcome of Du Bourg's trial.

While in prison, Du Bourg was not as isolated as his captors might have liked, nor as he would lead them to believe. He had contact both with the outside world and with other prisoners held for similar causes. One of these prisoners was Marguerite Le Riche, a coreligionist and wife of a Parisian bookseller.[75] Marguerite offered consolation and encouragement to Du Bourg though her corporeal encouragement was short-lived: she was executed in mid-August. But as a martyr-model, her influence continued to offer him hope and edification.[76]

Du Bourg's contacts with the outside world were more complicated, and often less than edifying. First, at some point near the end of his life, Du Bourg either dictated to a sympathetic ear or smuggled out (written in his own hand) his *Oraison au Senate de Paris*, confession, and interrogation. Though there has been some question as to whether this first work is of Du Bourg's hand, it is attributed to him in at least two other works.[77] Second, Du Bourg exchanged letters a number of times with the outside world. Although Du Bourg insisted that he had no contact with the outside world, he was apparently able to communicate until around December 21.[78] Most significantly the state uncovered a plot to free Du Bourg sometime toward the middle of September. A letter, written in code by Du

Bourg and containing plans for an escape, was intercepted after his servant mistakenly delivered the letter to a solicitor of the court, who had the same name—Durant—as the addressee. This unfortunate mistake led to a search of Du Bourg's cell, which uncovered the key to the code and many other letters addressed to or sent by the "Faithful and those of the Word."[79] After this discovery, the court moved Du Bourg to a cage in the Bastille.[80] Sometime in December evidence came to light of a second plot to free Du Bourg, involving a "Scottish Stuart, native of the Scottish nation."[81] Du Bourg was questioned about this plot before his execution, though he denied any knowledge of either the conspiracy or the Scotsman. Later, a Scotsman by the name of Robert Stuard would be arrested, accused of attempting to liberate Du Bourg, involvement in the assassination attempt on Minard, and plotting to set Paris on fire.[82]

These were not the only attempts to spare Du Bourg's life. Between the submission of the penultimate confession and the final judgment condemning Du Bourg to death, the Palatine Elector sent an envoy to the king proposing to settle Du Bourg as a professor at his university. According to the Protestant sources, once the cardinal of Lorraine (the source of all evil doing in their texts) heard of this offer, he pursued both the king and the Parlement to end the matter. He did so especially in light of the "offensive" confession "understood and heard [by the Parlement], and affirmed and confirmed by mouth of the said Du Bourg."[83] Regardless of the cardinal's alleged interference, the Parlement truly had no other option. The assassination of one of their own—Minard—probably at the hands of a Protestant understandably had a negative impact on the outcome of Du Bourg's final appeal. It would have put the magistrates on the defensive refusing to be threatened by such action, or the assassination would have made them even more fearful of Protestant extremism. Either way, forcing their hand even more was this now unrepentant heretic who, by recanting his more moderate confession, had disallowed any other outcome other than his own execution. It is not surprising then that on December 22 the Parlement declared Du Bourg's case "not receivable," ending his final appeal. That same day the elector indirectly got his answer in the form of a judgment read in the court condemning Du Bourg to be burned alive and his body reduced to ashes.[84] Inserted at the end of the judgment was a clause indicating that Du Bourg was not to feel the fire. In all likelihood, his former colleagues felt remorse for him, and determined that if he must die, it was to be as painless as possible.

Du Bourg was brought in front of his former colleagues at the chapel of the Conciergerie and the court clerk read the judgment, which was to be carried out the next day. In light of his confession, which ended with the words, "Here is the faith in which I want to live and die: and I have sealed this gift with my mark, ready to seal it with my own blood, in order to uphold the doctrine of the son of God," Du Bourg was more than aware of the probable outcome of his last appeal.[85] He certainly appeared prepared to embrace the title of martyr, even calling the situation a "gift." Some of the sources make reference to an address made by Du Bourg to his fellow magistrates.[86] If this address, as Lelièvre believes, is the *Oraison,* then Du Bourg chastised the court with the vigor and fearlessness of a dead-man-walking (or martyr) for disregarding the law of God and wrongfully punishing His faithful children.

Even on December 23, the day of his execution, Du Bourg's prosecutors had not given up their hopes of saving his soul and also of uncovering his co-conspirators. They questioned him not only about the conspiracy to free him, but again about the identities of his co-religionists, about which he remained silent. The notary, Simon Chartier, described how various members of the faculty of theology and other religious representatives sincerely attempted to bring him back to the Catholic Church and, in effect, obtain a recantation of his confession. He wrote: "[T]he abbot of Montebourg, curé of Saint Bartholomew, who by making many good admonitions and remonstrances to said Du Bourg in order to lead him back and bring him again to the way of good Catholics, quoting many passages of holy Scripture, offered him many times, as curé, to hear his confession, and to absolve him of sins by the grace and power that was entrusted to him by God."[87] But instead of returning to the fold, Du Bourg turned a deaf ear to their pleas and stated his willingness and readiness to suffer and die upholding the truth.[88]

As his execution was to be a public spectacle, Du Bourg was warned before leaving the prison against speaking against the church or dogmatizing in front of the crowds as it would cause a public scandal. Du Bourg responded that he had no desire to offend the honor of God or his church nor to cause anyone to be scandalized. He was then loaded onto a small cart and led to the Place de Grève, singing psalms and accompanied by four or five hundred

armed men. The spectacle of this procession testified to the importance of this execution—both as a possible flashpoint for the crowd,
and as a tribute to Du Bourg's celebrity as a heretic and judge in the
Parlement.[89] Once again, Du Bourg was warned that he was close to
death and to clear his conscience, to which he responded that he
was ready to suffer.[90] At the Place de Grève, Du Bourg stepped out of
the cart and walked to the gibbet where he was stripped down to his
chemise. The curé of Saint Bartholomew presented him with a cross
to kiss, which he refused. He addressed the crowd, clarifying his
"crime" and establishing his credentials as a martyr by explaining,
"My friends, I am in no way here as a thief, or as a murderer, but for
the Gospel."[91]

This claim was doubly important to Du Bourg. As with almost all
of the martyrs, the distinction between them and common criminals
who were also executed was essential. For Du Bourg, more so than
almost any other martyr, the point that his death was due to his beliefs alone reinforced his perception (and the perception of others)
that he remained a loyal magistrate (or subject, for the majority of
martyrs) to the crown.

The executioner then raised Du Bourg high on the gibbet and
with his last breaths, Du Bourg chanted, "My God, do not abandon
me."[92] In accordance with the judgment, Du Bourg died by strangulation, then the fires were lit beneath him. So he died without feeling the fury of the flames, and his remains were reduced to ashes.[93] It
is at this point that the legend of Anne Du Bourg was born.

It would not be Henri II, the king whom Du Bourg had so
grievously offended at the Mercuriale, who would see Du Bourg at
the stake. Henri II died of an infected eye caused by a jousting acci-
dent in July 1559. Ascending to the throne would be François II, a
minor (fifteen) at the time, accompanied by the regent, his mother
Catherine de Medici. It would be under François's watch, then, that
Du Bourg's body be reduced to cinders.

In response to a possible opportunity for change, a small band of
Huguenots led by a French exile from Geneva, La Renaudie, plotted
to "liberate" the minor king from the control of the Guise. While
this plot, known as the Conspiracy of Amboise, failed, it revealed the
very real threat the Huguenot movement could pose to the crown.
In response to this threat and the challenge posed by the growing
power of the Guise, Catherine crafted a policy that would play one

faction off the other, granting for a brief period some toleration to the Calvinists in France (after the execution of the conspirators). The policy eventually backfired as it hardened the extremists on both sides. With a female regent and a minor king, the crown was not in hands strong enough to withstand the hostilities that were spinning out of control. War would follow within two years.

Du Bourg's death, then, marks a turning point in the approaches and attitudes taken by the Huguenot movement. Coupled with outrage over the "massacre" of the conspirators, the death of Du Bourg led to a great out pouring of propaganda that put a new spin on the legitimacy of the persecution.[94] Now, with the new political reality of regent/minor king, Huguenot polemicists began to assert, cautiously, the importance of "traditional" councils to the king (e.g., the princes of the blood, the Estates General, the rights of "inferior magistrates") to counter the influence of the ultramontanes. No longer would the French Calvinists be satisfied solely with passive resistance. Instead, they would begin to take matters in their own hands. Martyrdom, however, and its accompanying rhetoric did not cease to be a primary weapon in this struggle for survival. The martyr would continue to be held up as the model for the ordinary man and woman, a model from which they could draw consolation, edification, and inspiration.

The story of Anne Du Bourg sheds light on the foundation of this model, the individual who would be executed for his convictions. More precisely, his case highlights the ambiguities of the identity of a martyr. A martyr is created after the fact, and his story is then reconstructed to conform with that image. Looking beyond that identity at the man and his trial, Anne Du Bourg was not an eager victim who willingly and enthusiastically embraced his fate from the beginning. His hagiographers would need to reshape his story so that he could become their most celebrated martyr. Most importantly, Du Bourg's story reveals much about the crisis of conscience —how a member of the most important court in France responded to the pressures exerted upon him by his church, his colleagues, and the state, while still maintaining his beliefs and identity as a man of the law.

This chapter has reconstructed Du Bourg's story through many different sources in an attempt to understand his motivations and beliefs. By presenting the complete story, we see Du Bourg as an ambiguous martyr, full of complexity and reconstituted out of the hagiographical symbol. Du Bourg did not embrace his fate without a strenuous internal and external struggle, and it was not until the very end (with the production of his final confession) that he willingly accepted his "responsibility" as a martyr—moving beyond the manipulation of rhetoric and law to preserve both his life and status.

3

The Making of
a Martyr

DU BOURG'S METAMORPHOSIS FROM AN ORDINARY MAN INTO A MARTYR
did not truly begin with the events described in the previous chapter.
Instead this transformation began in earnest with the reconstruction
of his story by Protestant propagandists after Du Bourg's death. His
actual execution and the events leading up to it, though moving and
dramatic, needed to be placed into a larger context, endowing his
"sacrifice" with greater meaning and significance. Protestant polemicists who wrote tracts and treatises on Du Bourg's "martyrdom" then
identified him as an uncompromising, willing witness who testified
for the truth with his blood. These often hagiographical texts not
only reveal or conceal details about Du Bourg, but more importantly,
they shed light on how the construction of a martyr transformed the
individual—cleansing him by fire, if you will—translating a complicated, unique individual into a venerated stereotype and larger symbol of the Reformed cause.

The martyr Du Bourg became greater and more germane than
the man. Du Bourg's significance did not arise simply because of his
own actions, but from how others perceived, used, and manipulated
his image. Thus, it is important that we look beyond the legal and political case of Anne Du Bourg to his transformation into one of the
Huguenot movement's most celebrated martyrs. Du Bourg's posthumous metamorphosis from man into martyr illustrates the process by
which an individual with all his human ambiguities becomes "per-
fected" through his death and according to the needs of his movement.

Before examining this transformation, we must look into the general nature of martyrdom. More precisely, a martyr is created after

the fact. Though martyrdom "occurred" with the shedding of blood, the identity of the martyr and its efficacy depended on two posthumous stages. First, there is confirmation (or conformation) of the subject's beliefs and actions to the ideology of the movement. And second, the new "witness" is memorialized within a larger context and tradition. An integral part of this process involves the construction of a narrative that inverted or challenged the persecuting authority or order that defined the subject as a criminal and/or heretic.[1] Thus the term "martyr," like "heretic" or "criminal," is a subjective rhetorical creation. The key to distinguishing between a criminal/heretic and a martyr is the cause for which the subject died. For example, even though Du Bourg "died well," according to Raemond he died a heretic—that is, for the wrong cause. What we are left with then, considering the various sources, are conflicting perceptions and representations. The identity of the executed became a battleground for those fighting the war over the "true faith."

The contemporary Protestant narratives attempted to reconstruct the martyr's actions, words, and indeed conscience, to produce a coherent and unambiguous representation of the experience. In this reconstructed form the martyr was, in its purest sense, a symbol; and this symbol was bigger than the individual who was executed. Regardless of whether the individual might have understood the implications of his act, he became a vehicle for issues that he might not have understood or recognized as part of his situation or sacrifice. Nevertheless, these issues were made manifest in the symbol. What this means is that the rhetoric surrounding the representation of a martyr and the general construction of his identity after his death are just as important as the actual details of their case.

This chapter focuses on Du Bourg the martyr, providing an analysis of the various reconstructions of his story and the messages disseminated through the narratives published for public consumption. More precisely it deals with how Anne Du Bourg conformed (or was made to conform) to the image or archetype of the martyr, and the ways in which he was used as a symbol This approach concentrates on the transformation of an individual (e.g., what happened after Du Bourg was executed, the roles and services he provided posthumously) and the generation of a specific rhetoric of martyrdom. More broadly, in conjunction with chapter 2, this study examines the problematic nature of martyrdom, the ways in which interpretation and contextualization of the individual's acts created a martyr, and the ways in which this identity was presented and transmitted to the "faithful."

MARKS OF THE MARTYR

Before examining the specific transformation of man into martyr, we must identify the traits or characteristics used to define martyrdom. Protestant usage of the term "martyr" is derived directly from the original Greek word for "witness." Whereas many Protestant writers described the martyrs as God's "champions," the main focus was the idea that they confessed and suffered willingly for the cause of God (i.e., *imitatio Christi*). A common reference for those who wrote on martyrdom or gave advice to the faithful regarding their responsibility to God, was the third-century church father Tertullian.[2] In referring to him, the Protestants were clearly laying the groundwork for modeling their martyrs upon those of the early church. This implied not only a direct lineage to a "truer" faith than Catholicism, but it alluded to the belief embodied by martyrdom and described by Tertullian: the mark of the true church was persecution, and its seed was the blood of the martyrs.

According to Crespin, there were five marks of a true martyr, the first and most important mark being that he has "held no other doctrine than that of the prophets and apostles, having drawn upon their holy confessions and writings."[3] In almost all of the accounts found in the martyrologies of Chandieu and Crespin, if no other information is given about a martyr (save the fact that he was executed), this mark is identified. Without this qualification, a "martyr" who might have otherwise died well for his beliefs was nothing more than a servant of the devil:

> When Satan has seen what true servants of God suffer for the truth, he has tried, like a deceiver, to have also martyrs for error and lies, pushing them forward next to the true witnesses of the gospel. This we see still practiced today by means of a sect of people who, suffering persecution under a label of the word of God, masked by an appearance of sanctity, obscure the truth in a remarkable way, so that it may not be discerned among the lies.[4]

The proper confession of the faith, then, was the defining mark of the martyr. The longer narratives in the martyrologies focused not on the death, but on the oral or written confession and/or interrogation—in other words, the statement of faith. The martyr himself often sent letters to friends, family members, or pastors containing his statement with instructions "to give word of" or "to make public" his confession. In other accounts a copy of the state's articles of condemnation or the *procès verbal* of the interrogation were included. With this information, the martyrologists were able to turn "criminality" into the mark of a martyr, thus inverting the justice of the state to display the constancy of the martyr. Additionally, in contrast to the profession (confession) of faith, the death of the martyr was described in a highly formulaic manner and almost as an afterthought. Truly the climax of the accounts was not the point of death (a trait common in Catholic hagiography), but the affirmation and confession of the proper faith.

The second mark was almost as important. The individual must have received from God the aid "that he gave long ago to all the others who suffered in His name."[5] This mark was proof of God's favor, as without such grace the martyr would not have been able to bear his burden. The martyr then became the vehicle for God's will as he transcended his human frailty only to serve God. This aid from God not only identified the martyr to believers, but also served to prove the righteousness of the cause to the persecutors. Reminiscent of Moses turning his staff into a serpent before Pharaoh, the martyr became a means through which God proved His power to the unfaithful. The weaker the vessel, the more mighty God's power (and hence, his favor) would appear.[6]

The aid from God enabled the martyr to display the next two marks: the patience to bear the horrors of prison, torture, and death, and to still praise God with joy; and the confounding and lack of successful intimidation by the persecuting (prosecuting) judges. The ability to subordinate bodily comfort to the salvation of the soul was an important lesson for the faithful; however, success depended on God's aid and deep commitment to His word. With regard to the fourth mark (standing up to the judges), again, God granted the martyr the ability to answer their questions with surprising knowledge and assurance. Like the second and third mark, this ability displayed God's power (and favor) in the described spectacle of the weak confounding and defeating the strong.

The final mark was the martyr's choice of God's truth and eternal life over terrestrial life and recantation: "the furnace was more agreeable to them, and they sang the praises of God in the middle of the flames."[7] This mark sealed the martyr's testimony with his own blood, binding him forever to God, the community of martyrs who came before him, and to the living faithful community as well. It was here that the martyr completed his final duty, and fulfilled the mandate given to him by God.

The martyr, if we continue to follow Crespin and Chandieu, was to be a mirror for the faithful, to inspire and educate as well as console. Chandieu, for example, instructed his readers to contemplate the zeal and courage shown by the martyrs and the vanquishing of their fears that proved their love of God over all else.[8] Others beyond the martyrologists prescribed the same approach to the martyrs as a source of inspiration to confess beliefs publicly and not to fear the repercussions.[9] It is here that we find the importance of Du Bourg's case. Readers of the accounts needed to see Du Bourg not as the unwilling victim of the state and the Reform movement, but as the sacrificial martyr who gave uncompromising answers to his interrogators, who wrote a final unambiguous confession, and who ascended the scaffold with his head held high.

NARRATIVES AND ACCOUNTS

After examining the marks that defined martyrdom, we now can return to the case of Anne Du Bourg and examine the texts that together created the martyr out of the man. While the pamphlets and martyrological narratives on Du Bourg are in accord with Crespin's model, it is not a perfect nor easy fit. Before analyzing the texts, however, it is helpful to establish a chronology and interrelationship among the works.[10]

The first account of Du Bourg's trial was published almost before the flames were extinguished under his gibbet. In 1560 at least three very different independent pamphlets appeared: *L'Exemplaire, et Forme du procez* (Envers, n.d.), *Chanson Spirituelle d'Anne Du Bourg* (Paris, 1560), and *Oraison au Senate de Paris* (N.p., n.d.). The two latter documents were purportedly of Du Bourg's own hand; the former anonymously recounted the *procès verbal* of his interrogation and also included his penultimate confession.[11] In 1561 the *Vraye histoire*, again penned by an anonymous Protestant, appeared with its own narrative of parts of the events, and it too incorporated the *procès verbal* of his interrogation and the confession. A year later, a second independent narrative appeared, *Histoire du procès fait à Anne du Bourg, conseiller au Parlement, de sa condamnation et de son exécution à mort, avec ses interrogatoires et ses responses, et de l'emprisonnement de quatre autres conseillers* (Lyon, 1562). Du Bourg's case was next memorialized in the martyrologies of Antoine de la Roche Chandieu (Lyon, 1563) and Jean Crespin (Geneva, 1564),[12] both of which incorporated the confession and interrogation into their narratives.[13] Crespin's version would be augmented in later editions. Another account of Du Bourg's martyrdom was produced in 1564, the anonymous *Confession sur les Principaux poincts de la religion Chrestienne. . .* (Antwerp, 1564), which, of course, contained that final confession, but also included a short narrative of the Mercuriale, trial, and execution. In addition there were other pamphlets and more general histories that recounted Du Bourg's case or used him as an example of the injustice of the persecution, but he was not an important focal point of these works.[14] Du Bourg's martyrdom was thus commemorated, recounted, and celebrated in numerous texts and forms which were circulated publicly for several years.

The publication of Du Bourg's own writings and the transcriptions of his interrogation and confession were among the first pamphlets produced after his execution. These texts, with little or no additional narrative, were published probably with the intent to counteract immediately the findings of the state—namely the accusations of heresy and *lèse majesté*. They attempted to de-criminalize Du Bourg by emphasizing his and the Huguenot cause's perception that he died for no other reason than upholding God's truth and the preeminence of that law over all others. The later narratives sought to do the same thing; however, they focused on presenting Du Bourg within a particular context, memorializing him within the tradition of martyrdom. The earlier transcriptions instead used Du Bourg's own words, with little or no editorial contextualization, to present the raw case: Du Bourg as a true witness for God's word, and his identity as a martyr, then, was implicit rather than explicit. More importantly the transcriptions worked as encapsulations and summaries of Reformed doctrine. These words, coming as they did from the mouth of Du Bourg the martyr, were powerful didactic tools, educating the reader with supporting chapters and verses from the Gospel. These earlier texts present the martyr at his purest, testifying with his own voice. Even without dramatic narrative they were powerful pieces allowing the dead to speak once again.

The sheer number of independent publications on Du Bourg as well as various compilations or histories that include an account of his martyrdom testify not only to the celebrity of his case, but also illustrate his erudition and eloquence. Unlike many of the martyrs in Crespin's and Chandieu's martyrologies, Du Bourg possessed a strong understanding of the subtleties of both theology and law due to his education and position as *conseiller-clerc*. He had studied jurisprudence and had published at least one legal commentary. Additionally, he was professor of civil law at the University of Orléans.[15] The education he received in law, his ordination as a deacon, and his experience in Parlement allowed him to approach his situation from an informed perspective. Understandably, his answers to his interrogators as well as his own views expressed in the *Oraison* and *Confession* were well argued, supported by both legal and biblical citation. These texts then were important to the Reform movement not simply because they were written by a martyr, but also because of the exemplary quality of the ideas and their expression.

While there is no solid evidence as to how the confession, the *procès verbal* of the interrogation, the *Oraison*, or the *Chanson* in general fell into the hands of the Reformed faction, the former two texts form the core of the contemporary narratives. Most notably, there is consistency regarding the various reproductions of these texts. The same version of the interrogation found in the *Exemplaire* is found in the *Vraye histoire*, and in the two martyrologies. The confession found in this early document is also reproduced verbatim in the same three works and in the *Confession*.[16] All these works were disseminated among the faithful; hence, the basic details of his trial, interrogation, and confession were circulated in a relatively consistent form in the public sphere.

While the conformity of the interrogation and confession throughout all the texts point to the use of shared sources, it also becomes obvious that the authors of the later texts used the earlier narratives and transcriptions for other information. For example, the author of *Confession sur les principaux poincts* created a truncated version of the *Vraye histoire*, a much larger and detailed work. And the *Confession* lifted chunks of prose from the latter work, but summarized most of the events. Borrowing also occurred among the French martyrologies as well.[17] Analysis of Du Bourg's account in Crespin's narrative from the 1570 edition reveals a conglomeration of Chandieu's account and Pierre La Place's history, *Commentaires de l'estat de*

France (1565). Crespin transcribed whole sections from both verbatim. While Chandieu did not include a copy of the *Oraison*, Crespin transcribed La Place's version word for word (with minor stylistic changes) complete with the same omissions and later commentary.[18] Hence, it appears that very few, if any, of the texts were produced in isolation.

The martyrological narratives augmented and complemented the earlier "transcription" pamphlets. We can divide these narratives into two types: first, the independent pamphlets (such as the *Vraye histoire* and the narrative found at the end of the *Confession sur les principaux poincts*); and second, the accounts found in the larger compilations (Chandieu's and especially Crespin's martyrologies). Whereas the first type of narrative explicitly identified Du Bourg as a martyr and focused solely on his case and the surrounding situations, the second type placed him within a broader context of persecution and among the larger constellation of martyrs.

In the martyrologies, Du Bourg took his place in the history of the fledgling church. Crespin's martyrology began in 1554 as a collection of letters and documents concerning the martyrdom of Protestants (or church reformers before Luther who espoused pseudo-Protestant views) with little or no editorial presence.[19] By his last edition in 1570, however, Crespin was writing the history of the Reformed faith, following the same type of format as Eusebius's *Ecclesiastical History*. The preface to this edition linked the contemporary martyrdoms to those of the early "true" church by beginning with the deaths of the first generation of Christian martyrs—John the Baptist, Jesus of Nazareth, and Stephen.[20] The title of the work itself also changed from the "Actes" (1554, 1564), "Livre" (1554), or "Recueil" (1554, 1555, 1556, 1557, 1561, 1563) to the "Histoire" (1570).[21] In a larger sense, then, Crespin's work underwent a transformation from a gathering of documents and stories to a work with a larger historical and geographical context, and sense of purpose.

This transformation is also evident in the changes to the accounts of Du Bourg's martyrdom from the 1564 to the 1570 edition.[22] The contrast between the two accounts in these editions is great, and a physical as well as a substantive description is necessary. Probably the most obvious change is in the format and particular content. In the 1564 edition, Crespin began the body of his account of Du Bourg with a brief description of the Parlement followed by a narrative of the Mercuriale. The account is self-contained, with all the information on Du Bourg found underneath his heading. This version is much shorter, compact, and lacking most notably the excerpt from the *Oraison* found in the 1570 edition. This particular omission, though, is hardly mysterious as Crespin's likely source, La Place, did not publish his work until 1565.

In the 1570 edition the account of Du Bourg's martyrdom is stretched out beyond its own narrative borders and indeed spills over both literally and figuratively into other sections. The Mercuriale has its own narrative separate from that of Du Bourg (complete with running head and section divider). Between the two accounts are historical sections of general persecution, the state of the French Reformed churches, and narratives of other martyrs executed around that time. The actual account of Du Bourg's martyrdom, then, begins with a description of him, and what happened after the Mercuriale. The introductory glosses of the two editions point out the difference. Whereas the 1564 edition introduced him as an example for other judges and lawyers, the 1570 edition included this recommendation and additionally explained: "What in the previous edition was not stated distinctly we have laid out historically in the present edition, according to the order of events, so that after having seen below the causes and circumstances of the imprisonment of M. Anne Du Bourg, there follow the proceedings against him and his final ordeal."[23] Crespin, then, in the later edition put Du Bourg in the larger context of the history of the Reformed church, while still emphasizing his individual role as a martyr.

Chandieu's history-cum-martyrology, unlike Crespin's, underwent only one edition, recounting (as the title suggests) the history of the persecution of the Parisian Reformed church from 1557 through 1561. The format of the work is similar to Crespin's later editions, with short sections on general events and persecutions between accounts of individual martyrs. His intent, like Crespin's, was to write a Eusebian type of history through the martyrs. Unlike Crespin's later editions, however, Chandieu's accounts run into each other, with only side glosses to direct the reader. Thus, the work visually presents itself as a continual history, rather than as individual biographies strung togther. The account of Du Bourg's martyrdom is only set apart from the surrounding text by the side gloss bearing his name, while the account of the Mercuriale is described separately. Hence, the effect is more similar to the 1570 edition of Crespin than the 1564 edition.

Whereas it is helpful to separate the two works in terms of the texts in general, more important (regarding Du Bourg) are their similarities—namely, that Crespin relied exclusively on Chandieu for his early accounts of Du Bourg, then added information directly copied from La Place. There is a conformity among the two major martyrological works, aside from the interrogation and confession, regarding the image and story of Anne Du Bourg. Concerning their intended audience, they presented a specific type of martyr who provided particular forms of consolation and education for the faithful.

THE GODLY MARTYR-MAGISTRATE

The central image of Du Bourg presented by almost all of these texts was that of the "godly magistrate"—a description crucial to understanding his representation and importance as a martyr. As the Huguenot movement protested its loyalty to the throne and the standing of their faithful as the king's most dedicated subjects, Du Bourg's story provided an exceptional vehicle by which the movement could demonstrate that they were being persecuted for no other cause than "upholding the Gospel." Du Bourg, as represented in each martyrological text, insisted throughout every stage of his trial and execution that his death was for no other "crime" than his faith. His position as a *conseiller* who had served the king loyally and honestly (as described in the martyrological narratives of the Mercuriale and of his reputation in general, even among Catholic writers) reinforced this perception. Du Bourg was represented as the righteous magistrate obedient and loyal to a deaf and misguided throne, and a defender of the prerogatives of a weak Parlement manipulated by the enemies of the Reform. This was at the heart of Du Bourg's symbolism to the movement. Indeed, his story could have been the embodiment of the movement's ideological struggle.

Du Bourg's role as godly magistrate was explicitly identified in Crespin's introductory gloss to Du Bourg's account which described him "as a special example to all persons placed in the role of judges that they should learn that all dignities and honors should be deferred before the word and doctrine of Jesus Christ."[24] Thus, Du Bourg was to be held as a model for those of his profession—a man loyal to the state, but above all to God.

The portrayal of Du Bourg as the godly magistrate is best understood through the analysis of three sources: the interrogation, the confession, and the *Oraison*. Whereas the martyrological narratives paraphrased or cited at least two of the three of these texts, the words attributed to Du Bourg dramatized this image without need of much contextualization or embellishment by the authors. Within the longer narratives (including those outside of the martyrological collections), the former two texts (and *Oraison* in Crespin), along with the accounts of the Mercuriale, were the most central. Not only did these texts fulfill the requirement of public confession, but they also testify to the importance of the godly magistrate role in Du Bourg's image as a martyr.

Du Bourg's case did pose somewhat of a challenge regarding this role for the authors of the martyrological narratives. Presenting Du Bourg as a godly magistrate was not simply a matter of transcribing his words. Complicating this image was his escalating criticism of the state, beginning in a subtle form found in the interrogation, and increasing in vehemence in the final confession, finally climaxing in the tyrannicidal remonstrance of the *Oraison*.[25]

In these texts, Du Bourg spelled out what he perceived as his mandate as both a man of faith and a man of law. Up until his last appeal was turned down, Du Bourg was careful to offer evasive and ambiguous statements (while declaring his obedience and loyalty to the authority of the church and state) regarding the areas where state authority came into conflict with his religious beliefs. In the end, however, Du Bourg had difficulty remaining evasive. In the *Oraison*, his final statement to his colleagues, he judged the king conditionally guilty of *lèse majesté*—that is if the king persisted in his error. Thus the king, as a traitor, theoretically deserved death. This statement of rebellion would appear to have conflicted with the image of a martyr put forward by both martyrologists. Since an important point for both Crespin and Chandieu was the innocence of the martyrs and their loyalty to the king (even praying for his health), Du Bourg appears problematic as he seemed to at least put the idea of regicide on the table. It is crucial then to trace how this issue can be reconciled with Du Bourg's image as the godly magistrate within the context of the 1560s, the rhetoric of martyrdom, and the more general ideology of the Reform.

In both the confession and interrogation, Du Bourg elucidated the heart of the Reformed doctrine: *sola scriptura*. This was the starting point for his religious statement. From here, he challenged Catholic doctrine on such issues as fasting, clerical celibacy, idolatry, purgatory, the mediation of the saints, the priesthood of all believers, and the sacraments. He argued that any alteration, augmentation, or subtraction from what is in the Gospel by anyone offends God. He stated, "I believe that it is not permitted to any person, of whatever estate or quality, to adjust or diminish this very holy word, whether by law, edicts or ceremonies, or in any other way involving the administration of Christian religion."[26] Explicitly he identified the papacy as the source of this offense, while implicitly he also included the monarchy through its use of laws regarding methods of worship employed by the Huguenots such as the prohibition against assemblies.[27]

Both the confession and the interrogation were essentially Du Bourg's religious statements; nevertheless, he could not separate out the political implications of the doctrines supported by him. As a man of the law and member of the Parlement, Du Bourg understood the responsibility of the state to defend the church against heresy. In both his confession and interrogation, Du Bourg refined this role. He identified in his confession the two swords of church discipline, one ecclesiastical and spiritual, and the other political. The magistracy, the political sword of Church discipline and "an institution of God in His church," must defend the Church and its faithful members, and punish the wicked.[28] It was the magistrate's duty to uphold and protect the true doctrine against idolatry, to promote the glory of God, and to punish false prophets who lead the people incorrectly, teaching stories and traditions of men in place of the word of God. He added, "All persons, of whatever estate, sex or condition, must be subject to this magistrate, and obey him in all honest and reasonable things, so long as he represents the person of the great Lord, and so long as he wants to follow Him in all of His ways and for us to live in complete peace and tranquility under Him."[29] Additionally, in his interrogation, Du Bourg gave the state the authority to persecute heretics: "the King has all power, for God has entrusted him with the sword in his hand so that he may preserve His church in all of its integrity and purity." Du Bourg qualified this statement, however, as he stated, "It is necessary to know who are the heretics, and which is the heresy, since one could punish too cruelly those who deserve a light punishment."[30] Again, here we find an allusion to his request to call a council to determine a useful definition of heresy.

These three issues laid out by Du Bourg regarding the role of the state in the matter of heresy were in complete accord with those laid out by Théodore de Bèze in 1554. Essentially, Du Bourg was the embodiment of the magistrate envisioned by Bèze. Bèze wrote: "Now, to come at last to the point, the question that we have to treat consists of three parts. The first: to know whether it is necessary to punish heretics. The second: if punishing them should be done by the magistrate who administers justice. The last, whether they should be condemned to death."[31] The position of magistrate, for both Du Bourg and Bèze, was a sacred responsibility—in both relationship to God and to the state. The godly magistrate, then, was required to recognize the truth and uphold God's honor.

Calvin also acknowledged this dual responsibility in his *Institutes*, when he limited resistance to the king to the magistrates. For Calvin, and the other two as well, it was not only the magistrate's right, but his *duty* to resist a tyrant who abuses and proposes things contrary to God's law.[32] In all likelihood, Du Bourg had read the *Institutes* and was well aware of Calvin's resistance theory. When asked in his interrogation "which works he has seen by Luther, Calvin and others . . . he said that he had read some works by Calvin and others . . . and that he bought them from those bearers of books who come and go throughout the country."[33]

REGICIDE AND THE *ORAISON*

To the equation of the godly magistrate we must now add the controversial *Oraison*. The *Oraison* was written by Du Bourg probably between the denial of his last appeal and the reading in Parlement of his death sentence, a period of a few hours.[34] It was an address read to his former colleagues (now judges), intended to remind them of their duties to the state and to God, and to chastise them for betraying both. This was his final statement as a man of the law, and his first as a self-ordained vehicle of God.

What makes the *Oraison* controversial for those recounting Du Bourg's martyrdom both in the present and in the past is one infamous passage which appeared in the independent publication in 1560. It was left out of La Place's account (1565) which Crespin copied for his 1570 edition. The *Oraison* is not the only text of Du Bourg's that La Place included in excerpt form. In his account of Du Bourg, La Place cited only parts of the confession and interrogation, relying on paraphrasing to give the reader the main points. While the primarily focus of this section is on the *Oraison*, and La Place's censorship of this text, we must recognize that he did not quote any of the interrogation and transcribed very little of the confession, the largest being Du Bourg's conclusion.[35]

In the controversial passage, Du Bourg clearly advocated tyrannicide in the instance of a king or prince who subverts God's law:

> For He who made a king of our prince, and who gave him authority over so many people, was that not the Great Lord of all kings? Would He have put him in such a place so that he might oppose Him, exempting him from observing what He commanded of all nations, of Heaven and of earth? From this I conclude that our prince is subject, and all his people are subject to the commandments of the sovereign King, and that he too may commit the crime of *lèse majesté*, if he decides something contrary to the will of his King and ours, and that he would be guilty unto death if he persisted in an error that he should have condemned.[36]

As martyrologists represented their martyrs as loyal subjects and not extremists in a political sense, a statement such as this would have been quite problematic regardless of how implicit or explicit its meaning.

The converse of Calvin's and Bèze's right of the magistrate to resist was that the common man had no right to resist the tyranny of an ungodly ruler. Calvin stated that ordinary people had no other option than "to obey and suffer."[37] Du Bourg, however, was no common man. Whereas an ordinary man would have been condemned by the reformers (and excluded from the list of martyrs) for advocating such a stance, Du Bourg was fulfilling his duty as a magistrate (as envisioned by Calvin and Bèze) in the face of a tyrant who made laws against and persecuted those who followed God's law.[38] The king that Du Bourg railed against tolerated and championed what the Reform (and hence Du Bourg) perceived as idolatry; in other words the king had committed *lèse-majesté* against God, according to the First Commandment. Ideologically, Du Bourg was on solid ground.

Whereas historian David El Kenz rightly notes that this was the first time a recognized martyr had actively advocated regicide, we must balance this seemingly extreme and incongruous stance (versus the image of the martyr as loyal subject) with Du Bourg's position as magistrate. Put into the context that Du Bourg was the first sitting member of Parlement to be executed for heresy in over thirty years, it is understandable why his stance appears incongruous. But in fact his unique position vis-à-vis other martyrs made this stance his responsibility. The conflict, then, lies within the context of the martyrological accounts and the rhetoric of the passive martyr.

While the tyrannicidal passage has been discussed by some historians in terms of its inflammatory nature (and thus its exclusion from the martyrological narratives), it has primarily been looked at in isolation. To examine at this passage outside the context of the other sections that were censured and other texts written by reformers presents only part of the picture and thus obscures the complex transformation of Du Bourg the condemned Parlementarian to Du Bourg the godly magistrate/martyr for the cause.[39] In addition to the tyrannicidal passage, La Place omitted the more vehement sections from his text that dealt with divine vengeance visiting upon the unfaithful king (as it had with the kings of Babylonia and Assyria). He also left out the passage that criticized magistrates who abused those faithful to God just to please their king. For example La Place omitted the following passage:

> I conclude, too, with what you have heard, namely that you should be held responsible, that your dissimulation should be exposed as a perjury by which you grievously enchant your king and abuse the people. Now why is the poor Christian burned alive for being so faithful both to God and to him whom He has given to govern us? I hold that not in a single point should God's honor be stained. Alas, is this so contrary to the hearts of men? I say that I do not oppose the king's decrees at all when I wish that God's law should march in front of them. Since this is reasonable, why do you oppose it?[40]

Additionally, he censored the following section: "You kings of today, do you expect to escape God's fury when you show no reverence for His word? Have the pride, the presumption and the ingratitude of the kings of Babylonia and Assyria not suggested themselves to you?"[41] Du Bourg's condemnations were venomous, full of the self-righteousness of a man who has very little left to fear. These were carefully thought-out excisions, intended to leave a message of unjust persecution and admonition, but to excise any hint of rebellion, violence, or outright condemnation. La Place then retained the sections that relate how the faithful could not resist suffering as it was sent by God, that charged unjust persecution by the state, and that chastised (less vehemently) the magistrates to uphold God's law above that of men.

Interestingly, these two sections cut by La Place were taken by Du Bourg almost directly from Calvin's *Institutes*. With regard to the magistrate's duty to counteract the tyrant, Calvin stated, "I am so far from forbidding them to withstand the fierce licentiousness of kings in accordance with their duty, that if they wink at kings who violently fall upon and assault the lowly common fold, I declare that their dissimulation involves nefarious perfidy, because they dishonestly betray the freedom of the people, of which they know that they have been appointed protectors by God's ordinance."[42] Additionally, Calvin described the divine vengeance wreaked upon tyrants in the past, using the same examples cited by Du Bourg, especially those of the Egyptians and the Babylonians: "Thus he tamed the pride of Tyre by the Egyptians; the insolence of the Egyptians by the Assyrians; the ferocity of the Assyrians by the Chaldeans; the confidence of Babylon by the Medes and Persians. . . ."[43] As stated earlier, Du Bourg had admitted possessing books by Calvin, and it appears, then, that he had a more than passing familiarity with his resistance theory and the responsibility of the godly magistrate.

The question remains, then, if these sections were in accord with Calvin's own writings, why would they be cut from the version of the *Oraison* included in La Place (and Crespin), and the text completely excluded from Chandieu, who had at least knowledge of the *Oraison*?[44] One possible answer lies in the one of the purposes of the martyrologies: to provide models for the faithful with regard to correct belief, behavior, and comportment in the face of persecution. Both Crespin and Chandieu considered their martyrs to be "mirrors" for the faithful. And although Du Bourg was held by Crespin as a model for men of the law, his assertions of tyrannicide and divine vengeance were not necessarily acceptable in terms of practice and emulation for the vast majority of readers. Though the rhetoric of tyrannicide and divine vengeance would eventually be employed by Protestant polemicists, the actual advocacy of tyrannicide and punishment of the king (even by God) did not fit with the image of the martyr forwarded by the martyrologists and the Reform before the St. Bartholomew's Day Massacre (1572).[45] Prior to the massacre, pamphlets advocating forms of "tyrannicide" and divine justice were directed toward the "wicked advisors" of the king, namely the Guise but not toward the king himself.

The martyr was to be a passive participant in the struggle against persecution. His active participation was limited to the public prac-

tice and confession of faith. His passive behavior in the face of persecution and torture made him a perfect vehicle for the legitimacy
of the Huguenot movement. Vengeance was not to be part of the
rhetoric of a martyr, nor was the advocacy or practice of violence or
destruction regardless of the martyr's office or position. Whereas Du
Bourg was given a special standing and prominence in the roll call
of martyrs due to his office and fame, his image still had to conform
to the model of martyrdom that most effectively carried the Reformed message. Though prominent and with many unique aspects
to his situation, Du Bourg the martyr was transformed into a stereotype. The passive martyr was the symbol of the unjust persecution of
innocents whose only "crime" was upholding the Gospel. They were
described as being the victims of the "ravenous wolves," blameless
"lambs" whose "innocent blood" was shed and who were devoured
and murdered. On his title page, Chandieu stated that "We are free
to die for Your sake every day, and we are counted like lambs for the
slaughter."[46] The lamb imagery reinforces the *imatio Christi* theme as
the lamb was often employed as a symbol of Christ, a reference to his
sacrifice as well as his passivity in the face of his judges and tomen-
tors. Apologists of the Reform repeatedly referred to lambs pastoral
sacrifice to describe not only martyrs, but the persecution of the
faithful in general.[47] Hence, innocence in the face of accusations of
sedition, rebellion, and passivity when confronted and persecuted
were essential elements in the image of the martyr. For example,
both Crespin and Chandieu excluded almost all Protestants who engaged in iconoclasm from their community of martyrs, even if they
died a martyr's death. Such behavior (which would also include violent acts or seditious language) would be a liability in terms of proving the righteousness of the cause with regard to obtaining recognition or tolerance from the throne—goals to which the rhetoric of
martyrdom prior to August 24, 1572, aspired.

An exception to this interpretation of the "loyal" martyr came
from Bèze, in his *Du Droit des Magistrats*. In this work he included
"not only those who have conquered without resistance, and by patience only, against tyrants who have persecuted the truth, but those
also who, authorized by law and by competent authorities, devoted
their strength to the defense of the true religion" in his definition of
a martyr.[48] This definition was certainly not acceptable prior to the
St. Bartholomew's Day Massacre, and it proved too radical even *after*
the massacre, when more aggressive resistance was advocated. Bèze's

work was censored by the Genevan Consistory due to its radical statements.[49] Thus, even up to 1574 (the year *Du Droit des Magistrats* was
written), passive martyrdom was still held as the model for the
Genevan Reform, though the rhetoric in France had begun to embrace a more active form of martyrdom.

The political context of the 1560s and early 1570s, the period
when the later narratives were written, is especially relevant to the
treatment of the *Oraison* in the narratives and its independent publication in 1560. Before the St. Bartholomew's Day Massacre, many reformers expressed hope of finding a way to soften the hearts of their
persecutors, of lifting the "veil of ignorance" from their eyes. For example, while this hope did wax and wane during the 1560s,
Chandieu still expressed this desire in the prefatory epistle to his
martyrology as he explained his reasons for writing it:

> The hope of the profit and happiness that this will bring to you, my
> very dear brothers, to see here an image of all the times that it has
> pleased God to test us together with tribulations, and then the desire
> I have to call back to examine our case anew the poor ignorant folk
> who have become our enemies in such numbers, to make them real-
> ize the injustices and the cruelties they have committed, and to bring
> them, if it is possible, by this means to some reasonable settlement.[50]

Many pamphlets of the early to mid 1560s, especially the *remonstrances* and *advertissements* which detailed and decried the persecution, reveal the hope to inform and sway the hearts the king and/or
queen mother, who were described as blinded by the influence of
the enemies of the Reform.[51] This was not an unfounded hope as
under the regency of the Catherine de Medici, the throne had been
more willing to compromise with the Huguenots as a way of counterbalancing the power of the Guise faction. The political situation
was more complex than this however, and the throne precariously
sat between the two forces.

More immediately, right before the Conspiracy of Amboise in
1560, religious and political tensions had reached a high point—
contributing not least of all to this was the death of Henri II and the
execution of Anne Du Bourg. The Huguenot movement was becoming restive. Exasperation with the determination of Henri II to exterminate the faithful, the dashing of hopes for a more tolerant new
king with assumption of power by the Guises after Henri's death, the
purposeful and well-organized campaign to hunt Parisian Protes-

tants in the summer and autumn of 1559, and finally Du Bourg's "unjust" death led to a movement ready to lash out in response. Discontent on the part of not only the Huguenots but also the lesser nobility over the influence of the Guises boiled over in the form of a plot to seize physically control of the court and king—to "free" him from the grasp of his "evil advisors."[52] Politically, this period witnessed a large influx of the lesser nobility into the Reform faction, whether it was due to opposition to the Guisards or to true religious conversion, the effect was the same: an increasing military character in the movement.[53] This was a relatively rapid response mostly on the part of the newer, more politically leaning members of the movement.

It was during this frenzied time that the *Oraison* as an independent pamphlet was published. This political context and the shifts that occurred in the following years shed some light on why the text was published, then suppressed or ignored. In the chaos immediately following Du Bourg's death, probably little was thought of the political implications of his statement. The rush to enshrine him among those who had received the "crown of the martyrs" and to protest the unjustness of his execution led to its immediate publication along with the rest of the early texts on his martyrdom. Additionally, as Raemond points out, Du Bourg's execution generated an enormous reaction in Paris, to the point that the crown ordered an accompaniment of four hundred horsemen to guard Du Bourg on his way to the gibbet. The tensions did not die down quickly, and in fact increased. Hence, the *Oraison,* with all its vehemence, expressed the frustration experienced by many in the French Reform (though not the Genevan—Calvin still counseled patience and passive martyrdom as the only righteous response except for the princes of the blood) in the direct aftermath of Du Bourg's death and the heightened political atmosphere surrounding the minor king.

The contemporary importance and influence of this text as an independent pamphlet are debatable. David El Kenz emphasizes it in terms of it ushering in a new type of rhetoric and trend in the Reform movement. More specifically he argues: "In this crucial year of 1560, the martyr no longer seems effective enough to outweigh a desire for the death of the sovereign."[54] However, this view is problematic regarding Du Bourg's qualified views on tyrannicide. Du Bourg's words and ideas as found complete in the *Oraison* indeed are echoed in the post-St. Bartholomew's Day pamphlets, but their weight dur-

ing at least the first half of the 1560s is uncertain. The *Oraison*, unlike the confession or interrogation, did not see print again until
1565 in its truncated form. Only Crespin cited the text later, otherwise it remained lost until the "discovery" of the independent pamphlet by Leliévre in the nineteenth century. Whether this was due to
purposeful suppression or simply that it was not widely disseminated
remains to be seen. It must be noted, however, that according to
Leliévre, the text of the *Oraison* was smuggled out of the Bastille the
same way as, and very soon after, the confession. If this is true, then
the document should have been as widely available as the confession
itself unless the text was found to be too subversive by editors to be
included in its complete form.[55] Hence, if the martyr had ceased to
be effective, then would not the polemicists and martyrologists have
at least celebrated and embraced more vigorously Du Bourg's views
on tyrannicide?

In the aftermath of the Conspiracy of Amboise (in which Chandieu himself had been implicated) the Huguenots declared their
loyalty repeatedly to the throne, though calling for a council of the
Princes of the Blood (especially Condé and Navarre—both with
Protestant sympathies) to aid the young king in governing. By
spring 1562 major shifts began on the parts of both the crown and
movement. First, religious and political tensions had again reached
their limit, and after the Massacre of Vassy in March of that year,
which tallied twenty-three Protestant deaths and over one hundred
injured (including men, women, and children), the Reform movement had shifted from a religious effort and coalesced into a military force, declaring its "true" intention to protect the king and free
him from his evil advisors—the Guise.[56] After war broke out, the
movement took up arms and proceeded to lay siege to Orleans and
threaten Paris itself. Even at war, though, the Huguenot faction still
clung to their stated loyalty to the throne and protest against the accusation of sedition.

With the Edict of Pacification of 1563, two additional shifts occurred, this time on the parts of the crown and the more resistant
magistracy and people. During this decade Henri's II zeal for Protestant blood gave way to the moderate stance toward the Reform by the
regency of Catherine. This was not due to a change in religious leanings, but to an effort to stabilize the throne, on which a vulnerable
minor sat, and to counterbalance the Guisard faction.[57] This peace,
however, was uneasy and difficult to enforce. Popular violence and re-

sistance on the part of many of the parlements—the Parisian especially—continued the persecution and prosecution of Protestants.
This resistance by the magistracy marked a third long-term shift: from
1562 on the prosecution of Protestants underwent a secularization.
Even the methods employed in the execution of Protestants illustrate
this shift: from this point on Protestants were hung as traitors more
frequently than they were burned at the stake as heretics.[58]

In the wake of all three of these major shifts, the Huguenot faction was not willing to alienate completely a throne which appeared
at times throughout the decade on the verge of toleration, though
the faction continued to clamor for more rights and recognition.
Nevertheless, it relied on a careful rhetoric that emphasized its loyalty and unjust suffering caused by lack of enforcement of the edict.[59]

It was in this political context that the later (censored) versions of
the *Oraison* appeared as well as the other major narratives on Du
Bourg's martyrdom. This context might explain both the publication of the independent pamphlet of the *Oraison*, and its censoring
later on. The passive representations of the martyrs, Du Bourg included, allowed the Huguenot faction to demonstrate its loyalty to
the throne even as it took to the battlefield.

The image of Du Bourg the godly magistrate/martyr presented a
complex problem for those who constructed narratives of his account. Whereas his own words provided substance to this image,
they also complicated it and at the heart of the problem was the
Oraison. Though conforming to the responsibilities of the godly/
magistrate, it conflicted with the image of the passive martyr—an
image made necessary due to the political and social context of persecution and the efforts to combat it.

APPEALS AND CONFESSIONS

The historical case of Anne Du Bourg presented two other major
sticking points for those who presented him as a true, constant martyr for the cause.[60] First, there were the repeated appeals by Du
Bourg, which stretched out his case a number of months. Second,
there was the issue of the "ambiguous confession," the text of which
was lost although there are numerous references to this vacillation.
In some ways these problems or "irregularities" testified to the hu-
manity of Du Bourg. Though problematic in terms of his representation as a constant martyr, the irregularities (especially his ambigu-

ous confession) revealed to the reader a side of the martyr that he or
she could sympathize with—the all too human desire to preserve
one's life. Ironically, it was exactly this desire that the martyr must
joyfully and triumphantly overcome. Thus it is important to examine
the ways in which the martyrologists and hagiographers of Du Bourg
handled these issues and conformed Du Bourg to the image of the
constant martyr regardless of these "ambiguities." These two issues
provide more precise examples of the ways in which the authors of
the martyrological narratives handled or shaped a situation that
might have adversely affected the "credibility" or reputation of a
martyr. Du Bourg's vacillation must have posed a dilemma for those
who sought to represent him as a constant, willing martyr. Much was
riding on the outcome of Du Bourg's case while he lived, but just as
crucial to the Reform movement was the posthumous image of this
important figure.

There were three ways in which the narratives (both independent
and those included in the martyrologies or histories) approach
these ambiguities. Some omitted them completely, out of ignorance
of the situation or due to self-censorship. It is impossible to discern
whether the cause is the former or the latter due to unknown authorship or the inaccessibility of information regarding the author's
motivations. Other texts made passing references to the situations,
while giving no description or explanation. In all likelihood this was
due to a desire to focus on those events (i.e., the final confession or
the interrogation) which supported a more positive representation
of Du Bourg. The third approach involved a defense of the events
and explanations that shed a more positive light on the situations.

The first example, then, of how his hagiographers dealt with a
problematic situation can be found in the descriptions of his appeals
process. After his initial condemnation by the bishop of Paris, Du
Bourg embarked on a number of appeals—five before his degradation and at least one more before his execution—to both ecclesiastical and secular authorities.[61] These appeals were described by the
martyrologists and pamphleteers, some in passing and others in
depth. Only a few sources expressed some unease with the number
of appeals and felt the need to offer some explanation. Among these
were Crespin, Chandieu, and La Place.[62] In contrast the *Vraye histoire*
and the *Confession* offered only relatively brief descriptions, with no
explanation save Du Bourg's protest of enmity on the part of the cardinals of Lorraine and Sens.

Why would these appeals be problematic? Appeals were common among the narratives of other martyrs. The problem here was the number of appeals as well as the notoriety of the case. According to La Place: "some councillors of the said court of Parlement, and also others, said that all of these delays were only postponements achieved by the said Du Bourg in order to gain time, and that they showed well that his zeal was not really for God and the religion that he believed in, and of which he made a semblance."[63] It was the matter of Du Bourg's sincerity that needed to be defended. But it was not only the enemies of Du Bourg that probably murmured about his sincerity in light of the delays. Crespin (Chandieu) described another group that Du Bourg himself felt deserved an explanation: the Reformed Church itself. He explained that Du Bourg wrote to the faithful, hoping not to offend them, reassuring them and explaining why he opened up yet another appeal.[64] Thus, these appeals raised the question for contemporaries of how dedicated Du Bourg was to both the faith and the embrace of his possible martyrdom. This question dealt directly with the image of Du Bourg the martyr—of how the reader might interpret the repeated appeals. Additionally, there was the question of the didactic function of the martyr's experience. What did this teach the reader about the behavior of a martyr and was this particular behavior to be emulated?

Chandieu and Crespin attempted to justify these appeals—not so much on the grounds for which they were opened, but in terms of the martyr's overall motivation. To do so they offered Du Bourg's explanation to his coreligionists: "That it was not at all that he wanted to gain time, and to prolong his life by subterfuges, but that it was in order to take away any reason for thinking that he had doomed himself, and that he was the cause of his own early death, if he had forgotten anything that might be used to justify himself."[65] Du Bourg himself, then, must have been concerned about how he appeared to the faithful. In offering this explanation in his letters to the Reformed Church of Paris Du Bourg appeared as a rational (not fanatic) adherent to the faith.[66] In this explanation, his end would be a passive martyrdom, brought upon him by God's grace and the intolerance of his persecutors rather than by any rash actions or neglect of his own.

Early Christian writers such as Origen wrote concernedly about the haste with which some Christians sought their own deaths. Here in Du Bourg's own words (according to Chandieu and Crespin) we find echoes of this sentiment. Du Bourg's martyrdom, as it is alluded to by both himself and his hagiographers, was a gift from God. As a martyr, he was God's vehicle and as such the timing of his death was not for him to precipitously decide. Rather, the more appeals he opened, so he explained, the more time he had to offer testimony of God's truth and possibly convince his persecutors of the justness of his cause. The recusation he had requested of the cardinals might have given Du Bourg a more favorable hearing and outcome in the Parlement, thus proving the righteousness of his cause and hopefully setting a precedent for the treatment of other Protestants, not to mention saving his own life.

Another problematic situation was that of the ambiguous confession. According to both Catholic and Protestant sources, Du Bourg wavered in his conviction at one point during the appeals process.[67] On December 13, after his degradation but before a final judgment was made on his last appeal to Parlement, Du Bourg submitted an equivocal confession. It gave hope to the court that he would return to the Catholic faith and avoid the death sentence. Six days later, after communicating with the pastor Augustin Marlorat, Du Bourg recanted this confession and returned to his earlier conviction, sending a newly written and firmly Calvinist confession to the court. In light of Crespin's first mark of the martyr (the unequivocal confession of the correct faith), Du Bourg's vacillation, though short-lived, complicated his image and needed to be addressed.

Among the Protestant narratives, we know of this ambiguous confession from Crespin (Chandieu), La Place, and de la Planche.[68] Neither the *Vraye histoire* nor the *Confession* made any mention of this vacillation. Whereas Crespin (Chandieu) and de la Planche gave great detail about the circumstances surrounding this confession, La Place briefly (almost furtively) mentioned it. La Place then moved on to describe and include excerpts from the final unequivocal declaration of faith that Du Bourg made a number of days before his execution. La Place wrote, "Du Bourg was presented to the said court bearing his complete confession, by which he declared that he wished to be correctly understood, revoking another ambiguous and doubtful confession that some of his close friends on the said court had counseled him to make that he might escape."[69] La Place's description, though short, gives us a common thread that was shared by all the texts that mention this confession. All of these texts attributed Du Bourg's momentary lapse (as it was described) to the influence of inconstant friends. Whereas Crespin (Chandieu) described these friends as "temporizers," de la Planche and La Place were more generous.[70] De la Planche, like La Place, did not make a judgment about Du Bourg's friends, and instead alluded to their concern for his life.[71] Regardless of how the friends were described, the responsibility of this confession was placed directly on them, not Du Bourg, thus lessening the negative impact of his semi-recantation and the undertones of Nicodemism.

The inclusion of a description of Marlorat's letter, found in Crespin (Chandieu) is an important aspect in the explanation of Du Bourg's vacillation. This letter explained to Du Bourg, as well as to the reader, the responsibility of the martyr not only to God but to the faithful as well.[72] It presented an opportunity to remind both audiences of the role the martyr played in the larger struggle of submission to God in the face of persecution. The martyr was part of a greater community, and his struggles were not simply his own. Hence, the inclusion of this letter turned what could have been seen as an embarrassment into a learning experience. Du Bourg then appeared refreshed and reinvigorated by the support of his community, enough so that he could embrace his fate unflinchingly. What appeared originally as a blow, turned into a victory.

The accounts of martyrs are almost written in reverse. The outcome of the stories is made evident in the identification of the subjects as martyrs, and the narratives of their martyrdoms follow a set path. The martyr himself, though unique in terms of the specifics of his case or experience, is transformed into symbol or stereotype with specific characteristics shared by all those who bear the title.

In Anne Du Bourg we see the transformation of a judge whose legal case, writings, and imprisonment involved aspects that did not quite conform with the image of the faithful, passive martyr established by the Reform before St. Bartholomew's Day 1572. This chapter, through the analysis of the Protestant texts that recounted his martyrdom, has examined the ways in which Du Bourg's case presented particular challenges for his hagiographers, and the ways in which these challenges were met.

The purpose of this study was not only to reconstruct a historical narrative of Du Bourg's case but also to examine the ways in which his posthumous image was shaped by his hagiographers. To obtain an understanding of the phenomena of martyrdom during the

French Reformation, a study of the rhetoric surrounding the representation of a martyr is just as crucial as the actual details of the individual's experience. As arguably the most celebrated martyr of the French Reform, Anne Du Bourg, both the martyr and the man, was a battlefield over which many political and religious forces fought. The use of his martyrdom as a weapon in the arsenal of the Reform was complicated, and it illustrates the complexity of martyrdom itself—both the act and the textual reconstruction. And while other martyrs' cases might not have been as well known nor as ambiguous, Du Bourg's transformation raises questions about the general nature of the martyr and the interpretation of the act.

4

Gender and
the Rhetoric
of Martyrdom

WHILE IN PRISON, ANNE DU BOURG CAME IN CONTACT WITH MAR-
guerite Le Riche, the wife of a Parisian bookseller and a fellow prisoner for the Calvinist faith.[1] Le Riche, Du Bourg explained in Jean
Crespin's account of her martyrdom, consoled, counseled, and exhorted him and others to be strong in their convictions and faith. Du
Bourg actually singled her out among his fellow prisoners for her
role in his journey: "A woman showed me my lesson and taught me
how I must carry this vocation."[2] This interaction was left out of Du
Bourg's much grander account, yet it is highlighted and celebrated
in Le Riche's narrative. This omission or the positioning of this interaction begins to allude to the ambiguous role of gender in the
rhetoric of martyrdom.

Among the most powerful images from the French Reformation
is a description by Catholic polemicist Florimond de Raemond of
the execution of Protestant women. He wrote how "simple weak
women seek out torments to prove their faith. Going to their death
they cry out only "Christ, Savior," and sing some Psalm. Young vir-
gins march most gayly to their execution, as if they were going to the
marriage bed . . . in a word, to die smiling, like those who eat the
Sardinian herb."[3] The impact of the spectacle was not lost on those
who witnessed it. Raemond continued his description by stating how
these demonstrations of constancy by the condemned women "cast
confusion not only in the souls of the simple, but also in those of the
greatest . . . [who] cover them with their cloak."[4] Most significantly,
these displays caused curious spectators to seek out the censored

Protestant books as a way of understanding the faith and motivations of these women. Raemond thus acknowledged the power of the female martyr, but he was not unique in this recognition. Early Christian martyrologists as well as those of the sixteenth century were well aware of the female martyrs' appeal and effect on both believers and nonbelievers.[5] The spectacle and theme of the small defeating the great appealed to and served the ends of persecuted Christians.

During its renaissance in the sixteenth century, martyrdom itself was not defined as a gendered act. In the prefatory epistle to the 1570 edition of his *Histoire des vrays tesmoins* the French martyrologist Jean Crespin did not differentiate between the sexes when listing the marks of a martyr.[6] The requirements were the same for all—the most subjective requirement consisting of assistance from God. This mark was most evident in the female martyrs, who, as the "weaker sex," could not have been constant and endured their sufferings without God's aid, which further legitimized the movement as favored by God. It denoted a type of election and created a division between ordinary society and the martyrs, though they were all bound by their common suffering. Along with election there was elevation—a rising above common men and women. Crespin, however, did construct the accounts of female martyrs differently from those of their male counterparts, and his instructions to his female readers hint at underlying issues of gender, authority, and social order. Thus while gender was not an issue in terms of identifying a martyr, the representation and interpretation of their act to an audience most certainly was.

The purpose of this chapter is twofold. The first goal is to address the concepts of martyrdom and martyrology, primarily the differences between the two. Second and illustrative of the first, the essay examines the problem of the textual representation of French female martyrs included in Crespin's *Histoire* in light of the sixteenth-century social and religious need to maintain traditional gender roles. More concisely it asks how these women, who deviated from prescribed behavior by engaging in social disobedience, by leaving their families, and by engaging in theological disputes, could be held as models for ordinary women. The answer can be found in the rhetoric surrounding their stories and their representation within them.

MARTYRDOM VS MARTYROLOGY:
DISOBEDIENCE TRANSFORMED

Anxiety over exemplary women in religious contexts is not a new theme in the historiography of antiquity through to early modern Europe.[7] In the study of martyrdom and martyrology much has been made of the female martyrs, mostly of those who met their deaths during the early Christian persecution.[8] Historians of antiquity and early Christianity have described how the female martyrs and their acts caused great discomfiture once the church was institutionalized, and the ways in which their narratives were shaped to ameliorate issues of gender. The accounts of female martyrs, such as Perpetua, Blandina, and Felicity, have provided historians with a rich resource from which to draw. A particularly pertinent study is Joyce Salisbury's examination of the martyrdom of Perpetua in *Perpetua's Passion: the Death and Memory of a Young Roman Woman.* Salisbury's work provides us with an example of the issues described above that begins with Perpetua's arrest and continues through her medieval representations. This study is especially useful in that it traces the evolution of her narrative from its origins through the ascendant church. Salisbury finds that the interpretations Perpetua's martyrdom were modified or reshaped to support the late antique/medieval interpretations of gender roles. Whereas the actual martyr abandoned her husband and child, rejected her father, and essentially led her fellow martyrs to their fate in the arena, a fourth-century representation plays down her leadership role and her agency in rejecting her family.[9] She notes that instead of rewriting the accounts, later commentaries emphasized certain aspects of the martyr that made them more appealing as role models for women, "and thus less threatening to the social order."[10] For example, Augustine and bishop Quodvultdeo wrote sermons dealing with Perpetua's abandonment of her family and role as mother and wife. These sermons reveal their unease with her rejection of traditional gender roles. In essence they attempted to ameliorate the upheaval of the social order celebrated in the account through the representation of the martyr.

Within the Reformation era, historians have recently turned to the female martyrs as a way of understanding larger issues of religiosity and narrative. Ellen Macek, Thomas Freeman, and Sarah Elizabeth Wall have examined Foxe's *Book of Martyrs* and the female mar-

tyrological narratives. Whereas Macek takes a broader cohort from
Foxe from which to draw her conclusions, Freeman and Wall focus
on the account of Anne Askew. Macek's study, "The Emergence of a
Feminine Spirituality in *The Book of Martyrs*," adopts a modern feminist perspective, seeking to locate women's spiritual agency through
the martyrological accounts.[11] Her concern is with the martyrs themselves, not larger messages of the martyrology within the context of
Reformed ideology. While it might be possible to glean instances of
female spiritual agency from Crespin's accounts of female martyrs,
my concern instead is not with the martyrs' experiences themselves
but how they are communicated to a specific audience. Freeman
and Wall in their essay, "Racking the Body, Shaping the Text: The Account of Anne Askew is Foxe's *Book of Martyrs*," address Askew's account not necessarily from a gendered perspective and instead focus
on the issue of authorial authority. The authors compare earlier accounts of Askew's martyrdom to Foxe's narrative and find that the
recent judgments of Foxe (that he is more "faithful" to Askew's own
words) to be imposing unfairly modern standards of authorship.
Their study is an analysis of the evolution of Askew's account, not
one that concerns itself necessarily with issues of gender, and in fact
they criticize feminist interpretations of "voice." While these studies
are useful in terms of raising questions of agency or the authorial relationship between martyrologist and martyr, neither is truly concerned with the larger messages being disseminated by the martyrologies regarding the gender roles of women within the Calvinist
faith.

To explore the problematic nature of female martyrs vis-à-vis
Calvinist ideology, it is helpful to place them in the broader theoretical framework of how martyrdom works. In doing so we can look beyond their particular individual deaths and begin to examine issues
of mandate, authority, and representation. This framework differentiates between the functions of "martyrdom" and "martyrology." Martyrdom, the act, occupies a separate created space and has a different function as a weapon than the martyrology, the text.

Martyrdom is a physical act of social disobedience and subversion: justified by her direct mandate from God, a martyr challenges
and inverts any authority or established order. By willingly renounc-
ing all that could be physically taken away from her—most importantly, her life—a martyr ascends beyond the reach and power of the
persecutor. Martyrdom is the act of an individual who defines herself

in terms of her responsibility to God, rather than to the temporal world. In essence a martyr reconfigures (though not reconstructs) society along different boundaries, based ostensibly not upon the values of the temporal world (i.e., wealth, intellect, and social standing), but upon the negation of those values. Thus, the power of martyrdom is primarily subversive and destructive—a self-justified ability to invert or destroy the worldly foundations upon which society is built. It is a potentially dangerous phenomenon when left on its own without any guiding interpretation. Martyrdom is the ultimate social disobedience.

A problem exists, however, when a persecuted faction cares also for social order and discipline. In the case of a newly evolving faith, these concerns are revealed in the attempts to institutionalize the faith, to create some sort of church discipline, and to move beyond its revolutionary phase.[12] The martyrology ameliorates the threats within martyrdom, transforming its destructive power into a formative one. In contrast to martyrdom, the martyrology functions to place the act in a framework that gives it meaning and significance.[13] The martyrological narrative textually interprets the act of martyrdom to be one supportive of order, community, and ideology. Martyrs' accounts are sanitized and contextualized by the incorporation of doctrine and propaganda in order to legitimate, support, and transmit the ideology of a persecuted faction. In many ways, this textualization rebuilds foundations destroyed by the act, but in accordance with the needs of a movement.

The female martyrs of the French Reformation embody this transformation, and in turn they became important weapons in the eschatological arsenal of the Reform movement. The use of women in the challenge to Catholicism solidified the perception that it was God's will being fulfilled through the martyrs. God's favor and support of the Reformed cause became much more evident as his victories and will were carried out by a "weaker vessel." By no means could women, seen as inherently weak and frail, have completed the task of martyrdom without God's aid and mandate. Through their perceived empowerment by God, female martyrs inverted the social order by confronting their powerful male persecutors and "triumphing" over them. Female martyrs' participation then served to support and further legitimate the righteousness of the cause. Therefore, these women fit into the first half of the paradigm—the use of social inversion to challenge the existing order.

As the martyrologies had an instructive function, the question arises as to how female readers were to perceive female martyrs and apply the lessons of these stories in their own lives. Actual female martyrs—versus textual constructions—had abandoned their sanctioned duties as mothers and wives and entered into public positions as religious agitators and rebels, challenging authority figures and accepted gender roles. Through their martyrdom women achieved the same "elevation" above ordinary society as male martyrs. In the attempt to reestablish social order, how was it possible to reconcile the accounts of these female martyrs with the socially (but not necessarily spiritually) subordinate position for women ordained by Calvin and other reformers?[14] The answer lay in the construction of the accounts and the representation of the acts themselves. Here we find the female martyrs incorporated into the doctrinal framework of French Calvinism—disarmed, so to speak.

CALVINIST PRESCRIPTIONS FOR WOMEN: DAUGHTERS OF EVE, PATRONS OF THE REFORM

Prior to and during the Wars of Religion, the Reform movement needed women's participation for propagandist purposes, as patrons, and as missionaries within their homes and environments. Their involvement in these areas has been noted not only by modern historians, but also by contemporary polemicists criticizing the Reform. Florimond de Raemond discussed the roles that women played in spreading the Reform, especially the influence of Marguerite de Navarre and other noble women as protectors and patrons of the reformers, and even listed their names.[15] He dedicated quite a bit of ink solely to women's involvement. They had been fooled, he explained, much like Eve in the garden of Eden, by the reformers whom he equated with the serpent. Raemond also described the influence of ordinary married women who act as "Eves," encouraging their husbands to convert: "He [the serpent/reformer] well knows that often man is an inaccessible place and cannot be taken by any other means except that of woman."[16] Widows and young unattached women, Raemond claimed, were the favorite targets of the reformers, as they did not have a husband who would keep them in line and give them good counsel.[17] Women's inherent weaknesses, whether they be noble or ordinary in status, made them vulnerable to heresy. Raemond looked to the church fathers and history to support his belief, citing Tertullian's admonishment, "You are the door of the devil." He also found resonance in Jerome's disdainful assessment of women, "It is the characteristic of the woman to allow herself to be deceived . . . and to deceive others."[18] Like the Protestant martyrologists, Raemond found legitimacy for his perspective among these early Christians, adding that even in the early Church, powerful women always protected heretics.[19]

Raemond, for all intents and purposes, gave us a somewhat accurate—albeit quite slanted—picture of women's involvement. There ware numerous examples of French noblewomen, informed by humanist educations, engaging in active careers within the Huguenot movement and evangelical reform efforts.[20] Their significance should not be underestimated. Nancy Roelker, in her study of these noblewomen, notes that while statistically their overall number is relatively low (she gives the number as "a few hundred at the height of the movement in the 1560s"), "the position of these women at the apex of the social and political pyramid in a markedly hierarchical society gives them an importance out of proportion to their numbers."[21] Not only did these women protect reformers in their courts and promote Calvinist teachings in their lands, but those who were the most politically prominent among them helped direct policy and negotiate with both the crown and foreign states. Raemond rightly pointed to Marguerite d'Angoulême, the sister of King Francis I and Queen of Navarre, as a significant force in the Huguenot movement. Marguerite sheltered numerous early reformers such as Gérard Roussel, and even gave safe harbor to Calvin at her estates.[22] Her circle of women spawned the next generation of female patrons and even gave birth to the male leaders of the Huguenot faction. There is also significant evidence that these women introduced their husbands and families to the faith, though many of the most active of these noblewomen were widows.[23]

What about common women? What type of Protestant activities did these non-noble French wives and mothers engage in? In her seminal study, "City Women and Religious Change," Natalie Zemon Davis examines these questions. Davis finds that Calvinism appealed more to the women from the artisan, merchant, and professional classes than from the unskilled masses.[24] These women knew scripture, confronted priests, defied Catholic traditions such as fasting, engaged in iconoclastic behavior, attended assemblies, and even participated in armed uprisings. "If she were a printer's wife or widow, she could help get out a Protestant edition to spread the word about tyrannical priests."[25] Additionally, women's homes were used for Calvinist services. In the Midi, for example, trials were held against two wives who allowed a Calvinist preacher to sermonize in their homes.[26] The activities of the female martyrs in Crespin's martyrology also reflect these activities.[27] And while Protestant women engaged in these efforts, Davis, unlike Roelker and Raemond, finds no evidence of a preponderance of common women leading their husbands to Calvinism rather than the other way around.[28] However, there is tremendous difficulty in discerning this information due to a lack of source material that specifically illustrates this causation.

Information from the heresy trials in France shed light on the number of women who were actually executed for their agitation on behalf of the Reform movement or their direct beliefs. With regard to the trials held prior to 1560, the number of women executed is relatively low. During this earlier part of the French Reform, "women accounted for less than 5 percent of all French martyrs. . . . Except for a few autonomous women in unusual situations, early 'Lutheranism' was overwhelmingly a man's crime."[29] The percentage does seem to correspond with the low number of French female martyrs included in the martyrologies even after 1560 though the overall number does rise.[30] This does not, however, mean that women were insignificant to the larger Calvinist movement. It simply reflects the legal reality that women received lesser punishments than men in cases of heresy. For example in the case of the Fourteen of Meaux (1546), out of the original sixty-one Protestants arrested for "reason of case and crimes of heresy, abominable blasphemy, private conventicles and illicit assemblies, schism and errors," nineteen were women.[31] Men, women, and children had gathered at the house of Etienne Mangin to celebrate the Lord's supper, sing psalms, and read scripture, rather than attend Catholic services commemorating the birth of the Virgin Mary. The assembly was denounced, and its attendees were taken into custody. Only fourteen of the sixty-one were condemned to be executed—all men. The women were given lesser punishments of the *amende honorable* or assisting in some capacity at the execution, though they, like the men, were all present at the Mangin house at the time of arrest.[32]

Ideologically, however, there was no permanent place for women within the formal structure of the French Calvinist religious movement. Women's salvation was closely tied to the household. Obedience, endurance, and duty were operative words in Calvin's commentaries on women. They reflected his concern for their proper order and placement within a patriarchy. The image of the Protestant female martyr, therefore, needed to be constructed so as not to be a threat to the gendered order, while still encouraging women's participation.

While Calvin was not the only reformer who helped shape the gendered order of Reformed theology, he nevertheless was one of the most prominent figures from whom advice was sought regarding issues concerning women, and his writings ostensibly defined the patriarchal nature of Calvinism in France. Testifying to his influence are numerous examples of Huguenot women seeking Calvin's counsel concerning their role and abilities to act within the constraints of their faith and the difficulties of marriage and family life vis-à-vis persecution.[33] Regarding the situation confronting Huguenot women, his was the voice resounded the loudest and most frequently.[34]

In his biblical commentaries, especially those on Genesis, 1 Corinthians, and 1 Timothy, Calvin addressed women's status and roles within the family and society. According to Calvin, though women shared spiritual equality with men there was an essential inequality between the sexes within society: "as regards spiritual connection in the sight of God, and inwardly in the conscience, Christ is the head of the man and of the woman without any distinction, because, as to that, there is no regard paid to male or female; but as regards external arrangement and political decorum, the man follows Christ and the woman the man, so that they are not upon the same footing, but, on the contrary, this inequality exists."[35] Hence, although women could stand beside men in the face of God, social distinctions had to be made so as to maintain worldly order. Understanding the problematic nature of female martyrs requires an awareness of the religious context in which they are situated.

The interpretation of Calvin's views of women is varied, so much so that one historian claims it is "up to the eye of the beholder."[36] Writing at a time when women played an integral role in the spread of the Reform, Calvin had to tread a fine line. Thus, there was an inherent tension in Calvin's thought between his assertion of the spiritual equality of men and women (reinforced by the need for the patronage of powerful women) and his insistence of the maintenance of the gendered social order.

Calvin's commentaries on women focused on women's inheritance from Eve, and followed the Pauline tradition of the subordination of women. Through obedience, submission, and the fulfillment of familial duty, women could be godly and redeem Eve's disobedience.[37] These three "requirements" were the penalties inflicted upon Eve by God after the expulsion, and were applied mainly toward a woman's relationship to her husband.[38] According to Paul, women's behavior was predicated upon the hierarchy of man (Adam) followed by women (Eve). He permitted "no women to teach or have authority over men; she is to keep silent. For Adam was formed first, then Eve" (Timothy 2:12–14, RSV). Calvin also emphasized that women were not to assume authority over men and he instructs them, that to be truly Christian, women had to "endure calmly and patiently the necessity of servitude, so as to submit willingly to their husbands."[39] He, too, associated this subordination with Eve's disobedience: "women, who by nature (that is by the ordinary law of God) is formed to obey."[40] This "ordinary law of God" referred to the curse of submission resultant of the Fall, a curse inherited in turn by all women. Calvin stated in another commentary that, just in case unmarried women did not think they were subject, "all women are born, that they may acknowledge themselves inferior in consequence of the superiority of the male sex."[41]

Eve was not an evil creature, however, just weak and vulnerable to her impulses. In his interpretation of the Fall, Calvin attributed responsibility to both Adam and Eve—not just Eve. She was not absolved, however, considering that "the woman through unfaithfulness to God's word by the serpent's deceit," caused the Fall.[42] Women in general, according to Calvin, were by nature "suspicious and timid" due to "the weakness of [their] sex."[43] He echoed Paul who noted that women were "burdened with sins and swayed by various impulses, who will listen to anybody and can never arrive at a knowledge of the truth" (2 Timothy 3:6–8, RSV). Their subjugation, then, was due not only to God's punishment described in Genesis, but also to women's inherent weaker nature and need for guidance. In following the Pauline interpretation, Calvin reminds the reader that Adam was created first, thus establishing the gendered hierarchy. Hence in light both of her weakness and of this hierarchy, subjugation was determined prior to, though it was exacerbated by, the Fall: "she was doomed to servitude before she sinned . . . that the subjection was not less voluntary [after the fall] and agreeable than it had formerly been."[44]

The duty of a wife to her husband extended beyond mere obedience. Eve was created as a helpmeet and companion for Adam, and these qualities helped to define women's role as much as subjugation and obedience.[45] This concept was at the heart of the Calvinist view of marriage. Calvin explained:

> Now since God assigns the woman as a help to the man, he . . . prescribes to wives the rule of their vocation, to instruct them in their duty. . . . We may therefore conclude, that the order of nature implies that the woman should be the helper of the man . . . that woman is given as a companion and an associate to the man, to assist him to live well . . . that women, being instructed in their duty of helping their husbands, should study to keep this divinely appointed order.[46]

As this was Eve's raison d'être ordained by God, women had to maintain this role. She had to remain with her husband even under trying circumstances such as difference in faith or abuse. Calvin's letters to Protestant noblewomen in France illustrated the practical application of his thought.[47] He did not advise divorce or separation, save in instances where the life of the woman was in imminent danger. Instead he counseled patience in the face of a husband's opposition, and perseverance in the faith—in other words a type of domestic or marital martyrdom.[48]

There were inconsistencies, however, in the application of Calvin's thought to the participation and leadership of and by noblewomen. Calvin's main interest was political in allowing women any agency at all as he "change[d] his emphasis [concerning women's capabilities and their proper roles] to fit particular problems or situations."[49] Thus by shifting emphasis, but not actually changing his stance, Calvin could successfully incorporate women into the revolutionary movement without endangering the patriarchy. These noblewomen, however, were not "ordinary" but women who possessed real power: their agency was based upon class, not action or gender. Thus allowances were made for them considering their ability to forward the cause. Lower-class women could not aid the cause in the same manner as the noblewomen, and hence their instruction needed to reflect their prescribed roles. The masses of women then, as readers of the martyrology, had to adhere to stricter, more limited roles so as not to threaten the patriarchy.

Calvin's pursuit of the patronage and support of noblewomen also conflicted with his interpretation of exceptional women in the Bible. In his study *Daughters of Sarah,* John Lee Thompson analyzed Calvin's exegesis of biblical women who had been elected by God to assume leadership or nontraditional roles. Thompson noted that Calvin's views tended to be harsher than his contemporaries.[50] According to Thompson, "Calvin does not allow for any exceptional behavior [for women] when that behavior violates moral laws" (i.e., the superior roles for men).[51] Additionally, he found that Calvin, even when discussing a woman as exceptional as the biblical Deborah, "takes pains to preserve nominal male leadership in or behind the picture."[52] Most importantly, Calvin generalized that women do not have the necessary abilities to assume such roles as Deborah. Thompson's analysis of Calvin's approach toward exceptional biblical women finds resonance in the martyrological narratives of these sixteenth-century female martyrs.

In sum, Calvin defines a woman's role in terms of her wifely and motherly duties—those which are not only ordained by God but are also described as a calling: a godly woman "submits to the condition which God has assigned to her, and does not refuse to endure the pains, or rather the fearful anguish, of parturition, or anxiety about her offspring, or anything else that belongs to her duty, God values this obedience more highly than if, in some other manner, she made a great display of heroic virtues, while she refused to obey the calling of God."[53] Her glory and most important role came through the fulfillment of this biological and religious role whose importance precede even a "heroic" act. It supported the patriarchal order and defined her sphere of activity.

RECONCILING THE FEMALE MARTYRS

In his martyrology, *L'Histoire des vrays tesmoins* (1570), Jean Crespin clearly directed his readers as to how they should understand and internalize its messages, and then how to put them into practice in their own lives. Most significantly, in his epistle to his readers Crespin addressed men and women separately: "You husbands do not make it difficult to leave behind your wives and children; for this is an exchange for the best condition for which you are prepared. You, wives, in order that the weakness of your sex does not turn your face away; there are virtuous women who by their example have paved the road for you."[54] There were two different messages or instructions for readers set in his address. The instructions to men were direct and practical, pointing out the sacrifice they must make. The legitimacy of their abandonment of family for the sake of religion was clear and unproblematic. Crespin admonished them to take an active rather than a passive role. Men's agency, then, was explicit and their position appeared inherently strong as difficulties would only have occurred if they themselves created them.

Women, however, were reminded of their weakness. Crespin's directions to them were much more abstract than the men's and gave no counsel except for observation and continence: actual instructions were unclear. There was no real encouragement to embrace the practical sacrifices of martyrdom. For men, although the abandonment of wives and children could have caused economic and emotional hardship, such a sacrifice posed no threat to the patriarchy or traditional social order. For women, however, the separation from the private sphere and the entrance into a public role *not* tied to the household (or that abandoned the domestic role completely) presented a problem. Desertion and abandonment could not be encouraged. Ordinary women could not have followed the type of directions given to the men without upsetting the social structure. Hence, their instructions were passive, demanding reflection rather than action. This created a distance between them and their situation, instead of the sense of immediacy implied for men.

While the overall ratio of male to female martyrs is vastly skewed to the males, Crespin worked hard to find female exemplars because "he was concerned to find examples of theologically correct heroism among persons of all nations, ages, and sexes."[55] Unlike the women Calvin turned to for patronage, the vast majority of French female martyrs came from the non-aristocratic classes.[56] Thus Crespin's representation of these female martyrs class-wise reflects the reality. Their socioeconomic status, if known, was defined through fathers and husbands: most female martyrs were identified as the daughter, widow, or wife of so-and-so, the apothecary, farmer, for example. Their non-noble status is paradoxical as it was both compelling and endangering. Part of the martyrology's appeal involved its ability to "enable ordinary men and women to participate vicariously in a great historic epic."[57] This "epic" involved "ordinary" people like the readers themselves challenging and confounding authority: hence, as propaganda directed toward the readers, it had a major empow-

ering effect. Images of rebellious women, however, could have en-
dangered the established hierarchy and social order if embraced as
a model by other common women.

As exemplary women the female martyrs had to appear as almost
a separate gender—female yet distinct from other women. One historian of late antiquity defined the early Christian female martyrs as
"subordinate heroes."[58] In the *Histoire*, however, the female martyrs
were not subordinate in heroism to the male martyrs—their deeds
were just as, if not more, exceptional. The gendered difference lay
not in their act as such but in how they were represented and constructed as models. To reconcile this role as model with their deeds
as martyr, the female martyrs in many ways had to remain separate
due to the implications of their behavior.

In many of the accounts it was noted how the women, "overcoming all weakness of [their] sex," were able to achieve martyrdom,
such as in the case of martyr Catherine Saube (1416).[59] In the account of the apothecary's wife (1540), the reader was told that "the
confession of this woman [had] all the lords equally amazed to see
that situation *against nature*."[60] Martyr Jean Bailly (1547) was described as "provided with grace and virtue unusual in her sex" that
allowed her to exhort others and remain strong herself in the face of
death.[61] Crespin related to the reader in the account of Philippe de
Luns (1557) how God changed "the foolishness of woman to a
courage more than heroic."[62] All women shared a common weakness—as it was inherent in their nature, just as in Eve's—binding
them together as a sex. As the female martyrs overcame this weakness (albeit as described with God's aide) at crucial moments, there
was an implied unbridgeable separation between ordinary women
and the female martyrs.[63] Though she might have been a "simple" or
"weak" woman, the female martyr rose above ordinary women and
achieved an unnatural state. She was not male as she retained those
feminine attributes praised by Reformed ideology, yet her nature
had been *transformed*—an alteration in the formula of her gender.

There is, however the issue of those women who gave in to the
weakness of their sex—those who had not "received God's grace." In
the case of Nicholas, a soon-to-be-martyr, he was questioned about
the identities of some Protestants who had stayed with him. As he refused, the magistrate who presided over the Nicholas's trial addressed and flattered the martyr's wife, Barbe: "Barbe, my friend,
think to save his life; you are still a young woman, if you want to tell

us those who you have lodged, I promise to deliver him from prison and give back his freedom."[64] She gave in to the flattery and false promises—a weakness of the female nature described by both Paul and Calvin. Hence, as a result of this shortcoming, the lodgers were captured and imprisoned. This too was a powerful lesson for women regarding what they must do for the faith; yet, Crespin did not decry Barbe. She was a "poor woman" who was "defeated." Her wifely concern for her husband's life compensated for her weakness, though it did not completely redeem her. In light of this example, it appears as if weakness was expected and bravery or courage were the exception.

Of particular importance concerning ordinary women is the message that only with God's will and aid could a woman have transcended her inherent frailty. This transcendence resulted from an election by God: it was his choice to empower a particular woman. By qualifying the female martyr's actions in such a manner, the actual deeds were not completely the woman's but attributed to God. There was a continual reinforcement of the idea that women might have needed *more* help as they were inherently weaker than men. The linking of the two (God's aid and the weakness of the female sex) differentiates the aid given by God to the male martyrs and that given to the female martyrs. In one example the martyr Marion (described rather vaguely as "the wife of Augustin") replied to her interrogators and "responded according to the measure of the faith & knowledge that God had given to her, of such strength that she did not once turn away."[65] Through their election female martyrs could be reconciled with the patriarchal order: they were not ordinary women as their nature had been divinely changed. In other words the emphasis on election and elevation created a boundary between the female martyr and the ordinary female reader.

The men had no such equivalent boundary. There was no mention of an inherent "weakness" shared by their sex. Though it was through God's will and help that they became martyrs, their "election" process was less of a transformation. Though a male peasant might argue theology and survive imprisonment and torture due to God's aid, the male martyr's nature remained untouched.

MARTYRLY MOTHERHOOD AND SPOUSEHOOD

The image of the female martyr had to embody the Calvinist vision of womanhood if she was to have a place within the framework of

Reformed ideology and be held as a model for ordinary women. Thus, the martyrological accounts of female martyrs were constructed as types of instruction manuals, balancing aggressive defenses of the faith with "proper" comportment and gender "appropriate" role fulfillment. This involved portraying the women as modest in their bearing, maternal or wifely toward others, obedient (in this case to God), and compliant. If married, they still had to maintain the companionate role wherever possible. Many of the female martyrs were represented or described in terms of "wifely" or "maternal" behavior through their encouragement and support or consolation to other martyrs—mostly male. As one example among many, female martyr Michelle de Caignoncle (1549), widow of Jaques le Clerc, was described as "exhorting the others to be constant," in this case Gillot Vivier and two other male martyrs with whom she was imprisoned.[66] Jean Bailly, wife of Simon Mareschal, "exhorted others, and principally her husband, to persevere" as she was led to her execution.[67] Anne Audebert (1549), widow of Pierre Genest, went so far as to exclaim "My God, the beautiful girdle that my spouse gives me! On a Saturday I was betrothed for my first wedding, but for this second nuptial I will be married this Saturday to my spouse Jesus Christ."[68] A married woman condemned to be buried alive shouted to the tower of Belfoi where she thought her husband Adrian (who had not remained firm in his faith) was imprisoned, "Farewell Adrian, I go to another wedding."[69] Philippe de Luns, before her execution, put aside her widow's weeds and donned her velvets in celebration of her martyrdom and impending "marriage" to Christ.[70] These female martyrs conformed to the ideal even if they were unmarried, widowed, or their marital status was unclear. Though the wedding trope is a common biblical descriptor for both men and women especially within Catholicism, in Crespin's *Histoire* it was reserved only for women for somewhat obvious reasons.

The family was central to a woman's salvation. In many of the female accounts, however, the family was nonexistent. Reflective of female involvement in the Reform, most of the female martyrs were identified as either widows or unmarried. If a female martyr was married, usually she had been imprisoned with her spouse, or the spouse had abjured.[71] Interestingly enough, in contrast to many of the accounts that focused on male martyrs, spouses and children were rarely described as being brought in as a factor in obtaining an abjuration during the trials. One interesting exception to this was the account of Hanon le Fevre. Hanon's death sentence had to be delayed until she delivered the child she was carrying, but her father, brother, and husband had already been executed. Immediately post-partum, her judges "begged" her to "save her life." She, of course, re-fused and expressed her readiness to join her father, brother, and husband.[72] There was no mention of the child she had just borne or its fate, or even if the judges had appealed to her maternal responsi-bilities to her newborn. Juxtaposed to the early Christian martyr Per-petua, whose account (not included in Crespin's martyrology, how-ever) also involved a newborn in prison and indeed highlighted her sacrificed relationship with the child in the name of her faith, Hanon's motherhood certainly received scant notice. The image of the sacrificing mother can be found throughout Catholic hagiogra-phy. For instance, in the letters of Jerome, we see him praising his friend Melania for abandoning her children, and extolling Paula for hardening her heart against her two children's pleas as she left them for the Holy Land.[73] Additionally, the accounts of Perpetua and Fe-licitas rejoice in the new mothers' rejection of their children and family in favor of their deaths: "maternal love must be crushed un-derfoot in the name of faith."[74] In these accounts, victory over famil-ial ties and emotion was celebrated, while in Hanon's case her ea-gerness and readiness, not her sacrifice, was highlighted.

In contrast, in at least three of the accounts of men—those of Pierre Mioce, George Charpentier, and Étienne Brun—the subject of the well-being of wives and children was questioned in front of the accused to tempt him to abjure. Though the men were aware of their family's possible fate—economic destitution, starvation, or worse—they persisted in their martyrdom. Both George Carpentier and Pierre Mioce were confronted with this situation and responded similarly. Carpentier explained: "My wife and my children are so dear to me, that the Duke of Bavaria could not buy them from me for all his goods; if it is for the love of my God and Lord, I leave them voluntarily."[75] Of Mioce, Crespin wrote, "Nothing known could di-vert him, not the weeping of his wife, nor the gaze of his family who they had placed before him."[76] These men were represented as aware of their responsibilities to their families; nevertheless, there was no difficulty in portraying them as voluntarily abandoning wives and children. Such abandonments were not described, much less celebrated in the same manner, in the accounts of the female martyrs.

CASE STUDIES

To illustrate how these themes work inside the actual accounts, we must turn to the narratives themselves. In this section we will examine the case studies of one female martyr, Marguerite Le Riche, and one male martyr, Étienne Brun.[77] Both accounts were of similar length and involved martyrs from social strata that were often grouped together and held as prime examples of inversion—of the "lesser" triumphing over their social and intellectual betters.[78] Brun is represented as a common farmer and yet he was wealthy enough to afford servants. Le Riche came from a similar economic background as a wife of an urban bookseller. Though neither were of an upper class, they both lived comfortably enough. Additionally, both martyrs had families and endured similar executions. Thus, while the individual circumstances of their lives differed (such as urban versus rural contexts, or with regard to conflict within the family), there is nevertheless enough commonality between the two for comparison. In these narratives we see how the martyrs were presented in a manner that took into account the gender roles embedded in the ideology of the Reform. Through the use of emphasis or downplaying certain situations, or by using gendered images or language, the narratives were constructed to support the patriarchal leanings of the Reform movement. Nevertheless, there was cognizance of the need for the support and involvement of women.

Marguerite Le Riche

The wife of a Parisian bookseller, Marguerite Le Riche originally followed her husband's lead in embracing the Reformed faith. Her conviction surpassed his, and unlike him she refused to attend Mass and dissimulate, preferring instead to worship at illegal Protestant assemblies. This in itself was problematic as her refusal to "play the good Catholic" caused much conflict and ill-will in their relationship to the point where he became abusive. Le Riche, however, was well aware of her marriage vows, and though she left the home to celebrate Easter with those who shared her belief, she returned to her husband afterward. Nevertheless her vows did not stop her from attending the assemblies, and there she resolved "to never go to Mass & sooner die."[79]

A short time after her return home, the local curé denounced her to the authorities after noticing her absence at Easter services. She was imprisoned at the Conciergerie, where she exhorted, admonished, and consoled her fellow prisoners, including Anne Du Bourg. During her imprisonment, both secular and ecclesiastical officials interrogated her numerous times in an attempt to first, discern her beliefs, and second, get her to recant. When asked about where she had spent the Easter holiday, she replied, "without any dissimulating, that she had been absent from her house, & had stayed at the home of her faithful [Reformed] friends so as not to be forced to profane the Communion of our Lord Jesus Christ in the fashion common to others but having properly made the Communion according to the ordinances of God in the assembly of persons who are faithful & Christian."[80] When asked about the secret assemblies and her views on the Mass, Purgatory, and auricular confession, she replied that all that she had learned was by the word of God.

Declared a "stubborn and obstinate heretic"[81] Le Riche was sentenced to be tortured to obtain the names of her "accomplices," then led in a cart to the Place Maubert where she was to be executed. Before she was taken from the Conciergerie, they gagged her, so that she could not speak to the crowds that had gathered for her execution. Again, she was asked to recant by the officials and told that if she did, she would be rewarded with a more "humane" death by strangulation before being burnt at the stake. To this she indicated no. As she was hoisted up onto the scaffold, the executioner repeated the question, to which she again responded negatively. At that point the fire was lit and she "thus returned her soul to the Lord."[82]

Le Riche's account was accompanied in *Histoire des vrays tesmoins*, by an introductory gloss in which Crespin addressed his readers: "Virtuous women, contemplate here the courage and zeal of this Marguerite your sister, who is placed before you as an example: make all your domestic disagreements an exercise of piety, both for the body as well as the spirit. She gave courage to persons great and small who at the same time were held prisoners."[83] The gloss itself deserves to be noted and contextualized as it set the stage for the account, directly addressing women in terms of how they should view Le Riche, her act, and how they should apply it to their lives. Within the gloss, Crespin emphasized three of Le Riche's characteristics: her courage, her forbearance of her domestic conflicts, and her encouragement of others in the pursuit of constancy and in the face of suffering. All three of these traits were gendered in one way or another within her account, pointing to particular issues that concerned gender roles. Most importantly, Le Riche was offered as an example for female readers, and her behavior in terms of the conflict with her Nicodemite husband was highlighted; thus, marital discord due to religious difference is addressed "correctly" through the retelling of her story.

To return to Le Riche's account, she fulfilled her duty to both God and to her husband by attending services as she "preferred to anger her husband rather than her God, to whom she was entirely consecrated." Nevertheless she returned home afterward as "she no longer wanted to be absent a long time from the house, but deliberated to return to that which God had placed and joined together, yet she foresaw the great conflicts & disagreements that she would have with him."[84] The first part of the description of her situation was essential to the representation of Le Riche. Her first responsibility was to God, a duty that she embraced fully; yet she did not neglect her commitment as wife. This was reminiscent of Calvin's admonishment that a woman's role within the family was more pleasing to God than any heroic role she might play.[85] In Le Riche's case both her duty to God and her duty to her husband were ordained: thus both roles must be represented as being fulfilled as much as possible, though the former must always precede the latter. Her efforts were aimed at remaining true to both even at the cost of abuse. Endurance and obedience rather than action and outright rejection were her path. She remained constant in her faith and persevering in God's commandment not to commit idolatry, while at the same time she respected the sanctity of her marriage as ordained by God.

In this way, Le Riche's account focused the reader's attention on the conflicts that occur within a marriage and the proper response to them. For Le Riche it was only after her husband threatened bodily harm and physically to force her to attend Easter Mass that she leaves him. Her "abandonment" of him, then, was not an attempt to avoid their discordant marriage (as she returns to him directly after the holiday), but an effort to avoid offending God. Her absence from her wifely duty was temporary, and her response was reactive and defensive rather than an active rejection. Hence, the narrative handled issue of the sanctity of marriage and familial duty versus obedience to God in a very different way than the narratives of the male accounts that dealt with the same issues. In the male accounts the abandonment of the family was celebrated, but in Le Riche's account there was an attempt to reconcile the duty that the Christian woman owed to God by avoiding idolatry, and her duty as an obedient wife. Le Riche's husband actually disappeared from her account; no mention of him occurs from her arrest on. On a literary level this removed the problem of abandonment from her act and sacrifice. Nevertheless Le Riche's example extolled forbearance and patience—not voluntary abandonment.

The portrayal of Le Riche and the emphasis placed upon her consolation and encouragement of her fellow prisoners also supported the Calvinist vision of women's salvation. The account told with great detail of her efforts to inspire and support those who were to share her fate: "She assiduously instructed the female prisoners with her & consoled them. The martyrs who left the Conciergerie to go to their deaths passed in front of her chamber and she was not discouraged to see them in the hands of the executioner, but crying to them and exhorting them to rejoice, and to patiently carry the burdens and afflictions of our Lord Jesus Christ."[86] In this representation she became almost maternal and a type of help-meet, providing comfort to others while putting aside her own situation. As an example to other women, she illustrated one particular way in which women could and should support the faith without assuming a role that was unfeminine or threatening. Their role should not be that of an instigator or agitator, but of a supporter. The most noteworthy aspect of this particular role was her interaction with Anne Du Bourg, arguably the most prominent Huguenot martyr of the sixteenth century.[87] Du Bourg and Le Riche were held in the Conciergerie at the same time in prison cells near enough to one another that they could see each other through a small window in the wall. Through this window they conversed with words and, when the situation did not permit words, they used signs.[88] Le Riche offered solace and encouragement to Du Bourg: she "served considerably to strengthen him . . . inciting him to persevere constantly, and consoling him."[89]

In the account Du Bourg recognized the role played by Le Riche and expressed his gratitude in a curious way: "A woman showed me my lesson and taught me how I must carry this vocation [he said], feeling the force and virtue of this poor woman."[90] In his words the reader could almost hear the surprise and astonishment in Du Bourg's voice. Additionally a particular intimacy could be found in this part of the account, most notably in their interactions through the window, their whispered words and secret gestures. And the reader saw her once again in an almost wifely role in relation to a more "significant" male personage. We are reminded that she is a "poor woman." Though extraordinary in her actions, she nevertheless fulfilled the duties of a "godly" woman.

Le Riche was a passive martyr. Her conviction, in the eyes of the reformers, was a model for the entire body of the Reformed faithful; however, her act and sacrifice was a different matter. Not everyone had the courage to withstand suffering, but everyone should aspire to live a "godly" life. The ability to undergo martyrdom was represented as a gift given by God, instilled within an individual at the time of his or her martyrdom rather than an inherent or preexisting quality. Whereas in the male accounts this gift was in accord with man's nature; for women, it transformed them by allowing them to overcome their inherent weakness. The female martyr, then, was the perfect vehicle for God to display his will and power. This was made manifest in the description of le Riche's appearance before her execution: her "clear and ingenuous expression" was attributed to God wanting to show the gathered crowd "the virtue of his [God's] spirit so miraculous in this woman."[91] The female martyr was then represented not as individual with agency, but solely as God's chosen weapon.

Étienne Brun

The martyrological account of Étienne Brun was intended to provide a model for the ordinary laborer. This narrative, designed to encourage and to exhort the common man to do his duty to God, explored the themes of social inversion, the significance of the Gospel, and the abnegation of worldly life (i.e., the family and familial responsibilities). It provides a contrast to the way in which the image and actions of the female martyr were constructed.

Brun was described as a farmer from the village of Reortier in Dauphiné, who possessed some intellectual ability.[92] Though not school-educated, he had taught himself to read and write. With this knowledge he came to notice the contradictions in the teachings of the priests and confronted them. As he did not know Latin, they admonished him that he could not know what he was talking about. Brun therefore took it upon himself to compare the Latin and

French Gospels and to memorize the relevant passages in the Latin so as to strengthen his arguments with the priests. The subsequent confrontation led to his imprisonment for heresy by the bishop of Ambrun. During his confinement, Brun signed a Latin document that amounted to an abjuration that in turn procured his freedom. Brun then returned home, only to fall into a state of despair over his lack of constancy.

Two years later, in 1540, Brun was again taken into custody and denounced by Gaspar Auger de Gap, a tenant farmer of the bishop who sought the reward of part of the confiscation of Brun's land. In an attempt to procure a second abjuration, Brun's jailers brought his wife and five children in front of him, reminding him of the poverty his death would inflict upon them. Brun, however, refused to recant, and instead left his family to their fate.

Brun was executed in June of that same year, though his execution did not proceed smoothly. The flames around his stake would not burn consistently, so the executioner knocked him on the head with a hook. Brun responded to this indignity: "Since I am condemned to be burned, why do you want to brain me?"[93] In response the executioner lanced him in the stomach. Brun's body was then burned and his ashes scattered in the winds.[94]

The account of Étienne Brun highlights a number of issues. Two sets of themes stand out, however, in terms of a gendered comparison with Marguerite Le Riche: the maintenance of his fatherly role prior to his arrest and his subsequent rejection of his family; and the acknowledgment of his agency and abilities as an individual despite the weakness suggested by his abjuration.

Before turning to these themes, we need to examine the ways in which Crespin directs the reader prior to the actual account. In his introductory gloss to Brun's account, Crespin identified the audience he wished to address: "There are, in the example of this martyr, certain peculiar things worthy of being noted, so as to know the gifts and graces that God gives to the people of the fields without observing human ways. This is the first, after Jean Cornon, that is given as a mirror for the tillers of the soil."[95] This introduction not only identified the martyr as an example for the common man who labors (just as le Riche's gloss presents her as a example for women) but also specifically located the lesson to be gleaned from the account. Crespin directed the reader to focus upon the "gifts and graces" ("les dons & graces") given by God and on how God worked through the martyr rather than completely attributing the exemplary behavior to Brun himself.[96] God's aid, however, was not linked to any specifically identified infirmity as in the cases of the female martyrs.

The account described Brun's search for knowledge as part of his effort to better his understanding and defense of the Gospel. Though he was "led by the mercy of God to the knowledge of his truth," it was Brun's own use of the truth that enabled him to "overcome the cunning and craftiness of the great people of Dauphiné."[97] There is a sense of the martyr's own agency through the knowledge he had acquired. In other words, though God led him to the truth, Brun himself used God's gifts to overcome his enemies; hence, he was not portrayed as solely a vehicle for God, but an individual graced by God. Though God's gifts allowed him to achieve enlightenment, especially in terms of acknowledging his mistake in abjuring, these gifts did not transform the makeup of his gender as they did with the female martyrs. Brun, a man, had no inherent weakness to overcome, and his elevation into martyrhood was less of a transformation. His nature remained unchanged.

Brun's temporary abjuration provided the only instance of weakness, but this should be qualified; the account did not show any attribution of responsibility to the martyr (be it through inherent weakness or individual whim). Brun was almost absolved of any accountability as Crespin placed the emphasis of the account on Brun's intellectual pursuits in the name of the defense of the Gospel. Whereas Crespin dedicated a paragraph and a half to describing Brun's laborious efforts of translation and memorization (thus extolling the martyr's personal exertion), he spent only a sentence on the abjuration, placing the responsibility squarely on the shoulders of the captors: "He [Brun] was circumvented & induced by lies and vain promises of support by the said Bishop to admit to a formula of abjuration that he [the Bishop] had written in Latin in their accustomed style, to obtain release."[98] Thus, unlike his agency in terms of supporting God's word, Brun was a passive participant in his abjuration; and when God made him aware of his inconstancy, it was described as "his error" ("sa fault") rather than weakness.

Another interesting counterpositioning is that of Brun the "good father" against Brun the martyr who rejects all concern and responsibility for the welfare of his family. In his initial description of the martyr, Crespin described Brun as he "devoted, . . . along with the working of the fields, to reading the New Testament translated into French: the one was for the nourishment of his family & the other for the instruction of them in all fear of God."[99] In this passage Brun was the caring father who provides for the spiritual and physical welfare of his family. This contrasts greatly with the scene where Brun rejected all concern for his wife and children's physical well-being. In an attempt to extract another recantation, Brun's prosecutors placed his wife and children in front of him, explaining that his children will starve after his death (if he persisted). Brun responded, "On condition that the food of the soul, which is the Word of God, does not fail them, I have no anxiety about the body's bread."[100] The scene was dramatic, and Crespin heightened the reader's sympathy for the children's fate by describing them as "the poor children" ("poures enfants"). Nevertheless, this scene was celebrated by Crespin as a sign of the martyr's dedication and constancy.

The main reason for placing these two images (the "good father" and the constant martyr) together in this analysis is to highlight how the family could be used in a male account. Within the narrative the two images heightened the notion of the martyr's sacrifice and the suffering endured for God's truth. The rejection of the family also evoked the oft-cited biblical passage of Matthew 10:37–39 (RSV): "Anyone who loves his father or mother more than me is not worthy of me; anyone who loves his son or daughter more than me is not worthy of me; and anyone who does not take his cross and follow me is not worthy of me. Whoever finds his life will lose it, and whoever loses his life for my sake will find it." The confrontation between Brun and his family was most significant in light of Crespin's prefatory address to men, the introductory gloss to the account, and the construction of the female martyrs. In the address Crespin admonished men not to hesitate to leave their families; while in the introductory gloss he instructed the "laborers of the earth" to reflect upon Brun's example. These were two clear encouragements to make the practical sacrifices necessary to defend the Reform movement. Regarding the female martyrs, however, there were no accounts that graphically described a similar active rejection or abandonment of the family. Rather, woman are portrayed as passive "abandoners." Women did not actively reject their families in the accounts, even if the husband was either not of the faith or a Nicodemite, as in Le Riche's account above. The female martyr was represented as remaining true to her role as wife (and/or mother) or performing that role for other martyrs.

During the conflict over religion in sixteenth-century France, women took an active role in the defense of their religious beliefs and affiliations. With regard to the Huguenots, women's participation regardless of class was necessary in the defense or aggrandizement of the faith, such as proselytizers within their families, as martyrs, or as actual participants in the physical defense during times of extreme need (for example, women in La Rochelle during the siege by royal Catholic troops [1573]). A problem existed, however, when such actions upset the social order and social discipline. Images of exemplary women therefore needed to be constructed so as not to pose a direct threat to the social order. Looking at gender roles in Jean Crespin's *Histoire des vrays tesmoins*, we can see how exemplary women and their actions could be incorporated into the larger ideological framework of the Reform movement.

Any type of martyrdom, whether it be of a man or woman, represents social inversion and social disobedience to at least some degree. The focus of this essay is how Crespin approached this issue with regard to women. More specifically, I have tried to identify the methods used to encourage women's participation in the movement, while at the same time maintaining the gendered social order. The key to this problem lies in the use of a gendered rhetoric of martyrdom. Through language, textual imagery, and shifts in emphasis, the female martyr could be recast as supportive of the social order. Although through their actions female martyrs flouted their prescribed subservience and inherent inferiority to men, the ways in which their stories were constructed within the martyrology transformed these acts so as to conform to the Calvinist image of the "godly" woman. It was this reconciled image that was presented to the female readers of the martyrology, and held up for them as exemplars for them to contemplate.

In exploring the difference between martyrdom and martyrology, many issues come to the fore—most significantly tension between the conflicting needs for subversion and order within a persecuted movement. By examining Crespin's female martyrs, we can see how these tensions are played out. While there were forms of religious expression and activism available to Protestant women, areas involving leadership and authority over men were, save exceptions for high noblewomen, proscribed by reformers such as Calvin. Protestant theology defined women's salvation through their obedience, submission, and familial duty. Female martyrs circumvented this definition, and moved toward a more active, confrontational position. Their acts of martyrdom, then, needed to be reconstructed and represented in such a way that the female martyrs were seen as still supporting and illustrating the gendered ideology of Calvinism. Their textualized accounts consoled, encouraged, and taught women, while also maintaining their subordinate position in society.

5

Nicodemism and
the Community

IN DECEMBER 1559 THE FRENCH REFORM MOVEMENT ALMOST LOST its most celebrated martyr. After six months of remaining firm in his faith, Anne Du Bourg submitted an "ambiguous" confession that would have saved him from the scaffold. Though the original confession is lost to us, sources allude to its compromising nature and describe the alarmed and motivated response of the Parisian Reformed community. Was it possible for the six days the confession stood, that Du Bourg had really changed his mind after remaining steadfast in face of the king and his interrogators, and after six months of prison? In all likelihood not. Rather, pressure from concerned friends and family (to which sources attribute the new confession) and the growing probability of execution as his appeals were running out had almost certainly shaken his resolve. His courage had faltered and he valued life over faith. Du Bourg's subsequent and last confession, which unambiguously asserted Calvinist doctrine, suggests that even during that six-day interim his interior faith did not change. For those six days until the passionate letter from the pastor Marlorat convinced him of his "duty," Du Bourg embraced a form of Nicodemism, a controversial type of religious dissimulation held in contempt by numerous Protestant reformers, by "compromising" externally. The pastor reminded Du Bourg that his struggle thus far had strengthened the weak and increased the size of the community, that "the eyes of all were upon him."[1] In other words, Du Bourg the Nicodemite would bring "ruin" to the community, while Du Bourg the martyr would embolden and strengthen it. Du Bourg's vacillation raises issues of community (its creation and

defense) and Nicodemism that intersect in the rhetoric of martyrdom found inside and outside the martyrologies.

In the prefatory epistle to his 1563 martyrology Antoine de la
Roche Chandieu told his readers that within the pages of his work,
"Some will recognize here the brothers and comrades who were
torn from their company to be cruelly put to death: wives will find
their husbands here, fathers their children, and children their fathers, tortured and murdered on account of the word of God. Others will see here the time of their imprisonment or of what followed.
Others will hear here of their losses, the theft of their possessions,
and the desolation of their families."[2] In acknowledging these connections, Chandieu drew his readers into the realm of the martyrs,
creating bonds between the living and the dead, and merging all
those who were persecuted into a community. The readers would
recognize their own world within the various accounts and identify
in some way with the martyrs' experiences. Such a connection reinforced the idea that all followers of the Reformed faith suffered for
and were bound by a common cause: being faithful to the "word of
God."

While providing this connection, the martyrologies of Chandieu
and Jean Crespin also introduced the martyrs as examples of correct
behavior in the face of persecution. Their constancy and faithfulness
were described as edifying to the community and their confessions
extolled and praised as evidence of God's favor and aid. Most importantly, their public profession of faith and steadfast adherence to
it above all worldly ties, needs, and desires strengthened the new
community in its struggle to survive and grow.

Just as the martyrs performed this service, drawing together and
embodying a community of suffering, the Nicodemite undermined
it. Théodore de Bèze described the phenomenon of Nicodemism as
a result of the persecution:

> At this time also there were some persons in France, who, having
> fallen away at first from fear of persecution, had afterwards begun to
> be satisfied with their conduct as the deny that there was any sin in
> giving bodily attendance on Popish rites, provided their minds were
> devoted to true religion. . . . The consequence was that from that
> time, the name of Nicodemite was applied to those who pretended
> to find a sanction for their misconduct in the example of that most
> holy man Nicodemus.[3]

The Nicodemite, then, was the antithesis of the martyr. And as the French crown stepped up its persecution of the Huguenots after 1540, the issues of martyrdom and Nicodemism became prominent topics in the works of many reformers.

In the writings of Jean Calvin and Pierre Viret the Nicodemite and the martyr were juxtaposed. Whereas the martyr was praised as a mirror in which the faithful saw amplifications of their own suffering as well as the triumph of God's cause, the Nicodemite was excoriated as a saboteur. The Nicodemite, then, was a type of anti-martyr whose actions subverted rather than supported, disheartened rather than consoled. The Nicodemite remained silent while others testified, clinging to earthly pleasures and fears rather than transcending them and fulfilling the responsibility to God. Thus, not only was the Huguenot community threatened without by persecution from the state and popular violence, but it was also, according to some reformers, threatened from within by the "perfidious" Nicodemites.[4]

This chapter examines the rhetorical building and defending of the Huguenot community prior to the St. Bartholomew's Day Massacre of 1572. Central to these processes is the general rhetoric of martyrdom, and its expression in the anti-Nicodemite texts. The first part of the chapter analyzes the ways in which the rhetoric helped create a larger sense of community by defining it as united by suffering in a universal and historical context. The second half of the chapter looks at the defense of this perspective, most notably through the anti-Nicodemite discourse. Nicodemism, as it was treated by the leaders of the religious Reform movement, especially Calvin and Viret, reveals more than a concern for the fate of individual souls. The spiritual health and cohesion of the community was at stake. Thus the reformers infused a type of social consciousness into the choices confronting the Huguenots in France.

The debate over Nicodemism is multifaceted. The purpose of this chapter is not to analyze the level of Nicodemism in the Huguenot community, or its origins, nor the varying attitudes of reformers, or even the response of the community to the reformers, all of which have been addressed by previous studies.[5] While the history of Nicodemism has been discussed by many historians, the position of the anti-Nicodemite discourses within the general rhetoric of martyrdom has been glossed over or neglected.[6] Most historians have done the opposite, placing the rhetoric within the anti-Nicodemite discourse. This has had the effect of taking Nicodemism out of the larger context of the literature of persecution, and isolating the Nicodemite from its counterpart, the martyr. While some of the analyses describe the option or representation of martyrdom in the discourses, they do not look at the ways in which the anti-Nicodemite texts use some of the same language, symbols, and images of the rhetoric of martyrdom, and indeed are vivid manifestation of this rhetoric.

This chapter, then, approaches the Nicodemite controversy from a new perspective by examining the connection between the anti-Nicodemite discourse, the communal identity, and the general rhetoric of martyrdom. Though William Bouwsma briefly touched on the connections when he noted that "His [Calvin's] insistence on the church as a functioning community was closely related to his rejection of what he called 'Nicodemism,'" his analysis goes no further.[7] Other authors have discussed the connections between rhetoric of martyrdom and the anti-Nicodemite literature. Peter Matheson's insightful article analyzes the reformers' varying degrees of advocating martyrdom vis-à-vis Nicodemism in building and defending the Reformed faith. However, Matheson's discussion neglects the prominent role that the rhetoric of martyrdom plays in the defending the church or community against Nicodemism. Carlos Eire's *War Against the Idols* alludes to the threat Nicodemism posed to the Protestant cause (i.e., community), but martyrdom appears tangential to his analysis, relegated to being one possible repercussion of "steadfastness: the other alternative."[8]

Brad Gregory, in *Salvation at Stake*, rejects a linkage between anti-Nicodemism and martyrdom in the minds of the Huguenots as not being "part of a collective Protestant *mentalité.*"[9] I agree with Gregory in that there was much resistance to Calvin's seemingly unrealistic demands and that many would abjure when pressured. The lack of constancy, however, does not preclude recognition on the part of the Huguenots of connection between anti-Nicodemism and martyrdom. In other words to choose a more pragmatic faith does not mean to lack awareness of or completely reject martyrdom. It only illustrates an inability or unwillingness to embrace such an extreme sacrifice.

The martyrologists and reformers, Calvin most notably, describe martyrdom as an election—a gift and ability granted by God. Hence, martyrdom was not advocated for all. And while martyrs were anti-Nicodemites, anti-Nicodemism was not necessarily a wholehearted embrace of martyrdom. Martyrdom was an ideal: the act of the martyr was not for everyone, but all could attempt to embrace or incorporate the qualities described by the martyrological accounts and not be a Nicodemite. Herein lies the linkage. The connection between anti-Nicodemism and martyrdom in the literature can be found, in examples placed directly in front of the faithful, and in all likelihood this linkage caused great discomfort. Hence, the desire to see and embrace areas of grey does not preclude the association of martyrdom with anti-Nicodemism in the mind-set of the Huguenot. The two issues were intrinsically linked through the rhetoric of martyrdom that pervaded most aspects of literature aimed at the persecuted French Protestants.

This serves to emphasize a more important difference in approach between Gregory and myself. Whereas Gregory finds paramount the importance of the individual conscience in the choice to embrace martyrdom, I would argue that the communal component of martyrdom is just as important in terms of the aims of the martyr. For example, as discussed later in the chapter, the letters written by the martyrs reveal a recognition that their sacrifice did not simply serve God but served the community of the faithful as well. Indeed, the community should *share* in the experience of the martyr. Many martyrs specifically stated that the purpose of their letters (including accounts of their interrogations and imprisonment) was for the "edification" and "consolation" of their brethren. One martyr went so far as to state in a letter that "I say Our [emphasis his] captivity, because you come to feel mine and I yours: for all good and bad are common among brothers."[10] The frequency with which the martyrs asked family members and friends to publicize their letters also reflects the communal concern and responsibility felt by the martyrs. The martyrs saw themselves not only as creatures of God, but as instruments for the community in the sense that they (through their acts and words) provided consolation, edification, and inspiration to the faithful; in other words their responsibility was to God but also to the community as well.

The creation of the Huguenot community and communal identity were intrinsically tied to the shared experience of persecution and suffering. Thus the perceived threat to the community by those who undermined this identity by avoiding or advocating avoidance of this experience should be recognized. The rhetoric of martyrdom forwarded this interpretation of community in its profoundest expression. Just as the advocacy of martyrdom as the ideal model and source of edification (and even augmentation) for the faithful is a sub-current in the anti- Nicodemite texts, so is the recognition of the particular communal threat posed by the Nicodemites.

BREAKDOWN OF
TRADITIONAL COMMUNITY

The Reformation brought about a type of social chaos, breaking down traditional bonds of family and parish, challenging notions of authority, hierarchy, and identity.[11] A declaration of faith was not solely a religious choice by an individual, but a political statement and a communal issue. The religious activities of late medieval Catholicism, such as processions, communion, marriages, funerals, and baptisms, bound the community together and displayed solidarity. These rituals were integral and regular occurrences in the life of the individual as well as in the greater life of the community itself.

With the growth of Protestantism in France from the 1530s on, these rhythms and traditional ties became disrupted, causing severe and distinct fractures in the structures and expressions of community. Most notably, the divisiveness over religion took the form of accusations of "pollution" and "infection."[12] Fear of pollution would ultimately lead to Catholic calls for "extermination" of the "heretics." Royal edicts speak of the "the sowers of this infection,"[13] while Catholic polemicists demanded that the king "no longer endure the impurity and wickedness of the guilty [Protestants]."[14] Pollution would bring about God's ire and punishment upon even the righteous if the offending parties were not dealt with appropriately. For example, one Catholic pamphlet, *Signes prodigieux*, referred to the spread of the Protestant doctrine as threatening the church and bringing about divine retribution upon the German territories.[15]

Some of the more extreme accusations regarding pollution levied upon the Protestants centered around charges of various sexual improprieties, including incest and licentiousness, that threatened the sanctity and tranquillity of the society and its very moral fabric.[16] Antoine de Mouchy, in the aftermath of the Rue Saint Jacques Affair, accused the Huguenots of engaging in secret orgies.[17] A Huguenot attorney and his family were charged with engaging in sexual misconduct after having been observed holding Reformed services at their home.[18] The common state condemnations levied

against the Huguenots of "disturbing the public repose" and, more
ominously, "sedition" reflect this concern for the health of the community.[19] This heresy, then, and its adherents were perceived as
threatening the larger national community on both the spiritual and
worldly levels, and thus in need of elimination.

On the Huguenot side, multiple treatises and sermons were produced, especially from the 1540s through the 1560s, advising "the
faithful man" how to live virtuously among the "papists" and casti-
gating idolatry as an "infection" or "pollution."[20] Understandably,
pollution by idolatry was a prominent theme in the prescriptive and
defensive works that attacked the rituals of the Catholic Church.[21]
Writers of the Reform movement, like the Catholic polemicists,
spoke of the threat of divine retribution if idolatry was tolerated.[22] It
must be said, however, that the reformers also recognized the communal repercussions of abstention from or participation in these rituals. For example, Calvin wrote, "Nothing is more infectious than association with the ungodly . . . especially when there is danger of
idolatry."[23] In another example, in his *Petit Traicté monstrant que c'est
doit faire un homme fidèle*, Calvin used the instance of the death of a father, neighbor, or friend to argue against performing acts of idolatry.
He pointed out the sinfulness of appearing to pray for the deceased's soul, of going along with the others to do so. Even more, it
would be wrong, and here he used the example of a deceased family
member such as a wife or father, to pay for a Mass.[24] In using these
examples, Calvin was referring to the traditional bonds within a
community, and the orthodox mechanisms by which these bonds
were expressed. Abstention from the offending idolatry, in these instances, would threaten that community. And by using such examples, Calvin aimed at the heart of the issue: a faithful man had to
break with the old community, including family, if it supported idolatry.

There are many examples of individuals facing familial or communal pressure to attend or take part in the Catholic rituals (or idolatry as defined by Calvin and others). Among Calvin's letters is correspondence from Huguenot women asking advice regarding abuse,
and in some instances forced attendance at Mass, at the hands of
their Catholic husbands.[25] The question that many of them posed
dealt with the legitimacy of leaving their spouses due to religious difference and the lack of freedom to practice their faith. Within
Crespin's martyrology there are also examples of tensions or differ-

ences among couples, most notably the example of Marguerite Le Riche and her husband.[26] In both the letters and the martyrological cases, we see families torn (or potentially torn) by the decisions of individuals to avoid being forced or pressured into idolatry. There were many other such examples, but nonetheless we are left with a picture of a fractured society, from its most basic level, that of the individual, to that of the family, and eventually to a national division resulting in civil war.

From 1534 on, the Protestants encountered a growing persecution by the state, and increasingly in many places, by the predominantly Catholic populace. Faced with this persecution, a Protestant had three options: to remain *in situ* and practice the faith as prescribed by the reformers, risking the possibility of losing not only land, home, offices, and wealth, but also life; second, to go into exile and still lose many if not all of his goods and lands, leaving behind family in many instances;[27] or third, to dissimulate. Each of these options had repercussions that threatened either the traditional community of parish and family, or the community of the faithful.

For those who chose the first option, the penalties were grave if an abjuration was not obtained, and even then punishment could not be completely avoided. Complete absolution was not a common occurrence in the judgment of heresy.[28] Punishment for recanted heresy ranged from performing an *amende honorable* and paying pecuniary fines, to the confiscation of goods, service in the galleys, and/or banishment. In cases of obstinate heresy the accused was sentenced to execution via the stake, or if he or she recanted, by the noose first.[29] In the *arrêts* issued against many Huguenots, often more than one penalty would be levied.

The use of the *amende honorable* is particularly telling about the communal implications of the Reformed faith in Catholic France, though it certainly existed prior to the Reformation, most likely dating from the eleventh century.[30] The *amende honorable* was a public penitential act dealing with honor, respect, repentance, and reconciliation. While it would accompany other penalties, it was a milder punishment levied upon those who wished to abjure and reconcile with the larger community, the state, and Catholic Church. It was usually imposed for lesser crimes that lacked true intention, such as unknowingly possessing censored books, though it also accompanied greater intention-driven offenses as well.[31] The penitent would appear in the main square or before the chief cathedral of the town.

His feet and head would be bare (signifying respect and contrition), body clothed in a white gown (signifying penitential status), and a lit candle or torch of a prescribed weight in his hand. There, he would kneel, confess his offenses out loud, and beg the forgiveness of "God, the King, and justice," though if he had blasphemed particular saints, such as the Virgin, she would be included as well. Often the penitent would then take part in a Mass, as the act was usually performed on a Sunday.[32] This was a public act of purification and a renunciation of the crime that offended the sacred. Both Crespin and Chandieu recount the *amende honorable* of martyr Geoffroy Guerin, which he committed "to the great regret of all those who knew him and had other hope for him."[33] Later, Guerin would recant this recantation and achieve recognized martyrdom.

While the ultimate price paid by many of those who stayed and confessed their faith was recorded, glorified, and memorialized in the martyrologies and other texts, the hardships and sacrifices endured by those who chose exile are not to be underestimated. Though the exiles would escape the persecution with their lives, they suffered many of the same losses as those who were caught. To flee to Geneva or any other territory in which Protestantism was accepted was defined by French law as *lèse majesté divine*, which brought about the same retribution as *lèse majesté humaine*. According to the edict of Châteaubriand (1551), any person caught corresponding with, sending money to, or otherwise having involvement with any persons in Geneva would be prosecuted. Additionally, the edict of Compiègne (1557) officially levied the penalty of death upon those who fled to the Swiss city. Both edicts demanded the confiscation of all goods and properties of these exiles.[34]

While many of the statutes were written with the express purpose of preventing the spread of Calvinism from its Genevan base, the burning in effigy of those who fled, the razing of the houses where "illicit" assemblies were held, and the language of the arrêts suggests a deeper sense of vengeance rather than simple preventative measures.[35] For example, in the case of Laurent de Normandie, the Parlement of Paris declared him and his companions,

> charged with contempt of court for the crime of *lèse majesté divine* for having withdrawn and fled from the city of Noyon, and gone voluntarily to the city of Geneva, a city suspect and receptive of heresy, to live there like the other infidels against the ordinances customs of

our Holy Mother Church and against the sacred sacraments, by this means voluntarily deserted and defected from the faith, to be dragged on a trellis, hung, burned in effigy, their goods confiscated by the king. . . .[36]

By burning in effigy those who willingly abandoned their homes and communities, the state enforced the perception that heretics could not avoid its justice.[37] This ritual act allowed the state to purify itself and the community of the contagion of these particular heretics, much as it does by the burning of the actual heretic. Exile, in light of its punishments, could be viewed in retrospect as a type of martyrdom—though the faithful testifies in absentia with symbolic blood.

Nevertheless, the punishments levied on the exiles brought about hardships upon their family and heirs who remained. As any offices, monies, or goods (both moveable and immoveable) were confiscated, any hope of inheritance or support would be dashed. The family then would come to be subject of suspicion, as if the heresy might have tainted it as well. Oftentimes, as Calvin himself suggested, the exile would have to leave behind weaker members of the family—which in turn encouraged Nicodemite behavior.

CREATING COMMUNITY

With the destruction of traditional ties came an effort to establish a new community based on a different collective self-consciousness and according to the needs and requirements of the new faith. At the heart of this effort to define and defend the increasingly besieged Huguenot community after 1540 was the rhetoric of martyrdom. The anti-Nicodemite works of Calvin and other reformers offered the blueprint for this new community, one untainted by idolatry and that would correctly worship together the true word of God. While the old institutions of Catholicism that expressed and supported community were to be excised from the new community, the survival and solidarity of the group still depended on outward expressions of faith. Though theologically it was the individual's relationship to God and not reliance upon ritual or outward acts that defined the path to salvation, much ink was expended by Calvin and others on the importance of outward expressions. The predominance of the invisible church of Luther had for the most part given way in Calvin's thought to the visible church on earth.[38] Attendance at assemblies where sermons were given, the Lord's supper reenacted, and psalms sung, were encouraged and insisted upon by many reformers.[39]

On a rhetorical level, Calvinist reformers often cited Matthew 10:37–39 (RSV): "He who loves father or mother more than me is not worthy of me; and he who loves son or daughter more than me is not worthy of me; and he who does not take his cross and follow me is not worthy of me. He who finds his life will lose it, and he who loses his life for my sake will find it."[40] Hence, the new community was based not only upon a shared religion but also upon a rhetoric of sacrifice and responsibility to God. A cornerstone in this building effort was the issue of martyrdom. While martyrdom has been described as "an assertion of individuality against the family and community,"[41] this argument fails to identify the community which the martyr reaffirms, edifies, consoles, and bonds together through his suffering and example. Though it applies to the former connections of the martyr, it overlooks the communally creative aspect of the rhetoric of martyrdom.

On an ecclesiastical and social level, the Huguenot community was bonded by the notion of "congregation."[42] However, during the years prior to the outbreak of the civil wars, from the late 1530s through the late 1550s, the identity of the "community of suffering" served to bond the community on a psychological level. The "suffering of the faithful" became a description that occurred in almost every sermon, treatise, or pamphlet written by a French Calvinist hand. At the heart of this reference was the dictum found in Crespin's prefatory epistle, that "Among the signs by which the true Church of God is known, it has been one of the principal ones, that she has always endured the attacks of persecutions."[43] Suffering marked the followers of the Reformed faith as God's chosen; and, as a trait that could be traced back to early Christianity, it provided a type of divinely sanctioned pedigree. Here the martyrologies and martyrological narratives functioned best.

The purpose of the martyrologies and martyrological narratives was not simply to recount individual martyrdoms; much more broadly, their aim was to respond to the needs of a fledgling community struggling for their existence and sense of identity. A particularly important expression of this can be found within the martyrological accounts: the letters written by imprisoned martyrs and sent to individuals or particular churches with the expressed purpose of wider dissemination. These and many other open letters to the Reformed faithful reflect the consciousness of the martyrs that their experience was not simply their own, but should be the spiritual "property" of the community in general. This suggests the perception that the road to martyrdom should not be traveled alone, but shared and benefited from by all. For example, martyr Pierre Bergier (1562), in a letter to his wife, instructed her to gather all his correspondence: "You will be able to distribute the said letters to many people, so that the Church may gather a greater harvest from them."[44] Another example is found in the account of martyr Richard Le Fevre (1564). Crespin, as editor, provided a brief introduction to Le Fevre's letters that included, "We have published his letters here so as to share them with all of the faithful."[45] In one of these letters, Le Fevre alluded to the reason for sending along information about his interrogation: "I shall report some of it, assuming that you don't ask for it out of curiosity, but only for the building of the Church."[46] The martyrs' experiences, as they themselves perceived it, would offer consolation, encouragement, and instruction to their audience—the entire community of believers, whose faith, rather than status or quality, marked them as God's chosen.[47]

This was a community based not so much upon the values and hierarchy of the past but upon a shared faith and worldview. The rhetoric of martyrdom offered an equal opportunity community, one where representatives of all ages, classes, and sexes would be recognized as equally valiant champions for the cause. Crespin stated in his prefatory epistle to the 1555 edition, "I hope that it will greatly serve, according to the needs of each of you, to console or to confirm. For you have here marvelous mirrors, and all sorts of examples from all classes, sexes, ages and nations."[48] In writing this Crespin rightfully acknowledged the universality of martyrdom—a phenomenon transcendent of the traditional boundaries and hierarchies within a community. Such a universalistic view recognized the theoretical equal value and importance of each individual member of the community and their participation.

The accounts within Crespin's work, while not numerically comprehensive, provide a relatively faithful representation of the universality of the persecution and the general composition of the religious Reform movement in France. Although Crespin's martyrology mentions only about 20 percent of those executed for heresy by the Parlement of Paris during the years 1540–1549, he is closer to the actual numbers for the latter decades up to 1570.[49] More important than numerical accuracy in understanding the broad makeup of the Reformed community is the diversity of the martyrs represented in the accounts.[50] There is a great disparity between the number of female and male martyrs (7 French women versus 157 French men—the proportion remains essentially the same when including non-French martyrs), especially considering the high level of involvement on the part of women in the religious Reform, but it reflects the actualities of the persecution: women usually received lesser sentences and were executed far less often than men.[51]

With respect to the martyrs' occupations, we find representatives from most professions, from peasant to merchant, from artisan to notable.[52] While the majority came from urban areas, the faithful peasant could have found exemplars in Estienne Brun (1540) and Jean Cornon (1535), each described as one who "is given as a mirror to the laborers of the earth."[53] Artisans and merchants found representation in the accounts of Etienne Bourlet (1534), Jean Du Bourg (1534), and Claude le Peintre (1540).[54] The martyrdom of Louis de Berquin (1529) gave the nobility their representative among those who received the crown of martyrdom, though for the most part, the nobility comprised very little of the total number of French martyrs. Students and priests, however, were well represented. This in part was due to their activism within the Reform.[55] For example, in the incident of Pré aux Clercs (1558), in which thousands of the faithful had gathered, it was a handful of students who initiated the assembly. While the students' dedication to the cause is represented most notably in the martyrdom of the Five of Lyon (1552), ministers, former priests, and monks could look to Jean Castellan (1524), Aymonde de la Voye (1541), and Augustin Marlorat (1562).

Chandieu also recognized the universal quality of martyrdom as he emphasized the courage of the lesser members of society and their value as models not just for their own class or gender but for the community as a whole:

> Do you want to learn to renounce yourselves, to carry your cross, to die with constancy to honor God? Here are your brothers in great number, and of all types, who have abandoned their lives for this and march today before you, to the end that you follow. . . . Here you read of simple weak women, of poor artisans, of young children, armed with the strength of the Holy Spirit, to have surmounted all the power of the world, and to gaily go to die.[56]

In acknowledging the accomplishments of the traditionally "weaker" members of the community, Chandieu not only gave evidence of God's favor but equalized the expectations for the community. All would be asked to sacrifice for the cause. Calvin too acknowledged how women and children also were included in the "army of martyrs": "We cannot allege that this was a small number of people; for there was on their side a great army of Martyrs. We cannot say that they were prophets that God had separated from the common people, for women and young children were among this band."[57] The diversity of the martyrs in the martyrologies reflected a community that extended beyond national boundaries. Not only were martyrologies also produced in Germany, England, and the Netherlands, but the martyrs were shared among the editors, presenting a larger vision of the community of the faithful.[58] Examples of those who testified for "God's truth" could be found in France, Spain, Italy, the German territories, England, and the Low Countries. These stories bridged the distance of time and space uniting the faithful in their experience of persecution and suffering.

COLLECTIVE MEMORY AND
THE HISTORICAL COMMUNITY

The martyrology also functioned as a vessel for collective memory. In the formation of the new community, the martyrology fulfilled the role of a depository for the memories of its community—the memories of persecution and victory that helped to shape its identity. Even more so, the martyrology served to define and shape the collective experience. It "furnish[ed] that sense of solidarity which is the prime essential of maintaining a group consciousness which has recently been achieved by which is in danger of disintegration."[59] Part of this group consciousness was the idea of a shared past, both recent and ancient, that reinforced the legitimacy of the movement.

Historians have examined the ways in which history and memory function to create communal identity. John Gillis puts it rather succinctly when he states, "the core meaning of any individual or group identity, namely a sense of sameness over time and space, is sustained by remembering; and what is remembered is defined by the assumed identity."[60] Many of these historians have focused on the link between national identity and memory. More specifically, they have looked at the French Revolution and World War II to examine this process.[61] What happens, though, when we look at this within an early modern (or early Christian) religious context?[62] Some of these approaches, then, prove problematic. Pierre Nora's influential work, *Les Lieux de mémoire*, identifies a modern separation between history and memory, indeed he sees them in an antagonistic relationship in the modern era. For those in the sixteenth century, however, history and memory were inseparable, functioning in tandem to create and support the identity of the Protestant community. Memory and history both helped them to make sense of persecution and suffering through the rhetoric of martyrdom. And it is in the martyrologies that we see this most clearly. The martyrology, as we shall see, tied the early church to the sixteenth century by declaring that the age of martyrs never ended. Yet, the martyrologies also helped to shape the present memory of persecution and memorialize the dead.

More useful for our purposes is Maurice Halbwachs' *Les cadres sociaux de la mèmoire*. Halbwachs argues that memory works through a social dynamic, that it is not simply an individual's psychological function. Memory, he claims, is inextricably tied to social contexts, rather than an original event that it recollects. Hence, memory does not truly exist without its present social dimension.[63] While individuals might have had their own personal memories of the persecution, the martyrologies collected these memories, contextualizing them and giving them a larger meaning than on an individual level. This would allow the individual reader to understand the events on a larger scale, making sense of the persecution and even ameliorating some of the psychological trauma experienced.

Halbwachs' examination of tradition is just as significant in terms of the relationship of memory to martyrdom. Tradition, he argues, is the past as "appreciated relative to present need, and the similarities rather than the differences between them are therefore emphasized."[64] And here the early Christian model is especially useful. Elizabeth Castelli's insightful study, *Martyrdom and Memory: Early Christian Culture Making*, combines a rethinking of Halbwach's theory with a close analysis of early Christian martyrdom. Castelli finds that, "memory work done by early Christians on the historical experience of persecution and martyrdom was a form of culture making, whereby Christian identity was indelibly marked by the collective memory of the religious suffering of others."[65] This provides a useful starting point from which we can build an examination of the Reform movement's use of tradition, history, and memory that would serve to create their communal identity. As Christianity's early history was written with the blood of the martyrs and the suffering of the faithful, so would its later history in the persecuted Reform movement. These later Christians would share, through the rhetoric of martyrdom, in the collective memory of suffering that defined early Christianity. It would provide solace, meaning, and a sense of community.

For the Reformed faith, there were no sacred pilgrimages or acceptable relics to venerate as there were for Catholics, thus the martyrology functioned as a "place" of commemoration.[66] Yet unlike Pierre Nora's "lieux de memoire," memory was not simply relegated to the martyrology, to be distinguished from the present. While it did help to create an "official" memory of the persecution, the memorialized martyrs were still a part of the community, not separate from it. For the martyrologists there was no difference between history and memory. The martyrs of the present were the martyrs of the past, set on the same continuum and embodying the same values and goals.

Though the individual dead could be visited and acclaimed in the accounts, it was not the martyr as an individual that was focused upon. Instead, the martyrs' sacrifices and the meaning of those sacrifices were paramount. Now, what gave that sacrifice meaning for both the individual and the community depended upon its contextualization, especially regarding its historicity and tradition. Much was at stake in this effort. While martyrologies on the surface appear to be compilations of accounts, a closer look reveals the construction of an entire history of a movement that transcended simple commemoration.

By evoking the legacy of martyrdom, the martyrologists and polemicists of the Reform addressing the subject purposely drew on the martyrological genre and tradition of the early church that, during the late medieval era, was transformed. As much as the notion of shared suffering identified the Reformed faithful, the construction of a shared history gave this new community grounding and a communal past from which they all might draw. Essential to this purpose, and the creation of their identity, was the separation of the Catholic version of the history of the church from the Calvinist view. In rejecting the traditional rites and rituals that formerly united the community, and supporting the pared down versions that they associated with the early "true" church, the Reform movement needed to reconceptualize their history. An important part of this history was martyrdom, and while the reformers reclaimed and appropriated both the early Christian martyrs and martyrdom itself, they presented them differently than the medieval era. During the Middle Ages, the sacrifices of the early martyrs became signs of the sanctity of the individual, not the particular righteousness of a cause. The suffering of the martyrs was about imitating Christ, bearing his cross, but paramount were the martyrs' paths to salvation through spectacular martyrdoms and the accompanying miracles. As the Catholic church claimed it had entered the "Age of Confessors" as the "Age of Martyrs" and persecution had passed, individual piety would be the focus in the hagiography. Accompanying this shift was an intensified reverence for the relics of the martyrs (and saints in general). Relics and their emergent cults could be viewed as means by which people could associate themselves and empathize with the experience of the martyrs even though the direct connection with suffering through persecution was no longer likely in western Europe.[67]

The Calvinist martyrologists directly attacked the validity and efficacy of the changes and proceeded to offer corrections that would restore the martyrs to "the correct practice" ["leur droit usage"].[68] But they and others did more: they were reclaiming the history (vis-à-vis the martyrs) of the church. As martyrdom continued to be an option for Protestants, and persecution continued to define the church as "true," polemicists challenged this Catholic chronology of the church. For example, in the French translation of 1564 of Tertullian's *Letter to the Martyrs*, the translator and editor, Jean Saugrain, wrote in his prefatory epistle that the Age of Confessors, as defined by the Catholics, never occurred and that the Age of Martyrs never ended as the true church is always persecuted.[69] Hence, the martyr's suffering was not about the individual, but the defining feature of the true faith or church in a contested age.[70]

This reconceptualization of church history extended to the interpretation of the "use" of martyrs by the martyrologists. Both Chandieu and Crespin criticized Catholic "corruption" of the early martyrological accounts. Crespin called the Catholic works "a treasury, in no way a confession of their faith, of their sacred words, of their constancy, but of some worthless tatters, of some old rags, of some bones of horses or asses."[71] Instead, he said, "we do not at all beguile ourselves to keep their [martyrs'] ashes, or their bones, these are mortal things: but see them living again in their responses, letters & arguments, with the recollection of their constancy for the purpose that we will be edified."[72] Additionally,

> The [Catholic Church] thinks [the martyrs] have been so suffocated that their memory has been forever extinguished and that of the whole nothing at all may be perceived. But what happens is completely the opposite of her plans. For behold a good part of them restored, since these latest times, to a condition better than when they shared in the course of this human life. Now, as I have been explaining for a long time, it is not their bones, nor their hair, nor the limbs of their bodies, nor certain rags or pieces of their clothing, nor fables from Golden Legends that recommend them—and turn them into reliquaries, in the manner of the party that opposes you and of its accursed Synagogue; rather it is they themselves, speaking through their writings, consoling and teaching those who still remain in this course [i.e. alive].[73]

Here were see the differentiation between the perceived Catholic veneration of martyrs and their relics, and the self-described Protestant focus on the larger meaning and purpose of the martyrs and martyrology. Suffering, for Protestants, when placed in its historical perspective, was not just a matter of individual salvation, but a key feature of community and identity. And this superseded the medieval focus on individual suffering. Hence, persecution and martyrdom, within a historical context, were used as a way to understand and shape the evolving memory (and practice of that memory) of the present, giving their suffering a larger meaning.

The genre of martyrology-cum-history, as established by Eusebius, played an important role in linking memory and history that would benefit the movement. Controversy over the title of Crespin's work reflects concern with distinction between Catholic hagiography and the Protestant revival of the martyrological tradition. In August 1554, Crespin asked the Genevan Council, which either denied or allowed all legitimate publication in the city, for permission to publish his martyrology.[74] The work was reviewed by the council, which then suggested minor modifications as well as a change in title that originally included the words "Le Livre des Saints" to a less Catholic sounding *Le Livre des Martyrs*.[75] But the title continued to evolve as the editions grew. The 1555 edition bears the title of a *Recueil*, while the 1564 edition was called the *Actes des Martyrs*. Eventually the title would stand as *Histoire des vrays Tesmoins*.[76] What do these changes tell

us? Based on the differences among the editions (such as growing
numbers of martyrs, and the acquisition of new sources), the earlier
versions were truly more commemorative with less contextualization
by Crespin in terms of contemporary events other than the martyrs'
deaths. The term "receuil" would translate as compilation or collection, certainly highlighting the memorializing nature of these early
editions. "Actes" continued to focus attention on the martyrs' deeds,
rather than the broader context. But the 1570 edition, bearing the
title of a "Histoire," is a full-blown polemical martyrology-cum-history, cast in the same mold as Eusebius's *Ecclesiastical History*, functioning in the same way and tracing the foundations of the Church
that were built with the blood of the "righteous."[77] Crespin (and to
some extent Chandieu), then, based his last edition of his martyrology on the *Ecclesiastical History*, using the same format, narrative
techniques, and account constructions. Like Eusebius, he (and Chandieu) focused on the martyr's words, and whenever possible, let the
martyr speak for him/herself through letters, providing editorial di-
rection where necessary. Again, like Eusebius, Crespin interspersed
historical events between the accounts, providing a context for the
martyrs that, in Crespin's case, traced back to the persecution of early
Christians. These techniques helped both Eusebius's and Crespin's
martyrologies become more than just commemorative or resuscita-
tive works. Placing Crespin within the martyrological tradition reveals his purposeful imitation of Eusebius's techniques. The imitation
was an effort to create a continuum not only between the martyrs
past and present, but to establish a rhetorical link and legitimacy for
Crespin's own history. But, to claim that Crespin's work was simply a
Eusebian history would be a disservice to the Calvinist work. As Daniel Woolf points out in his study of the Foxe's rhetoric, "such a flat assertion of the genre provides little aid in understanding some of the
problems that Foxe faced in writing the lives and deaths of several
hundred men and women, ancient and modern, linked solely by
their willingness to suffer for their faith." Eusebius, Woolf continues,
did not have to deal with such large numbers, nor did he have the
problem of "twelve hundred years of medieval literature."[78]

Those "twelve hundred years" of martyrological and hagiographical writings, however, would in the end actually benefit the readers
of the Calvinist martyrologies, with the caveats described by the authors above. In identifying the martyrs as such, Crespin and Chandieu invoked an archetype that would be familiar to all their readers.

The narrative would be familiar, beginning with the capture of the martyr, his or her confession, and eventual execution. The actual event and situation are secondary to the topos and the label, as evidenced by the very short accounts in Crespin that merely identified the martyr as such. These shorter accounts provided scant information about the individual and details about the experience save the acknowledgment of a confession of faith, and the date and place of execution.[79] Hence, the stereotyping in the accounts served to focus the reader's attention not only away from the individual (i.e., away from the Catholic sense of venerating the martyr as an individual) but toward the function of the martyrs' confession, conviction, and purpose. It also evoked a type of social memory of martyrdom, as the significance of martyrs would be well known to the reader already. The reader, already sensitized through his or her prior indoctrination of Catholicism, would have recognized the significance of the martyr's act and more importantly, of his or her label as such. It is a narrative technique as well as a theological imperative.

These martyrological works and histories identified the Protestants as God's "chosen ones," though as part of a continuum, with persecution as God's mark. The examples of the Israelites, whose election by God and suffering were compared to the modern faithful, and of the early Christian martyrs, who were presented as the spiritual ancestors of the persecuted community, were plentiful in both the works of Crespin and Chandieu.[80] Though the Israelites were condemned and punished for their ingratitude and temporary fall into idolatry, nevertheless the identification with them served to form the impression of the inheritance of their election by God, creating a type of "super-community" of God's chosen who have suffered persecution.[81] The martyrology, as a tool of memory and history, would offer the means by which the faithful would not fall into the same forgetfulness that led to the downfall of the Jews. It would serve as a "memory aid" ("comme d'une aide à votre memoire") so that the persecution would not be forgotten and the faithful remain grateful.[82] The salvation and success of the community was directly tied to the very act of remembering and suffering. After discussing the plight of the Jews, Chandieu admonished, "if by his grace he spared us from even a light affliction, it would still be ingratitude if the memory of this benefit was not preserved."[83]

Outside of the martyrologies, references to this "super-community" of sufferers exist in numerous places. One example of this is in

Heinrich Bullinger's sermon "De la fin du siècle, et du jugement à venir de notre Seigneur Jesus Christ." Bullinger traced a history of the "chosen ones," beginning with the persecution and enslavement of the Jews in Egypt, through the martyrdoms of the early Christians, up to the reign of the papacy which had engaged in "perpetual ambushes, cheating and torments."[84] In tracing this lineage, Bullinger raised the ante for Protestants as he listed out the years of persecution: two hundred years for the Jews in Egypt and seventy under the Babylonians, three hundred years for the early Christians under the Romans, but seven hundred for the church under the dominion of the papacy.[85] Thus, he elevated the Protestants in terms of their suffering in relation to their predecessors.

The early Christians and their martyrs were also part of this "super-community." The martyrologists and Reformed polemicists worked diligently to create a sense of conformity and continuity between the early Christian persecution and the affliction of Huguenots. The purpose of this was to create a sense of legitimacy for the cause and contextualize the contemporary persecution in the larger history of the church. Crespin even entitled his preface "Preface Showing a Conformity of persecutions, and Martyrs of recent times to those of the early Church . . ." ("Preface Monstrant Une Conformite des persecutions, et Martyrs de ces derniers temps a ceux de la premier Eglise . . ."). This introductory section (much of which was taken from Chandieu's epistle) begins the history of the "true" persecuted church with martyrdoms of John the Baptist, Jesus, Stephen, and the suffering and/or martyrdoms of the Apostles. Next he discussed the specifics of the conformity with the early Christian persecution and martyrdoms, including issues of perceived criminality. The "crimes" of Jesus and the early martyrs are associated with the "crimes" of the Huguenots: "In summary, they only accused him [Jesus] of the greatest crimes of all, namely blasphemy and sedition." The accusations against the Apostles? Sedition and mutiny, "making particular assemblies, finding fault with the great Prelates of Jerusalem. . . . If it is a question of others, you will find, in effect, the same procedure."[86] This approach, however, was not unique nor limited to the martyrologies in general. It was an important component in the larger rhetoric of martyrdom. Pamphlets such as the *Juste Complainte des Fideles de France. Contre leurs adversaires Papistes, & autres. Sur l'affliction & faux crimes, dont on les charge á grand tort* (Avignon, 1560) describe a direct link between these two eras in terms of the accusations and defenses. The author stated, "Those of the ancient church acted similarly, as the Ecclesiastical histories testify, and the defenses that the ancient doctors made for them, for they were accused with the same calumnies that are charged against us up to the present."[87] Larger histories, such as Jean Sleidan's *Oeuvres. . . qui concernent les Histoires qu'il a escrites* (Geneva, 1566) also employed this technique. Sleidan, when discussing the persecution of the faithful innocent in Magdeburg in 1549, compared it to that of the early church, claming, "Their condition is the same today."[88] However, the connection is not just backward-looking. The historical perspective of a community bound by suffering leads, implicitly within the Christian tradition, to an ascendent church. Chandieu gave hope to the faithful, predicting that the persecutions will subside as they did for the early Christians, and if war happens (which it did), they will be the victors as champions of Christ. Persecution for the faithful, he claimed was not a curse, but blessing from God to help them find their way much as it had been for the early Christians.[89]

The Calvinists were not the only ones making use of historical precedent from antiquity to legitimate their cause or response. Catholic polemicists responded to the Calvinist use of the early church with their own examples and citations. For example, Claude de Sainctes, in his pamphlet *Discours sur les moyens anciennement practiquez par les Princes Catholiques, contre les sectes* (1563), described how the first Christian Emperors had treated or defined heresy, citing Theodosius and Honorius. Essentially the purpose of this pamphlet was to turn the Calvinist strategy of identifying themselves with those of the early church against the pagan emperors into associating them with the early heretics who were persecuted by the early Christian emperors.[90] While de Saincte dealt primarily with legitimating the legal prosecution of Calvinism in France, Florimond de Raemond, another Catholic polemicist, directly challenged the Protestant claim to the tradition of martyrdom. After naming the works of Crespin, Foxe, and other Protestant martyrologists, Raemond pointedly cited Eusebius on identifying proper martyrs versus heretics.[91] Raemond also quoted Augustine on how the ways in which false martyrs (read Protestants) were not dying for the truth, but for lies: "wretched men, says Saint Augustine . . . they live like reprobates, die like Heretics, and are honored like martyrs."[92]

Up to this point, I have focused primarily on the ways in which the community was defined and identified through their collective suffering. There was, however, in the rhetoric of martyrdom from the 1560s onward, an increasing reference to the community as bound together as warriors of Christ.[93] As the conflict between the Huguenot and Catholic factions in France escalated after 1560, the rhetoric of martyrdom shifted from a passive form of a didactic and emulative nature to a rallying call. God was now called upon to avenge the blood of the innocents[94] and the prayers written for the Huguenot soldiers exhorted them to fight to the their last drop of blood, to prefer death rather than shame and humiliation by betraying their consciences.[95]

Again, at the heart of this particular rhetoric were the martyrs, the "valiant champions, who have been through their battles, and by their death surmounted all afflictions, who are remarkably useful and necessary."[96] This language and imagery is firmly rooted in the early Christian era, though the image of the Christian soldier certainly could be found during the Crusades. The martial imagery was, however, a crucial component in the rhetoric and culture of early Christianity that arose out of their history of martyrdom. The spectacle of martyrdom transformed the victim into victor, and the weak into athletes. For Origen, Tertullian, Eusebius, and others, the martyrs were athletes in the arena, Christ's gladiators and warriors. For example, Tertullian, in *To the Martyrs*, described the impending executions as a "noble contest" in which "the living God acts the part of superintendent and the Holy Spirit is your trainer, a contest whose crown is eternity. . . . And so your Master, Jesus . . . has brought you to this training ground [prison]."[97] Origen explained that "The person who does not refuse the 'affliction upon affliction' but welcomes it like a noble athlete,"[98] and again compared martyrdom to a "contest." Yet Origin considered the contest taking place not just in the arena; for him the contest had a greater setting including the whole world and the angels in the audience.[99]

During the sixteenth century, whereas the martyr had been described occasionally prior to 1560 as "champions" of God—individual warriors who fight for His cause very much in the image of the medieval champion representing his king—this martial imagery began to be applied to the community in general, even by the martyrs themselves, sometime after this point. The combat of the martyr became the battle of the faithful. For example, martyr Claude Monier (1561) addressed his brethren:

Up, then, my warrior comrades, to the attack! Courage, soldiers, courage! March hardily! Do not fear them! They are not people for us, for Jesus Christ our captain has defeated them all. The hope for His victory will serve to arm our head. Let us not forget our shield, which is to have a living faith, powerful and virtuous, to ward off the blows of our enemies. Watch lest the sword slip from our hands, this blade of the Holy Spirit that cuts on both edges, which is that living word of God that pierces hearts and souls and thoughts and intentions.[100]

In another letter martyr Geoffry Guerin (1558) wrote that "under the protection and defense of [the Church] we must all fight, like true champions and soldiers faithful to our captain."[101]

The writings of the reformers also referred to the community in terms of this martial imagery. Jean L'Espine wrote: "Let us also realize that it is not a great honor for a Christian if, when he departs this world to return to Heaven to see his Father, he does not bring Him his shield, which is faith, and his lance, which is the word, and all the rest of his arms, red and stained, both with his own blood and with that of the enemies of the Church, for there is no order of knighthood more beautiful."[102] Calvin also described the community in similar terms in his sermon on suffering persecution, that "it is necessary for a Christian, even when he is resting, to keep one foot always raised to be able to march to battle."[103] This image of the community existed concomitantly with the "community of suffering," which, like the martyrs, did not lose its significance or efficacy even as the Reform movement went on the offensive in the civil wars. Nevertheless, as the movement became increasingly frustrated, culminating in the Conspiracy of Amboise (1560) and the outbreak of heated warfare in 1562, the "community of suffering" underwent a subtle transformation from passive sufferers to active militants on a number of levels.

Whether united in suffering or battle, the identity of the community of the faithful was defined through the rhetoric of martyrdom. The survival of this community depended on its solidarity and the outward expressions of faith that bound it together. The martyrologies and martyrological narratives provided exemplars for the community and created both a new vision of the past and social memory, while uniting the persecuted and victorious martyrs with the living community, and providing a common bond among the faithful. This was a community whose fate depended not only on the physical survival of its members but also on their unambiguous adherence to the doctrines of the faith regardless of the consequences.

DEFENDING THE COMMUNITY:
THE ANTI-NICODEMISM OF CALVIN AND VIRET

The fear of idolatry was not simply a matter of an individual polluting him or herself. Idolatry by an individual among the faithful had distinct communal repercussions. As the martyrs represented cases of the heroic avoidance of idolatry, the Nicodemite blurred the lines, allowing and even rationalizing the acceptance of idolatry in the name of self-preservation or pragmatic faith. For the sake of the preservation and augmentation of the community of the faithful, this was behavior that the reformers could not excuse nor allow.

A relationship exists between the martyrologies and the anti-Nicodemite discourses. Not only did they both present martyrs as exemplars of proper behavior,[104] but they also addressed similar issues and concerns: offering consolation and instruction to those living in hostile territories, extolling the triumph of the soul over the desires of the flesh, emphasizing the importance of orally confessing of the faith, and defining the community of the faithful and their responsibility to God. In essence the anti-Nicodemite texts used the same language of responsibility and sacrifice, of creating a separate community based not upon the traditional ties of parish and family but upon the cross that the faithful must bear as God's chosen. This cross was their responsibility to God to uphold unambiguously and confess the faith even while suffering persecution.

The avoidance of this cross, in the form of Nicodemism, had repercussions within the community of the faithful, according to Calvin and Viret. This avoidance and its impact on the community became the topic of numerous treatises written in the vernacular by them (i.e., intended for a popular audience) beginning in the 1540s, the period in which the French state began its active pursuit and persecution of Protestants within its boundaries.[105] These reformers imbued a type of social consciousness in the choices made by the Reformed faithful in light of the negative repercussions, as they perceived them, brought about upon the community by the actions of the Nicodemites. In other words just as the rhetoric of martyrdom created a sense of community among the faithful, the anti-Nicodemite treatises reflected a concern for this community, calling upon its members to acknowledge their responsibility not only to God but to the community itself when negotiating the hazards of persecution and living "among the papists."

Whereas both Calvin and Viret expressed sympathy for the suffering of the French community and the situation it was in, they both nevertheless demanded that the faithful abstain from idolatry in any form, whether through removing oneself from the territory or refusing to participate in any Catholic rites or rituals.[106] While Calvin was not the first to write on the subject, he was certainly one of the most prolific.[107] He spent a great amount of time on this issue from the 1540s on, coinciding with the stepped-up persecution of Protestants in France. Indeed, almost all his work on the subject addressed the Huguenots.

It is in the *Excuse de Jehan Calvin* that Calvin first used the term "Nicodemite," though in this work he used many of the same arguments and images as he does in the earlier *Petit traicté*. The main difference between the two texts is the degree of harshness—his anger over the complaints about his severity revealed itself in the later work. Previously, in the *Petit traicté*, he had broadly defined those whom he would later call Nicodemites as those who "simulate." In the *Excuse de Jehan Calvin*, Calvin refined his definition of Nicodemite, breaking it down into four categories. His four main types, then, consisted of false evangelists who claim to preach the gospel, but are concerned more for their positions;[108] evangelists at court and the ladies that patronize them that take the Gospel too lightly;[109] those who treat Christianity as a philosophy; and finally the common folk and merchants who dissimulate out of fear and weakness of the flesh.[110] He reserved his greatest disdain for those who tried to defend their actions, rather than asking for forgiveness of their weakness.[111]

Viret's most comprehensive work on anti-Nicodemism is a collection of five treatises entitled *Traitez divers*, published in 1559, consisting of one original and four previously published treatises.[112] His definition of the Nicodemite was less precisely outlined than Calvin's, and the "sin" more sympathetically presented. Viret divided the Nicodemites into two categories: those who mislead purposely, and the commoners who fall prey out of weakness. Viret referred to the former as "advocates and procurers,"[113] who have created a "pernicious doctrine" and lead men astray through sly arguments.[114] He essentially equated them to Satan or servants thereof, convincing men that simulation is but a small sin.[115]

While Calvin saw no difference in degree or sinfulness among his Nicodemites, Viret reserved his vitriol for those who preached Nicodemism and his pity for those who succumbed. Viret was much more understanding and less judgmental than Calvin toward the common folk who "succumb to the weakness of the flesh." Viret's admonitions to common folk took a more sympathetic tone than Calvin's, as Viret himself questioned whether he would be able to remain constant if he lived under the same conditions as the persecuted Huguenots.[116] And unlike Viret, Calvin's black-and-white stance on the issue earned him accusations of being unreasonable and unsympathetic from both his sixteenth-century audience and modern historians.[117]

Regardless of the differences in the degree of sympathy they expressed, both reformers expended much ink and time to counter Nicodemite arguments. Whereas Calvin's works after the *Petit traicté* were chiefly attacks on Nicodemism, Viret's were more consolatory and instructional, though his message was no less uncompromising or demanding than Calvin's. His sympathy was for the suffering, but it did not extend to the excuses and arguments put forth by Nicodemites (especially those who preached compromise from the pulpit) which he refuted with all the vehemence expressed by Calvin. The severity of their admonitions and the sheer number of pages they dedicated to the issue testifies to both their frustration and the pervasiveness of Nicodemism.[118]

The number of anti-Nicodemite treatises aside from Calvin's and Viret's is quite large, the most important of which being *Le Temporiseur* (originally published in Latin in 1549 as *Proscaerus,* then in French in 1550), by Wolfgang Musculus. Its four dialogues addressed the main arguments of Nicodemism, namely conformity out of fear. The text was reproduced in numerous editions and languages.[119] The French translation contained an important anti-Nicodemite collection, the pamphlet *Conseilz et Advis de Plusieurs grands & doctes personnages sus la même matière contenue au précédent Livre du Temporiseur* (published independently in 1565), comprised of numerous epistles and excerpts from previously published anti-Nicodemite tracts that offer consolation and advice. The contributors included: Oecolampadius, Melanchthon, Bucer, Peter Martyr, Calvin, Simon Sultzer,

Jean Lason, Bernardin Ochino, Celius Secondus, Viret, Martin Bor-
rahus, Oswald Mycone, and Zwingli. Nicodemism was of great concern, then, to a number of reformers, all of whom advocated the
same uncompromising stance of the importance of oral confessions
of faith and refraining from idolatry. It is important to note here that
the editor of the *Conseilz et Advis,* Jean Saugrain, was also the editor of
the French translation of Tertullian's *To the Martyrs* and his *Letter to
Scapula.*

Nicodemism troubled these reformers on numerous levels. One
of the most important areas of concern in which it inflicted damage
was the community. The threat Nicodemism posed to the individual's soul was of great concern. Viret especially paid much attention
to the suffering of individuals and how fear and pain could lead to
Nicodemism. But even here, both Viret and Calvin pointed out how
the weakness of an individual could threaten the community as a
whole. Both reformers wrote considerably on the individual's responsibility to God and the rewards that would be attained for faithfulness, and concomitantly the spiritual penalties for idolatry. However, the survival of the Reform movement in France hinged upon
the resolve and congregational discipline of the community. Hence
from 1540 on, the community of the faithful, not just the individual
believer, became a focal point for the leaders of the Reform as the
Huguenot struggled for survival. The threat Nicodemism posed was
not just to the salvation of individual members, but also to the community's physical and spiritual health, and its identity (as it was defined through the rhetoric of martyrdom). And while general attention has been paid to their discussion of this threat, many of the
analyses have overlooked the ways in which both reformers attempt
to make the faithful aware of their responsibility to the community
to avoid Nicodemism.

Calvin and Viret had similar interpretations of what the community was, and its significance. On a practical level, Calvin saw "community" in its traditional sense: made of neighbors and house-
holds.[120] While this interpretation held true in areas like Geneva,
where the faithful could live and worship together without the pressure of persecution or the yoke of a Catholic state, it did not do justice for the community in France. There, his association of the "community" with the "church of the faithful" was more applicable.[121]
Calvin and Viret both insisted on the separateness of this community
from that of the idolaters, and the maintenance of its purity. Hence,

the community in France for both reformers was based on faith: the community was the faithful. Calvin and Viret emphasized the importance of not just the individual worshipping God properly, but also the entire community. This, Calvin claimed, was his intention in writing on Nicodemism: "For I can truthfully protest, before God and his angels, that my intentions is no that than to obtain, insofar as I am able, that we should all serve God together purely."[122]

The proper edification of the community was a theme expressed throughout both reformers' texts on Nicodemism. Each member of the community had a responsibility to provide a good example for his or her neighbors. "It is to give no cause to our neighbor to be displeased with us, to give him no poor example, and to neither say nor do anything that would corrupt them."[123] This example involved confessing the faith and avoiding idolatry in any form. Both reformers postulated that proper worship and confession of the faith by individuals had a positive impact on the community, thus fortifying it.[124]

The Nicodemite, on the contrary, provided a bad example for the community, infecting it with "a venom so powerful and so dangerous that one must draw back from it as far as possible."[125] Not only did one particular type of Nicodemite infect them but actively tried to corrupt them and so lead them into the same sin: "Moreover he moves us to induce others to dissemble."[126] Calvin also described these particular simulators as bad influences on the community as they "induce others, by their example, to idolatry."[127] Both reformers, in these instances, were referring to Calvin's first type of Nicodemite (or according to Viret a type of "Satan"), those who claim to preach the Gospel, but nevertheless cling to idolatry.

The Reformers also gave the example of those within the community who dissemble by attending Mass and thus induce others by their example to do the same. Do they think that "They do not scandalize the weak, by giving them a poor example or by giving them doubts and scruples that they do not know how to resolve?"[128] In an analysis of 1 Corinthians, Calvin discussed how Paul related the communal impact of someone who "quibblingly pretend[s] innocence of conscience" and commits idolatry so that "they invite them [neighbors], by their example, to do the same things; and they do them, not because they understand them to be lawful, but because they see an authority in the individual whom they imitate, though he is acting not only with a doubtful, but an opposing conscience."[129]

Through passages such as these Calvin instilled a communal dimension into the choice made by the individual. Calvin firmly believed any Nicodemite behavior on the part of individuals to be just as detrimental to the health of the community as that of those who actively proselytize its arguments. The decision to engage in Nicodemite behavior impacted the community by posing a negative example, leading others into the same sin. The reformers attacked not only the Nicodemite arguments but also Nicodemite behavior that could enfeeble the community. The wrong choice by an individual threatened not only the spiritual health of the community but also their physical health by bringing down God's ire upon both the righteous and idolaters together.[130] Instead of supporting a community of the faithful the Nicodemite undermined it, be it intentionally or unintentionally. Calvin pointed out a type of domino effect that such behavior could potentially have upon the community:

> And it is no small thing to give a poor example to one's neighbors, to confirm the ignorant in their error and to trouble the weak or to scandalize them. But when with all this we add an impudence, and like shameless whores we set our own mouths on fire in order to say that we have done nothing wrong, that is to despise God openly and as if with deliberate intent to provoke Him to combat, and to arm Him to take His vengeance on us.[131]

The individual then as part of the community had a responsibility, beyond his own salvation to the welfare of all.

The physical threat to the community posed by the Nicodemites took on another form in the reformers' thoughts. According to Calvin, the Nicodemite, in going along with the idolaters, not only posed a bad example for the faithful but confirmed the "idolaters'" [Catholics'] superstitions and hardened them in their errors by not showing them the right way.[132] In doing so, the Nicodemite betrayed the faithful, condemning them to further persecution and causing the deaths of others. Viret described this betrayal in vivid terms:

> And what is more, we [who might embrace Nicodemism] inflame the fury of tyrants, and we betray our brothers, and we are oftentimes the cause that they are put to death. For if we were to declare ourselves openly, or at least if we did nothing to approve the false religion of the idolaters, we would sow confusion among them, where now we confirm them in their error and tyranny and arm them with our authority against our brothers.[133]

Calvin viewed this issue a bit differently and less clearly than Viret. Though the Nicodemites might not bring down persecution upon themselves, "they nourish all idolatry with their dissembling, become the reason that the necks of some men are broken and that others are wounded grievously, and that some are butchered and others are lamed, or stray from the right road."[134] The decision to dissemble, then, was infused with the responsibility of the physical harm of others. No longer was it simply a matter of the individual and his God or the individual and the reformer, but the welfare of others is factored into the equation.

Calvin also countered the argument put forth by the Nicodemites that they simulate so as to lessen the danger of persecution and help the church to grow, otherwise it will perish. Calvin argued that if we all dissemble as they do, "the countries where God has planted many seeds would remain deserted."[135] In other words the seed of the church, the martyrs, who cause the church to grow, will cease to be produced and hence, the church cease to thrive. As the martyrs were an essential influence on the community in terms of the examples of their sacrifices and confessions, the argument of the Nicodemites fell flat on both Calvin and Viret. Instead, they contrasted the constancy and sacrifice of the martyr with the "scandalousness" of the Nicodemite.[136] Just as the martyr was the source of augmentation of the faith, the Nicodemite caused it to decrease. In equating the situation of the early Christians to that of his time, Viret admonished, "If they had been as afraid for their skins as we are, the Christian religion would not have grown so much in so little time."[137] Calvin also argued that without the willingness to suffer of the early Christian martyrs, or if they had believed Nicodemite arguments, there would never have been a Christian Church.[138]

The martyrs were held as examples of those who overcame their worldly ties and desires, sacrificing their own lives so as to avoid idolatry. They, unlike the Nicodemite, provided true edification. The establishment of the priority of upholding the Gospel over all else, which in turn brings about suffering and persecution, was a prominent theme in both the martyrological accounts and the anti-Nicodemite texts. This suffering and persecution helped to define the community as chosen by God. The Nicodemite refused to accept this suffering, and instead chose to value earthly comforts. He was not willing to follow the admonishments of Matthew 10:37–39 and hence, in refusing, undermined the identity of the community so as to retain a comfortable and safe life. In a particular passage Calvin noted the Nicodemite argument that if God sent persecution, then it must be borne in patience, but it is good to avoid it as much as possible. Calvin admitted this was true, but argued that if one endures nothing for God's word, "Is that not to want to transform Jesus Christ to have him just as our flesh would like him to be?"[139] Viret associated some suffering and sacrifice with the believer's responsibility to God, that to be a true Christian one must endure. To support this argument he cited Luke 14:25 (RSV): "And he who would like to be my disciple must renounce himself and he much carry every day His cross on his shoulders, and he must follow me."[140] The willingness to suffer some degree for God's truth, then, was essential to being a good Christian.

Calvin's strongest assertion of this theme can be found in the second of the *Quatre sermons*, an "Exhortation to Endure Persecution to Follow Jesus Christ and his Gospel" ("Exhortation à souffrir persecution pour suyvre Iesus Christ et son Evangile"). The corpus of the *Quatre sermons* is essentially an anti-Nicodemite text, exhorting the faithful to avoid idolatry in the first sermon, asserting the importance of external worship and church discipline in the third, and extolling the privilege to hear freely the Gospel preached (i.e., an argument for exile) in the faith. The second sermon, however, is a specific argument for the responsibility of the faithful to endure suffering if it means upholding God's honor in the face of idolatry and superstition. Calvin, like Viret, described the path that Christians must tread to be full of suffering: "Although it may seem rough to us at first glance, we must content ourselves with this word of Saint Paul (1 Thess. 3:3) that we are called upon and created to suffer, since he said that the condition of our Christianity is such that we must travel by this road if we want to follow Jesus Christ."[141] Suffering, then, was a mark of the true church and of God's chosen ones: "Saint Paul shows us by his own example that we have to glorify ourselves with the stigmata of Christ, which are the marks by which God recognizes us and acknowledges us as his own." Additionally, Calvin stated that God uses persecution to discover which are his faithful.[142] The acceptance of suffering, then, in this and other anti-Nicodemite texts, was a key ingredient in defining God's faithful, just as it was in the general rhetoric of martyrdom.

Suffering martyrdom, however, was not for everyone. Whereas Calvin and Viret extolled martyrdom in terms of its edification of the faithful and embodiment of true Christianity,[143] neither advocated martyrdom wholesale. One must be willing to suffer even to the end in defense of God's honor, but it must be done carefully and correctly. Confessions were to be made with "Christian modesty," and martyrdom was not to be actively sought out. Both acknowledged how foreign martyrdom was to human nature, and to that extent, Calvin and Viret counseled exile as the most realistic response to the persecution. If one was forced to stay due to weakness or circumstances that could not be overcome, then they recommended steadfastness. Viret, in particular, directed those who could not "attain to this high grade and to the Christian perfection of the martyrs." Instead, he offered, "let us be secret disciples with Nicodemus and with Joseph of Arimathea. And if we do not show ourselves clearly, let us at least not do anything that would dishonor Jesus Christ, and let us not agree with his adversaries by sharing at the table of the devils."[144] He qualified this concession, though, with the demand that those who must do this must also confess their weakness to God and beg for his forgiveness. Viret's sentiments were echoed in Calvin's *Petit traicté*, though Calvin added at the end of his recommendation that "the glory of God, which is what is at question here, should be more precious to us than this fallen and transitory life, which, to speak truly, is no more than a shadow."[145]

The choices of the faithful persecuted in France were not simply a matter that affected the individual. Reformers such as Viret and Calvin imbued these decisions with a social consciousness: choice of behavior had communal repercussions ranging from providing bad examples and leading others to the same sin, to bringing about God's ire upon them all, bringing physical harm upon others, and finally to undermining the efforts of the martyrs. As the martyr supported and edified the community through his suffering and sacrifice to uphold the Gospel, the Nicodemite damaged and subverted it.

Just as the breakdown of a community is often based upon difference, the creation and identification of a community is based on similarity. With the rise of Protestantism in France in the 1530s, the old institutions of Catholicism that bound the community together were challenged. Reformers insisted that the faithful abstain from any and all forms of "idolatry." In doing so, they attempted to create a separate community, one that was pure and untainted.

From the 1540s on, as the repression of heresy by the state and hostility from the predominantly Catholic populace increased, the rhetoric of martyrdom took central stage. It reassured the faithful that persecution and suffering were the marks of the true church. The new community, then, was bound not only by their common faith but by the shared experience of suffering and sacrifice. The rhetoric, through the martyrologies and martyrological narratives, provided examples to which all could relate, and representations that would reinforce the notion that they all suffered for a common, righteous cause—rather than the accusations of blasphemy, heresy, and seduction put forth by the state. Martyrdom became a vehicle by which the Reform could reconceptualize the past and create an interpretation of history (both ancient and contemporary) that would legitimate the new community. It was through the rhetoric of martyrdom that the Reform created a sense of universality, that the fight for which they all suffered transcended geography, time, and traditional hierarchies.

The imagery and language used in the anti-Nicodemite texts are specific examples of the rhetoric of martyrdom in terms of defining and supporting a community based upon suffering and the fight against the superstitions and idolatry of their former community. Reformers such as Calvin and Viret considered it the responsibility of the faithful to support this new community rather than undermine it due to human frailty or desire for earthly comfort. To endure suffering for the cause was to bear the cross of Christ, and to avoid this cross, was to deny him. They imbued this argument with a social consciousness, making the faithful aware of their responsibility not only to God, but to the community as well. This was done through the same images, language, and symbols of the larger rhetoric of martyrdom.

The proper functioning of the community of the faithful was integral to the success of the Reform in the minds of many of its leaders. A shared faith, however, was not enough in terms of psychologically and emotionally binding the persecuted community in France together. Thus, the rhetoric of martyrdom, which further defined the community through suffering, provided the means by which the faithful could make sense of a world of violence and dislocation.

Epilogue:
St. Bartholomew's Day,
1572

HISTORY SOMETIMES PROVES TRUE THE OLD QUIP, "JUST BECAUSE you are paranoid does not mean they are not out to get you." For the Huguenots nothing illustrated this more than the events surrounding the St. Bartholomew's Day Massacre of 1572. The blood had not dried on the streets of Paris before Calvinist conspiracy theories were out and about, but these were different from the theories that preceded them. Before the massacre, Huguenot polemicists from about 1550 to 1572 developed various conspiracy theories involving "wicked advisors" to the crown or conniving Catholic bishops and judges bent on usurping royal power and exterminating Protestantism.[1] Events such as the massacres at Mérindole and Cabrières in 1560 and at Vassy[2] in 1562 provided fuel for these theories.[3] Rumors of conspiracy had surrounded previous attacks and would be used to justify the use of force against the monarch, who, according to the Huguenots, was being ill-advised, left in the dark, or pressured by "evil-minded" forces.[4] This nicely constructed scapegoat of the "king's wicked advisors" essentially excused the king from complicity and allowed the Huguenot faction to maintain their proclaimed loyalty to the crown. The failed Conspiracy of Amboise in 1560, in which the Huguenots attempted to "liberate" the king, illustrates this perception.

After the dust settled from Vassy it became crystal clear that the crown did not have control over the ultramontane faction of the Guise family. Apparently the Huguenots were paranoid for good reason. The Guise, Anne de Montmorency (the constable of France), and Marshal Saint-André had united to counter the policy of toleration temporarily embraced by the regent, Catherine de Medici. During her regency in the 1560s, Catherine had been relatively willing to compromise with the Huguenots as a way of counterbalancing the growing power of this ultramontane faction. But on March 1, 1562, François de Guise, with over two hundred armed men, attacked a group of Huguenots who were legally (according to the edict of January of 1560, which granted some toleration) conducting services in a barn in Vassy. Guise and his men killed men, and unarmed women and children. In the aftermath, Calvinist polemicists claimed it was a premeditated attack and outside of legal justification. Guise claimed he had only been passing by and that he and his men had been provoked. The massacre at Vassy was the final straw that led to open civil war. Calvinist resistance theory, then, justified the taking up of arms in defending the crown from tyranny and the "evil advisors."[5] Thus the Huguenot faction was not willing to alienate the monarchy even as it technically bore arms against it.

Martyrdom and its accompanying rhetoric played an important role in this schema. Calvinist polemicists and martyrologists emphasized time and time again that the deaths of the faithful were due to religious conviction, not any secular or political crimes. The deaths of the martyrs proved the righteousness of the cause and would—as it had for the early Christians, it was thought—lead to triumph. Their blood was that of the innocent and their passivity in the face of persecution proved their status as loyal subjects. Even during the wars, Calvinist "Christian soldiers" also fought and/or died not as traitors to the crown, but as its saviors. In their prayers, soldiers were to ask God "to have mercy on our King, to illuminate him in the knowledge of your truth, and not implicate him at all in the tyrannies that are committed in this Kingdom under the pretext of his name. And give him wisdom and discretion to be able to recognize his faithful servants, those whom he has been persuaded, in hatred of his Church, to be his enemies."[6]

This all changed in the wee hours of August 24, 1572, the St. Bartholomew's Day Massacre. While in some respects, the massacre is the story of a wedding celebration gone horribly wrong, it is also a major turning point for the French Calvinists and their struggle to survive. All their caution and paranoia did not prepare them for what was to come. Both the Huguenot and Catholic leadership had gathered mid-August in Paris to celebrate what was to be a type of

peace treaty between the factions, the wedding of Henri, King of
Navarre, a Prince of the Blood and Huguenot leader, and Marguerite Valois, the Catholic sister of King Charles IX. The event was
not met without some suspicion on the part of the Huguenots as
Henri's mother, Jeanne d'Albret, had died two months prior. Later,
rumors of assassination would abound, most notably that Catherine de Medici had sent poisoned gloves to dispatch this Calvinist
queen.[7] Nevertheless, the wedding was held on August 18. On August 22, a failed attempt had been made on the life the leader of the
Huguenot faction, Gaspard de Coligny. Given a royal guard to keep
him safe, Coligny was confined to bed rest. But early in morning of
August 24, sometime before dawn, a second and successful attempt
was made on his life, setting in motion a massacre that would first
take the lives of just about the entire Huguenot leadership, then extend to the Protestant population of Paris, and finally engulf many
of France's provinces. The massacre began with a decision that had
been made the evening of August 23: the Huguenot leadership must
be eliminated out of fear of an attack. Once Coligny was dead and
his body mutilated, the violence took on huge proportions pro-
pelled by the rumor that the king himself wanted the extermination
of all Protestants in the city.[8] No longer was it simply the assassination of the leadership, but a massacre bringing about the violent and
gory deaths of men, women, and children. The Seine, it was said, ran
red with the blood of innocents. And the violence was not confined
to Paris, but quickly spread outside of the city. Contemporary esti-
mates of the dead ranged from 50,000 to 765,000,[9] and polemicists
and artists would depict the atrocities committed against men,
women, and children in all their gory detail. Just who was the instigator of the massacre? Protestant sources invariably pointed to the
Guise, to the queen mother, to the king himself. Regardless of the
authorship of the larger massacre, we do know that Charles IX did
make the final order for the annihilation of the leadership.[10]

What can be said with certainty is that the event transformed the
rhetoric of martyrdom and removed any barriers to a direct attack
on the French monarchy. In the aftermath of the massacre, Protestant polemicists went on the offensive attempting to identify the re-
sponsible parties and decrying the event. Within the realm of political theory, some of these polemicists even implicitly advocated
regicide, an act considered much too radical in Calvinist circles
prior to the massacre.[11] More influential, however, were "historically"

based explorations of the nature of royal authority and the role of the king's "traditional" advisors. After the massacre, treatises such as the *Reveille-Matin* (1573), *Francogallica* (1573), *Du Droit des magistrats*[12] (1574), and the *Vindiciae contra tyrannos* (1579), implicitly or explicitly legitimated aggressive resistance to the crown, rejecting the passive or conciliatory approaches favored prior to 1572. Beginning with the *Reveille-Matin* each of these works declared in one way or another that the monarch was not the sole possessor of sovereignty and could be rightfully overthrown. The unquestioned authority of the king, then, was fair game. For example, the *Francogallica*, penned by François Hotman, found that in its earliest days, the monarchy shared sovereignty with an elite council, the predecessor of the Estates General. It followed that this council, representative of the people, had the power to dethrone a monarch if he proved tyrannical.[13] And in *Du Droit des magistrats*, Calvin's moderate resistance theory, focused originally upon obedience to authority, was vastly extended and reinterpreted by Théodore de Bèze, to be a "considerable theory of revolution."[14]

So while the St. Bartholomew's Day Massacre created more "martyrs" for the Calvinist cause, there is a distinct change in the rhetoric surrounding them. The call was not for martyrly forbearance but for vengeance and action against a tyrannical monarch. Crespin's martyrology continued to grow after his death in 1570, under the editorship of Simon Goulart, with the incorporation of the massacre's victims and others who were to follow them. Goulart even produced an account of the massacre under his own name, *Mémoires de l'estat de france sous Charles IX*. But there is a profound difference in the purpose of his text, versus the earlier stated aims of Crespin as martyrologist. Robert Kingdon identifies three key goals of the work: first, to describe and memorialize the event; second, to bring international attention and involvement in the French conflict; third, "to challenge received ideas about the very nature of contemporary government, in particular the notion that absolute monarchy was the best and most natural form of government."[15] This last aim highlights one of the chief differences between the rhetoric of martyrdom prior to St. Bartholomew's Day 1572 and after it. Whereas the martyrs and the rhetoric of martyrdom focused on duty to God, responsibility to the community of the faithful, sacrifice, suffering, and loyalty to the king, after 1572 martyrdom became a rallying cry for political change on the part of the Huguenots. After the massacre, the illusion of a king led astray or manipulated by enemies was shattered. It became crystal clear to the Huguenots that they were not simply in danger of persecution—they were in danger of extinction at the hands of the king himself and a populace that had "innocent" blood on it own hands. The passivity of the martyrs was no longer efficacious in the struggle against a king now proven to be hell-bent on the extermination of the faithful.

Conclusion

Traditionally martyrdom has been viewed as the choice of an individual to sacrifice knowingly and willingly his or her life rather than betray a belief or principle–be it religious, political, social, or philosophical. This choice, however, has many implications that resound beyond the individual. Once a martyr has been recognized as such, his or her identity as an individual and the specific context in which the martyrdom has taken place is subsumed by the associated role as a witness for the cause and is set in a larger eschatological or moral context. In other words, the individual becomes a symbol of the belief system, and is then incorporated into a tradition that is used to console, exhort, edify, unite, and defend the faithful followers of a movement. This interpretation of martyrdom becomes especially clear when we look at the persecution of Protestants and the rhetoric that surrounded it during the French Reformation.

In 1523 the first alleged "Lutheran" was burned in Paris. Although this execution was not necessarily remembered by Protestants in their collections recounting the history of the persecution of the true faith, it does mark the beginning of a course of action on the part of the state to "exterminate" the heresy not only being imported from the German territories but also being nurtured in its own lands as well. As the persecution of French Protestants increased during the 1530s, a tradition and a language were reborn: the act and rhetoric of martyrdom. This tradition and imagery would reach its pinnacle in the 1560s, only to be rejected for a more aggressive approach after the St. Bartholomew's Day Massacre of 1572. But during the period from 1530 through to 1572, martyrdom and its corresponding rhetoric provided the French Reform movement and community with its rallying call, its source of solace, its edifica-

147

tion, and its identity. By looking at the chaos that evolved into the Wars of Religion through this particular lens, the violence, the hatred, the suffering, and the passion of the period jump out in high relief.

Although the details of individual lives and events should be by no means ignored as a way of obtaining a good picture of the experiences of sixteenth-century Huguenots, the images and language that populated the works written, read, and absorbed by this community are just as integral to the understanding of their worldview. While we will never know the individual circumstances that led many French Protestants to choose to sacrifice their lives for their faith, we may look at the general and central role martyrdom played in the movement. Many of the faithful did not have to make a decision of life or death, but this does not mean that they did not share in the peril or turmoil that the persecution and the fracturing of society engendered. Martyrdom and its surrounding rhetoric played an essential role in both the understanding and self-representation of the French Protestant community and its context. More specifically while the martyrological narratives provide material relevant to the lives of individuals, they reliably reveal much more about the values, the needs, and the ideology of the Reform movement. The story of the martyr is often multilayered and the actual details of their experience can be subsumed by the needs of the movement. Thus the accounts, in many ways, tell us more about the ideology of the Reform than they do about the individuals themselves.

As this study has shown, the rhetoric of martyrdom was used to define, delineate, and describe not just the stories of individual martyrs or the persecution but also many of the problems faced by this newly conceived community. It permeated many of the theological, political, literary, prescriptive, and historical works penned by French and Genevan Protestants from the 1540s through to 1572. The pervasiveness of the rhetoric, which was not confined solely to the martyrological accounts, illustrates the centrality of the theme of martyrdom to the Reform movement. It became the defining feature and the focal point of numerous works in almost every written genre, extolling or illustrating the themes of duty, sacrifice, and the heroic endurance of suffering—all traits embodied or exemplified by the martyr.

The rhetoric of martyrdom functioned in a number of ways from the level of the individual to that of the greater community, and in the larger struggle against external persecution. As the conflict between the Reform movement and its Catholic persecutors involved political, spiritual, and emotional factors, the rhetoric of martyrdom provided the imagery and language that supplied inspiration and consolation, while also offering absolution and legitimization for resistance to the state in the form of the martyr's (or potential martyr's) mandate from God. Indeed, from a spiritual and emotional standpoint removed from legalistic appeals to the French constitution and magistracy in Protestant resistance theories, the rhetoric of martyrdom supplied the Reform with both a sense of duty and with legitimacy in its struggle against repression.

Through the language of common suffering and the universalization of the example of the martyr, the rhetoric of martyrdom shaped the Reformed community's identity. It bonded this persecuted minority through their shared experiences (of varying degrees) of disenfranchisement and suffering. The rhetoric universalized the experiences, and the literature, in its various forms, and allowed the community to live the experiences of individuals as if they were their own. This in turn eventually produced a revised history that defined the Reformed community as inheritors of the title of God's chosen or the true church: God's faithful always experienced persecution. In other words, the language and imagery of martyrdom incorporated their individual experiences in a larger, more profound, and meaningful context. This rhetoric emphasized the faithful's responsibility not only to God, but the individual's responsibility to the community as well.

As a multipurpose tool, however, this rhetoric and its accompanying textual images also provided a valuable way of harnessing the potentially disruptive power of martyrdom. While the acts and experiences of the female martyrs without any interpretation could have been threatening to the gendered social order espoused by the reformers (Calvin in particular), the framework in which these martyrs were placed in terms of language and imagery, recast their acts to be supportive of this order. It is here that we find the rhetoric of martyrdom being used to reinforce the theologically ordained inferior position of women, while still employing them as challenges to the church and persecuting state essentially by placing all the agency and ability in God's hands. The female martyr's strength was solely attributed to God, while her example was held forth for women only after being qualified.

The conflict that was born out of attempts to reform the Catholic Church left France a physically fractured, spiritually wounded, and psychologically scarred nation up through the seventeenth century. The sense of dislocation and disenfranchisement as well as the fear of persecution (and prosecution with all its consequences) forced the Huguenot community to reinterpret the bonds that originally held the national and local communities together. The rhetoric of martyrdom and the examples of the martyrs offered a weapon against persecution, but they also worked as a force within the movement, providing it with its identity and sense of community. Most importantly both the rhetoric and the act were powerful expressions of and vehicles for the ideology of the Reform movement itself.

While this study has focused on seemingly abstract concepts, such as "rhetoric," "identity," "language," "ideology," and "representation," it would be a mistake not to acknowledge the horrific realities brought about by religious persecution. The division of Christendom not only divided the community, it brought out the worst in it. The particular viciousness of the violence, whether perpetuated by the state or populace, created a permanent scar on the psyche of early modern Europe, and it would take nearly two centuries for the argument for religious toleration to be heard and be legally acknowledged by a broad swath of "enlightened" Western society.

Notes

1. The Rebirth of the Rhetoric of Martyrdom

1. Jean Crespin, *Histoire des vrays tesmoins de la verité de l'Evangile, qui de leur sang l'ont signée, depuis Jean Hus jusques au temps presente* (Geneva, 1570; reprint, Liége: Centre national de recherches d'histoire religieuse, 1964), 522: "porte son affliction avec une joye indicible."

2. *Exhortation et Remonstrance aux Princes du Sang, et Seigneurs du privé conseil du Roy, Pour obvier aux seditions qui occultement semblent menacer les fideles pour le faict de la Religion* (n.p., 1561), 7: "que la mort de l'un, a été renouvellement de vie a cent autres."

3. See David Seeley, *The Noble Death: Graeco-Roman Martyrology and Paul's Concept of Salvation* (Sheffield, UK: JSOT Press, 1990); and Arthur J. Droge and James D. Tabor, *A Noble Death: Suicide and Martyrdom among Christians and Jews in Antiquity* (San Francisco: HarperSanFrancisco, 1992).

4. Droge and Tabor, *A Noble Death*, 20–22.

5. Ibid., 29–36.

6. Seneca, "On Providence," 2:10–12. In *Moral Essays: Volume I*, trans. John W. Basore, Loeb Classical Library (1958).

7. Robin Lane Fox, *Pagans and Christians* (New York: Knopf, 1989), 420. See also Droge and Tabor, *A Noble Death*, and W. H. C. Frend, *Martyrdom and Persecution in the Early Church: A Study of a Conflict from the Maccabees to the Donatists* (New York: Anchor Books, 1967) for an analysis of the Judaic interpretation of martyrdom through the Maccabean tradition.

8. Frend, *Martyrdom and Persecution*, 34.

9. Ibid., 34–39.

10. Glen Bowersock, in his work, *Martyrdom and Rome*, looks at the linguistic origins of the term "martyr." Lucy Grig argues, however, that the absence of this term does not preclude Judaism from having its own sense of the concept prior to the use of the term. See Glen Bowersock, *Martyrdom and Rome* (Cambridge: Cambridge University Press, 1995), chap. 1; and Lucy Grig, *Making of Martyrs in Late Antiquity* (London: Gerald Duckworth, Ltd., 2004), 9.

11. Tertullian, *Flight in Time of Persecution,* in Tertullian, *Disciplinary, Moral and Ascetical Works,* trans. Rudolph Arbesmann, Emily Joseph Daly, and Edwin A. Quain (New York: Fathers of the Church, 1959), 7.1.

12. See Ignatius of Antioch, *Epistle to the Romans,* 6. This passage is discussed by Grig in *Making Martyrs,* 17–18.

13. See for example, Origen, *Exhortation to Martyrdom* in *Origen: An Exhortation to Martyr, Prayer, and Selected Works,* trans. Rowan A. Greer (Mahwah, NJ: Paulist Press, 1979), chaps. 11 and 39, and Tertullian, *To the Martyrs* in *Tertullian: Disciplinary, Moral and Ascetical Works,* trans. Rudolph Arbesmann, Emily Joseph Daly, and Edwin A. Quain (New York: Fathers of the Church, 1959), 2.1.

14. Tertullian, *To the Martyrs,* chap. 2.

15. See Origen, *Exhortation to Martyrdom,* chaps. 1, 18, 21, 36, and Tertullian, *To the Martyrs,* 1.3–6, 3.3–5.

16. Tertullian, *To the Martyrs,* 3.1–2.

17. For a short summary of the history of martyrology, see my entry in *A Global Encyclopedia of Historic Writing,* ed. D. R. Woolf, vol. 2 (New York: Garland, 1998), 595–97.

18. Eusebius, *Ecclesiastical History,* 5.1.

19. The sources on martyrological inversion in antiquity are numerous. See for example, Grig, *Making Martyrs in Late Aniquity;* Francine Cardman, "Acts of the Women Martyrs," in *Women in Early Christianity,* ed. D. M. Scholer (New York: Garland, 1993); Stuart G. Hall, "Women among the Early Martyrs," *Studies in Church History* 30 (1993): 1–22; Rachel Moriarity, "'Playing the Man'–the Courage of Christian Martyrs, Translated and Transposed," in *Gender and Christian Religion,* ed. R. N. Swanson (Suffolk, UK: Ecclesiastical History Society / Boydell Press, 1998); Joyce E. Salisbury, *Perpetua's Passion: The Death and Memory of a Young Roman Woman* (New York: Routledge, 1997).

20. Elizabeth Castelli, *Martyrdom and Memory: Early Christian Culture Making* (New York: Columbia University Press, 2004), 24–26.

21. See Peter Brown, *Augustine of Hippo* (Berkeley: University of California Press, 1967), chap. 21. Brown cites Augustine's letter to Marcellinus (*Letters,* 139:2), expressing this concern.

22. See Augustine, *The city of God against the pagans,* ed. and trans. R. W. Dyson (Cambridge: Cambridge University Press, 1998), bk. 19.

23. W. H. C. Frend, *The Rise of Christianity* (Philadelphia: Fortress Press, 1984), 668–73.

24. Thomas F. Mayer and D. R. Woolf describe "Pure hagiography, with its stress on the supernatural, on the signs of divine favor meted out to hermits and clergy and demonstrated by irreproachable lives, by conversion experiences, and by miracles . . . was certainly the most influential and popular of all medieval biographical genres." "Introduction" in Thomas F. Mayer and D. R. Woolf, eds., *The Rhetoric of Life-Writing in Early Modern Europe: Forms of Biography from Cassandra Fedele to Louis XIV* (Ann Arbor: University of Michigan, 1995), 12.

25. See Hipolyte Delehaye, *The Legends of the Saints,* trans. Donald Attwater (New York: Fordham University Press, 1962; originally published as *Les légendes hagiographiques* [Brussels, 1905]).

26. Ibid., 11.

27. *Dictionnaire de droit canonique,* ed. R. Naz, vol. 6 (Paris: Librairie Letouzey et Ané, 1957), 838.

28. Alison Knowles Frazier, *Possible Lives: Authors and Saints in Renaissance Italy* (New York: Columbia University Press, 2005), 59.

29. Ibid., 64–77.

30. Ludwig Rabe, *Der heiligen aus erwohlten Gottes Zeugen Bekennen und Martyren* (1552); John Foxe, *Acts and Monuments* (1554); Jean Crespin, *Livre des martyrs* (1554); Flaccius Illyricus, *Catalogus testium veritatis* (1556); Antoine de la Roche Chandieu, *Histoires des pérsecutions, et martyrs de l'Église de Paris, depuis l'An 1557, jusques au temps du Roy Charles neufviesme* (1563); Heinrich Pantaleone, *Martyrum historia* (1563); Adrian Cornelis van Haemstede, *De Gheschiedenisse ende den doodt der vromer Martelaren* (1559). For an analysis of these martyrologies in their national contexts, see Brad Gregory, *Salvation at Stake: Christian Martyrdom in Early Modern Europe* (Cambridge, MA: Harvard University Press, 1999), 187–96.

31. David El Kenz, *Les bûchers du roi: la culture protestante des martyrs (1523–1572)* (Paris: Champ Vallon, 1997), 72.

32. Nancy Lyman Roelker, *One King, One Faith: The Parlement of Paris and the Religious Reformations of the Sixteenth Century* (Berkeley: University of California Press, 1996), 189–91. Roelker also discusses the differing opinions of historians regarding the degrees of sympathy held by the members of the royal family toward religious reform.

33. "Edit qui enjoint expressement a tous baillis, senechaux, procureurs, avocats du roi, etc . . . , sous peine de suspension et privation de leurs offices, de rechercher et poursuivre les lutheriens, et de les livrer au jugement des cours souveraines," June 1, 1540, no. 305, in Francois-André Isambert et al., eds., *Recueil general des anciennes lois françoises depuis l'an 1420, jusqu'à la Revolution de 1789,* vol. 13 (Paris, 1822–33).

34. See Nathaniel Weiss, *La Chambre Ardente. Étude sur la liberté de conscience en France sous François Ier et Henri II (1540–1550)*(Geneva: Slatkine Reprints, 1970). Also see Roelker, *One King, One Faith,* 214–222.

35. See Origen, *Exhortation to Martyrdom*; Tertullian, *Apology* and *Letter to Scapula,* in *Tertullian: Apologetical Works and Minucius Felix Octavius,* trans. Rudolph Arbesmann, Emily Joseph Daly, and Edwin A. Quain (New York: Fathers of the Church, 1950); Tertullian, *To the Martyrs.*

36. Foxe's *Acts and Monuments* has generated significant works in this area. For example, See D. R. Woolf, "The Rhetoric of Martyrdom: Generic Contradiction and Narrative Strategy in John Foxe's *Acts and Monuments*" in *The Rhetoric of Life-Writing in Early Modern Europe,* 243–82, and John R. Knott, *Discourses of Martyrdom in English Literature, 1563–1694* (Cambridge: Cambridge University Press, 1993).

37. Gregory, *Salvation at Stake.* See also Luc Racaut, "Religious Polemic and Huguenot Self-Perception and Identity, 1554–1619," in *Society and Culture in the Huguenot World, 1559–1685,* ed. Raymond A. Mentzer and Andrew Spicer (Cambridge: Cambridge University Press, 2002).

38. Catherine Randall Coats,*(Em)bodying the Word: Textual Resurrections in the Martyrological Narratives of Foxe, Crespin, de Bèze and d'Aubigné* (New York: Peter Lang, 1992), and Frank Lestringant, *La cause des martyrs dans "Les Tragiques" d'Agrippa d'Aubigné* (Mont-de-Marsan: Éditions InterUniversitaires, 1991).

39. An example of a work that balances historical context with a textual analysis is John Knott's valuable study of the British martyrologies and rhetoric. See Knott, *Discourses of Martyrdom in English Literature, 1563–1694*. See also an older, but useful, work also on the British martyrologies and identity, William Haller, *Foxe's Book of Martyrs and the Elect Nation* (London: Jonathan Cape, 1967).

40. See chapter 4 for a more complete discussion of history and martyrology.

41. For example, in the anonymous pamphlet *Remonstrance à tous estats [en faveur sur le huguenotisme ou protestantisme]: Par laquelle est en brief demonstre la foy & innocence des vrays chrestiens: Les abus ausquels font detenus leurs ennemis & persecuteurs: Et le jugement que Dieu en sera* (Paris, 1560), the author points out the effect that persecution has on the church, "car tant plus ils persecutent, tant plus croist le nombre des Fidèles, & multiplie tellement cette sainct semence. . . ." See also *Prières pour les soldats & prisonniers de l'Église reformée* (La Rochelle, 1568). The prayers offered in this pamphlet use the same martyrological rhetoric.

2. THE TRIAL AND DEATH
OF ANNE DU BOURG

1. Florimond de Raemond, *L'Histoire de la Naissance, Progrez, et Decadence de l'Heresie de ce siecle* (Arras, 1616), 1284: "Il me souvient que quand Anne du Bourg Conseiller au parlement de Paris, fut brule: tout Paris s'étonna de la constance de cet homme. Nous fondions en larmes dans nos Colleges au retour de ce supplice & plaidions sa cause apres son decez, maudissant ces Juges injustes qui l'avoient justement condamne: Son preche en la poteance & sur le buchier, fut plus de mal que cent Ministres n'eussent sceu faire." The first edition of this work was published in 1606, posthumously. See Barbara Sher Tinsley, *History and Polemics in the French Reformation: Florimond de Raemond, Defender of the Church* (Selinsgrove, PA: Susquehanna University Press, 1992).

2. Matthieu Lelièvre, "Anne Du Bourg avant son Incarcération à la Bastille," *Bulletin de la Société de l'Histoire du Protestantisme français* 37 (1887): 569–90; "Le Procès et le Supplice d'Anne Du Bourg," *Bulletin de la Société de l'Histoire du Protestantisme français* 36 (1888): 281–95; "Les Derniers Jours d'Anne Du Bourg," *Bulletin de la Société de l'Histoire du Protestantisme français* 37 (1888): 506–29.

3. David El Kenz, who wrote one of the most recent studies of Du Bourg in his *Les bûchers du roi: la culture protestante des martyrs (1523–1572)*, (Paris: Champ Vallon, 1997), does not cite any of Lelièvre's works.

4. William Monter, *Judging the French Reformation Heresy Trials by Sixteenth-Century Parlements* (Cambridge, MA: Harvard University Press, 1999); Nancy Roelker, *One King, One Faith: The Parlement of Paris and the Religious Reformations of the Sixteenth Century* (Berkeley: University of California Press, 1996); Donald R. Kelley, *Beginning of Ideology: Consciousness and Society in the French Reformation* (Cambridge: Cambridge University Press, 1981).

5. El Kenz, *Les bûchers du roi*, 182: "le martyre ne semble plus assez efficace pour compenser un désir de mort contre le souverain."

6. See the epilogue, below, for a discussion of the changes in resistance theories after 1572.

7. Roelker, *One King, One Faith*, 194.

8. Ibid., 203. Crespin includes Berquin's account in his martyrology from the 1555 edition on. See Jean Crespin, *Recueil de Plusieurs Personnes qui ont constamment endure la mort pour le Nom de notre Seigneur Jesus christ, depuis Jean Wicleff, & Jean Hus jusques a ceste annee present MDLV* (Geneva, 1555), 758–59.

9. Kelley, *Beginning of Ideology*, 13.

10. Roelker, *One King, One Faith*, 205.

11. N. M. Sutherland, *The Huguenot Struggle for Survival* (New Haven: Yale University Press, 1980), 338–39. In her appendix, Sutherland lists and gives a summary of all the major edicts of religion from 1525v to 1598.

12. Barbara Diefendorf, *Beneath the Cross: Catholics and Huguenots in Sixteenth-Century Paris* (Oxford: Oxford University Press, 1991), 49. See also Pierre de la Place, *Commentaires de l'estat de la religion et republique soubs les rois Henri et Francois seconds et Charles neufviesme*, in *Choix de chroniques et mémoires sur l'histoire de France*, ed. J. A. C. Buchon (Paris: Desrez, 1836), 14–16 on the establishment of the church and church discipline.

13. Francis Higman, *La Diffusion de la Réforme en France, 1520–1565* (Geneva: Labor et Fides, 1992), 226.

14. Assemblies such as this were defined as illicit and illegal in various edicts, in relation to caused a "scandale publique" and disturbed "la repose publique." See especially, "Lettres patentes enjoignant aux parlemens de royaume de rechercher et punir les lutheriens," Lyon, August 30, 1542, no. 352, and "Edit qui porte peine de mort contre ceux qui publiquement ou secretement professent une religion differente de celle catholique," Compiegne, July 24, 1557, no. 382, in François-André Isambert et al., eds., *Recueil Général des anciennes lois français depuis l'an 420 jusqu'à la Révolution de 1789*, vol. 14 (Paris, 1822–33). Cf. Raymond Mentzer, *Heresy Proceedings in Languedoc, 1500–1560*, Transactions of the American Philosophical Society, vol. 74 (Philadelphia, 1984). Mentzer points out that French criminal law did not embrace a sizeable corpus relating to religious offenses until the sixteenth century: "The enactment of these measures by the royal government corresponded approximately to the rise of French Protestantism and the increased activity of secular courts in the adjudication of heresy . . . and, for the most part, were directed against overt acts which might disrupt public tranquillity and threaten political and social accord . . . ," 131.

15. Jean Crespin, *Histoire des vrays tesmoins de la verité de l'Evangile, qui de leur sang l'ont signée, depuis Jean Hus jusques au temps presente* (Geneva, 1570; reprint, Liège: Centre national de recherches d'histoire religieuse, 1964), 492–93: "ne pensans point inciter les autres à faire le semblable."

16. John Viénot, *Histoire de la Réforme française* (Paris: Fischbacher, 1926), 245; E.-G. Léonard, *Histoire générale du protestantisme*, 2nd ed., 3 vols. (Paris: P.U.F., 1980).

17. See Isambert, ed., *Recueil Général*, vol. 14, no. 382.

18. Crespin, "Les assemblées du Pre aux clercs." See also Roelker, *One King, One Faith*, 233.

19. *Mémoires de Claude Haton*, vol. 1 (Paris: Imprimerie impériale, 1857), 47–48: "Les hereticques de France, qu'on appelloit lutheriens, faisoient grand debvoir d'acroîstre leur nombre et de gangner quelques princes ou grands seigneurs, pour les soustenir et deffendre en tout et partout, envers tous et contre tous. . . ."

20. Crespin has a vivid account of the threat posed by the crowd in his narrative of the *affaire*, describing the decision they faced: "attendre la venue des juges, & une mort certaine en faisant une ouverte confession de sa foi: ou rompre ceste multitude furieuse qui tenoit la maison affliegée . . . ," Crespin, *Histoire des vrays tesmoins*, 474.

21. For a summary of the legal shifts in jurisdiction, see Sutherland, *The Huguenot Struggle for Recognition*, 42–48, 54–57, and appendix; El Kenz, *Les bûchers du roi*, 33–35; and Mentzer, *Heresy Proceedings in Languedoc*, 46–51.

22. For example, in the case of the clergy, the Edict of Fontainebleau recognizes *cas privilegié* "as an offense which causes or is accompanied by open scandal or popular unrest [i.e., preaching] . . . under jurisdiction of royal courts," while the lesser *delit comun* was a "common misdemeanor, where public order remained undisturbed." See Mentzer, *Heresy Proceedings in Languedoc*, 45.

23. See "Edict of Châteaubriandt," Châteaubriandt, June 27, 1551, in A. Fontanon, ed., *Les Édits et ordonnances des rois de France*, vol. 4 (Paris, 1611), 252–57.

24. See "Edit qui porte peine de mort contre ceux qui publiquement ou secretement professent une religion differente de celle catholique" Compiègne, July 24, 1557, no. 382, in Isambert, *Recueil général*, vol. 12. For a discussion of this law see note 14.

25. Sutherland, *The Huguenot Struggle for Recognition*, 345.

26. Roelker, *One King, One Faith*, 235–36. See also Kelley, *Beginning of Ideology*, chap. 5.

27. "Lutheriens & contraires a l'Eglise Romaine: que cela estoit un scandale au peuple & aux subjets du Roi," X2a121, AN (cited by Monter in *Judging the French Reformation*, 166). The anonymous pamphlet *Confession sur les Principaux poincts de la religion Chrestienne. presentée à la Cour de parlement de Paris, Par Anne du Bourg, conseillier de la ditte Cour: estant pour lors prisonnier pour la defence de la Parolle de Dieu* (n.p., n.d.), and Jean Crespin's martyrology, *Actes des Martyrs deduits en Sept livres, depuis les temps de Wiclef & de Hus, jusques a present. Contenans un Recueil de vraye histoire Ecclesiastique, de ceux qui ont constamment endure la mort es derniers temps, pour la verité du Fils de Dieu* (Geneva, 1564), give this number as four. *La vraye histoire, de la fausse procedure contre Anne Du Bourg, Conseiller pour le Roy* (Paris, 1559), in *Mémoires de Condé, servant de'Eclaircissement et de Preuves à l'Histoire de M. De Thou, Contenant ce qui s'est passe de plus memorable en Europe*, vol. 1 (London, 1743), 219, incorrectly lists the number as two. See also El Kenz in *Les bûchers du roi*, 176.

28. *Vraye histoire*, in *Mémoires de Condé*, vol. 1, 219: "Lutheriens" who "persever- ans en icelle, & qu'il faut ainsi juger."

29. Ibid., 220: "les erreurs & heresies qui polluloyent en l'Eglise."

30. Interestingly, in his interrogation, Du Bourg states that "il n'est d'avis de suffoir l'execution, sous correction: ansi qu'il est d'avis de puir les hérétiques . . . selon la qualité de l'hérésie. . . ." *Vraye histoire*, in *Mémoires de Condé*, vol. 1, 235.

31. La Place identifies President Minard as the informer (see *Commentaires*, 12); the *Vraye histoire* identifies them as Minard and First President Le Maistre (in *Mémoires de Condé*, vol. 1, 220); and the author of the narrative contained in the *Confession sur les Principaux poincts* describes the situation as some conseillers tipping off the cardinal of Lorraine, who informed the king.

32. Rolker, *One King, One Faith*, 71. Also described in Jaques-Auguste de Thou, *Histoire universelle de Jaques-Auguste de Thou*, vol. 2 (The Hague: Henri Scheurleer,

1740), 670. See also Kelley, *Beginning of Ideology*, 171–72. Sources such as the *Vraye histoire* recognize the king's attendance as a *lit de justice*, though it does not describe the required ceremony. On the origins and evolution of the *lit de justice*, see Sarah Hanley, *The Lit de Justice of the Kings of France: Constitutional Ideology in Legend, Ritual, and Discourse* (Princeton: Princeton University Press, 1983).

33. The *Confession sur les Principaux poincts de la religion Chrestienne* describes the Parlementaires' right to speak freely: "que puis que par droict divin & humain, & toute ancienne coustume, & observation de la court de parlement, les opinions des conseilliers estoyent libres, & devoit un chascun parler selon sa conscience: mêmes que la presence de la majesté du Roy le confermoit en ceste liberté . . .," Dij.

34. De Thou, *Histoire universelle*, vol. 2, 670: "Ce qui fait qu'on les regarde comme des hommes seditieux, n'est-ce pas, parce que la faveur de la lumière de l'Ecriture, ils ont decouvert & révéle la turpitude de la puissance Romaine, qui panche vers sa ruine, & qu'il demandent une salutaire reformation?"

35. Francis Throckmorton, English ambassador to the French court, quotes the king as saying "Je verrai de mes yeux brûler cet Anne du Bourg." See Micheline Dupuy, *Pour Dieu et pour le roi: la montée de l'intolérance au XVe siècle* (Paris: Perrin, 1984), 229. Many of the sources repeat this quote. See also *Vraye histoire*, in *Mémoires de Condé*, vol. 1, 223; La Place, *Commentaires*, 14; Crespin, *Histoire des vrays tesmoins*, 521.

36. Ibid.: "pour estre spectacle au people."

37. De Thou, *Histoire universelle*, vol. 2, 673.

38. *Vraye histoire*, in *Mémoires de Condé*, vol. 1, 224: "Juge naturel, qui estoit la cour de Parlement . . . suivant l'ancienne coustume qu'ils dient avoir été tousjours observée." The interrogation was also published separately as *L'Exemplaire, et Forme du procez commis, Faict par les commissaires du Roy Contre Maistre Anne de Bourg, Conseiller en la Court de Parlement de Paris. Luy estant detenu Prisonnier pour la Religion, Contenant au vray les Interrogations à lui faicts: Et les responses & confession de sa Foy. En laquelle Dieu le veuille maintenir & fortifier* (Envers, 1560). See chapter 3 for a discussion of the sources.

39. *Vraye histoire*, in *Mémoires de Condé*, vol. 1, 224: "sur peine d'etre declairez attains & convaincus des cas á eux imposez, & de rebellion au Roy."

40. Ibid., 265–74. See below for a discussion of Du Bourg's legal strategy.

41. Ibid., 237: "il ne pense rien avoir dit contre l'ordre de sa profession, les Commandements de Dieu & de l'Eglise, ce qu'il ne voudroit faire."

42. Ibid, 237: "il faut obeir aux Ministres de l'Eglise, Curez & autres, qui ont charge de noz ames, en ce qu'ils commandent, qui est conforme à la parole de Dieu."

43. Lelièvre claims that this was a major mistake of Du Bourg's, that "sa conscience ne lui permettait pas de taire un principe qu'il croyait vrai, simplement parce que l'application de ce principe pouvait lui nuire" ("Le procès et le supplice d'Anne Du Bourg," 288). This was not just a matter of conscience, but part of Du Bourg's legal strategy. See below.

44. *Vraye histoire*, in *Mémoires de Condé*, vol. 1, 235: "de nommer ceux qui sont de son opinion qu'il a declairée ce-dessus, qui ne reverent la Saincte Messe . . . & autres Sacremens . . . qu'il ne peult juger de la conscience d'autry."

45. Ibid., 242: "il fait bien par les Loix Civiles, qu'il est loisible á un chacun de racheter son sang par tels moyens dont il s'advisera."

46. Ibid., 243: "il fait bien qu'il l'a offensée & offense de moment á autre: mais croit que Sa Majesté aura mercy de son ame, par le mérite du precieux Sang de son Fils."

47. Ibid., 235: "qu'il luy pleust de sa benigne grace [the king], pour la charite qu'il porte a ses subjets, pourvoir les moyens d'assembler un Concile pour extirper les hérésies qui sont pour le jourd'hui: & pour determiner par iceluy d'aucuns doubtes qui peuvent rester en la Religion, entre les ignorans: ainsi que sa Majeste même a promis par le premier article du Traitté de la Paix." The "Traitté de la Paix" here refers to the Treaty of Chambord (1552) between Henri II and the Protestant princes. At this time Henri needed their aid, and such a promise to convene a council would make him seem more sympathetic to them and less hostile to their co-religionists in France. Hence, the princes would be more likely to help Henri's cause.

48. El Kenz, *Les bûchers du roi*, 180.

49. De Thou, *Histoire universelle*, vol. 2, 691: "un tres-grand concors de personnes des deux sexes . . . & qu'ensuite les chandelles ayant été eteintes, chacun avoit satisfait ses desirs . . . qu'un d'entre eux avoit eu alors un commerce criminel avec la fille de l'Avocat, & avoit même content sa passion jusqu'a trois fois."

50. Ibid.: "l'imposture trouva facilement créance dans l'esprit du peuple & augmenta la haine contre les Protestans."

51. Crespin, *Histoire des vrays tesmoins*, 530.

52. Ibid. See also *Vraye histoire*, in *Mémoires de Condé*, vol. 1, 254; La Place, *Commentaires*, 20; Regnier de la Planche, *Histoire de l'estat de France, tant de la republique que de la religion, sous le regne de Francois II* in *Choix de chroiniques et Mémoires sur l'Histoire de France*, ed. J. A. C. Buchon (Paris: Desrez, 1836) 209–10; and Brulart, *Journal*, in *Mémoires de Condé*, vol. 1, 5–6. See also Monter, *Judging the Reformation*, 173.

53. Crespin, *Histoire des vrays tesmoins*, 530.

54. See Mentzer, *Heresy Proceedings in Languedoc*, 46.

55. "Arrêts du Parlements de Paris, rendu pendant l'instruction du procès d'Anne Du Bourg, Conseiller en cette cour; & l'Arrêt de mort donne contre lui, le 23 Decembre 1559," in *Mémoires de Condé*, vol. 1, 270: "l'Estat, vie & honneur . . . l'on n'a pas accoustummée en appeller les Chambres."

56. Roelker, *One King, One Faith*, 236. Roelker cites Throckmorton's letter to Queen Elizabeth "which states that of one hundred twenty persons, only Le Maistre and fourteen others supported the death sentence."

57. "Requête d'Anne Du Bourg, Conseiller au Parlement. A Nosseigneurs de la Court de Parlement," in *Mémoires de Condé*, vol. 1, 272.

58. Ibid., 271: "si ladicte Sentence estoit executée, ce seroit en consequence le priver de son Estat de Conseiller Clerc, lequel il ne pourroit tenir sans les dicts Ordres. Voila une ouverture faicte á l'Evesque de Paris ou autres Juges d'Eglise, de pouvoir en consequence de ladicte degradation, priver un Conseiller Clerc de son dict Estat de Conseiller, qui est un vraye entreprinse de Jurisdiction. . . ."

59. Lelièvre attributes Du Bourg's appeal on this ground to his desire to stay in the Catholic Church—to reform it rather than separate from it. See "Le Procès et le supplice d'Anne Du Bourg," 294–95. This seems to be an awkward fit with what Du Bourg is attribute to having said at the degradation ceremony—by both state

documents and Protestant pamphlets: that he was relieved to be stripped of the Orders and that he had only taken them to obtain his seat in the Court. When this ground for appeal is looked at in conjunction with the rest of the Requête, it becomes clear that it is part of his legal strategy, rather than a spiritual decision.

60. See Kelley, *Beginning of Ideology*, 5.

61. See *Remonstrances de la cour de Parlement a Paris, l'un sur l'Inquisition pour le fait de la Religion Chrestienne. L'autre touchant la jurisdiction, de ceux que l'on nomme Hérétiques, donne par Edit, aux Evesques & Ecclesiastiques de France* (n.p., 1561). In these remonstrances, especially the second one, Du Tillet focuses on the notion that the Parlement should reassert their position as the dispensers of the "king's justice," that by giving away the Parlement's authority to the church, the king is giving away his own. He suggests that royal justice (i.e., of the Parlement) is better qualified and manned to judge the cases. Though not referring to Du Bourg's case, these remonstrances reveal the overall tensions over jurisdiction and sovereignty of the Parlement regarding ecclesiastical authority.

62. "Requête d'Anne Du Bourg," in *Mémoires de Condé*, vol. 1, 271–72: "Sa Majesté n'a entendu par icelles deroger audict privilege; & ou la clause derogatoire y seroit, (que non) ladicte Court a accoustume de deliberer sur semblables Lettres toutes les dictes Chambres assemblées, & faire Remonstrances, voire les reiterer selon l'importance des cas avant que frapper coup á rompre tels priviliges & de telle consequence que celluy qui s'offre presentement, qui vous touche tous Mes dicts Seigneurs, & duquel vous-memes été Conservateurs." Italics are mine for emphasis.

63. Roelker cites their involvement in the Chambre Ardente (*One King, One Faith*, 218). See also Nathanaël Weiss, *La Chambre Ardente. Étude sur la liberté de conscience en France sous François Ier et Henri II (1540–1550)* (Geneva: Slatkine Reprints, 1970), xxxiv, lxxvi. Saint-André, however, had signed relatively few death sentences, though according to Weiss, he "servait avec zèle, d'obtenir leur rétractions sous la forme d'amende honorable aggravée de peines diverses probablement précédées d'un ensemble de procédures destinées à intimider les prisonniers" (lxxvi–lxxvii).

64. Crespin gives this date as November 20, while Brulart gives it as November 21. The *procès verbal* of his degradation lists the date as "Lundi XXe jour du mois de Novembre." See Procès verbal de la Degradation d'Anne Du Bourg Conseiller en la Cour, November 20, 1559, Collection Brienne, BN. Also, Crespin identifies the bishop as the "evesque de Lautreger" while the *procès verbal* identifies him as "Mre Jehan Juvénal des Ursins, evesque de Treguyer."

65. Procès verbal de la Dégradation d'Anne Du Bourg, Conseiller en la Cour, November 20, 1559, Collection Brienne, BN.

66. *Confession sur les Principaux poincts de la religion Chrestienne*, Diij. See also *Vraye histoire*, in *Mémoires de Condé*, 246: "que par ce moyent le caractère de la beste, dont il est parle en l'Apocalypse lui estoit osté: & ne tenoit plus aucune tache de l'Antechrist de Rome." The text is identical in both. See Chapter 3 for a discussion of the sources.

67. De Thou, *Histoire universelle*, vol. 2, 701: "d'adoucir ses juges par des responses moderées & d'eviter par-la un Arrêt rigoureux." See also La Place, *Commentaires*, 20; de la Planche, *Histoire de l'Estat de France*, 210–11.

68. Brulart, *Journal*, in *Mémoires de Condé*, vol. 1, 7: "abjura tous les propositions Hérétiques & erronnées qu'il avoit tenues, & ce en la presence de ses Juges." See also de la Planche, *Histoire de l'Estat de France*, 210, who attributes the confession to Marillac while pleading the appeal. De la Planche claims that Du Bourg wasn't given the opportunity while in court to deny the confession. The sincerity, timing, and method of this abjuration is controversial and debated or overlooked in the sources. See chapter 3.

69. De Thou, *Histoire universelle*, vol. 2, 701: "Qu'il devoit donc rejetter les laches conseils de ses amis, qui vouloient lui persuader de menager sa vie, au prejudice de sa reputation & de son salut éternel, & se preparer avec un grand courage, & une conscience pure, á soutenir le combat." Though the letter is lost, de Thou records the tenor of the message. The language that de Thou uses in relating Marlorat's message is consistent with Crespin, Pierre Viret, and Jean L'Espine especially when they talk about the rewards of martyrdom versus nicodemism. Thus, I tend to believe that de Thou's paraphrasing is probably close to the original letter. See also Chandieu, *Histoire des pérsecutions, et Martyrs de l'Eglise de Paris, depuis l'An 1557. jusques au temps du Roy Charles neufviesme* (Lyon, 1563), 422.

70. De Thou, *Histoire universelle*, vol. 2, 701: "apres avoir laisse aux hommes cette grande leçon."

71. Chandieu, *Histoire des pérsecutions*, 422: "Que les nouvelles de sa constance estoyent non seuelement en toute la France, mais en tout la chrestienté, et avoyent confirmé beaucoup d'infirmes et esmeu les autres de s'enquerir de leur salut. Que les yeux de tous estoyent sur lui . . . s'il faisoit par crainte chose contraire à sa première confession, il seroit cause d'une merveilleuse ruine."

72. M. l'Abbe Brulart, *Journal*, in *Mémoires de Condé*, vol. 1, 7–8. See also La Place, *Commentaires*, 20. This final confession was published multiple times in different sources. It was published separately as *Confession sur les Principaux poincts*. See chapter 3 for a discussion of the sources.

73. Kelley identifies the point of no return for Du Bourg as the interrogation (*Beginning of Ideology*, 173). However, it appears that with the ambiguous confession, Du Bourg and his friends in Parlement still held out hope for a positive outcome—until Marlorat's remonstrances (which led to the final confession) and the execution of Minard.

74. *Vraye histoire*, in *Mémoires de Condé*, vol. 1, 246–47; De Thou, *Histoire universelle*, vol. 2, 702.

75. While the account of the exchange between Marguerite and Du Bourg is found only in the martyrologies of Crespin and Chandieu, archival documents identify her as a prisoner in the Conciergerie at the same time. See Henri Bordier, *Copie des Extraits fait par le greffier Dongois mort en 1717 des Registres Criminels du Parlement de Paris, en ce qui se rapporte aux Protestans (1534–1584)*, MS 486, Bibliothèque de la Sociètè de l'histoire du protestantism français; and U/2505, Le Nain collection, Tournelle Registers, AN.

76. Ibid.: "Une femme m'a monstre ma leçon, & enseigne comment je me doi porter en ceste vocation-ci: [he says] sentant la force & vertu des admonitions de ceste poure femme." See also Chandieu, *Histoire des pérsecutions*, 337–42. Chandieu and Crespin are almost identical in their narratives of Marguerite le Riche, except

Chandieu curiously leaves out (or Crespin adds) the description of how they conversed through the "petite fenêtre."

77. Both La Place and Crespin include excerpts from the *Oraison* in their works. See Crespin, *Histoire des vrays tesmoins*, 534–35; La Place, *Commentaires*, 22–23. See chapter 3 for a full discussion of the *Oraison*.

78. Crespin, *Histoire des vrays tesmoins*, 530.

79. Brulart's Journal, in *Mémoires de Condé*, vol. 1, 4–5: "Fidèlles & à ceux de la parolle." Crespin also states that during Du Bourg's appeals, he had "moyen de faire entendre de ses nouvelles à l'Eglise, pour l'advertir de l'estat auquel estoyent ses affaires: des demandes qu'on lui avoit faites . . . C'estoit la teneur de ses lettres." *Histoire des vrays tesmoins*, 530. Regarding this attempted escape, Leliévre believes that Du Bourg was framed and really had no knowledge of any attempt to free him. See Leliévre, "Les Derniers Jours d'Anne Du Bourg," 508 n.3.

80. Crespin, *Histoire des vrays tesmoins*, 530.

81. Procès verbal of Du Bourg's execution, U/2505, Le Nain collection, Registers of the Tournelle, AN: "Stuard Escossois nature de la nation escossoise." See also Monter, *Judging the Reformation*, 173. Monter investigated an accusation originally levied in the *Procès Verbal* of Du Bourg's execution. He traces Robert Stuart's involvement and proves the escape attempt did occur. See also de Thou, *Histoire universelle*, vol. 2, 402–5, 504, and Diefendorf, *Beneath the Cross*, 55.

82. Diefendorf, *Beneath the Cross*, 55.

83. *Vraye histoire*, in *Mémoires de Condé*, vol. 1, 262: "entendue et ouye, et par ledict Du Bourg, de bouche affermée & confermée." See also La Place, *Commentaires*, 21–22. The two sources have an almost identical description of the event.

84. This date is variously given as December 27 by La Place and December 24 by the *Confession sur les principaux poincts*. The arrêt found in U/2505, Le Nain collection, Registre de la Tournelle, AN, is dated December 23.

85. *Vraye histoire*, in *Mémoires de Condé*, vol. 1, 262: "Voici la Foy en quoy je veux vivre & mourir: & ai signe ce present de mon signe, prest a le seeller de mon propre sang, pour maintenir la doctrine du Fils de Dieu. . . ."

86. See Lelièvre, "Les Derniers jours d'Anne Du Bourg," 514–15 for a discussion of Chandieu and De Thou's descriptions. El Kenz, in his *Les bûchers du roi*, only states that the work is attributed to Du Bourg and considers the pamphlet on its own without tackling the question of whether it was simply printed from a copy "il l'aurait écrit ou dicté à des compagnons de cellule and transmis secrètment à des coreligionnaires" or if it was actually read to the court by him. See 180–82. Du Bourg, after the failure of his last escape attempt (or plot to spring him) was held in a cage alone at the Bastille, thus it could not have been transmitted by his cellmates. See Crespin, *Histoire des vrays tesmoins*, 530.

87. Procès verbal de l'Execution, U/2505, Le Nain Collection, Registers of the Tournelle, AN: "l'Abbe de Montibourg cure de Sainct Barthelemy faisant plusier bonnes admonitions et remonstrances audit du Bourg pour le remettre et reduire en la voye des bonne catholiques lui alleguant plusiers passages de la saincte escriture l'offrant par plusiers fois comme cure l'ouyr en confession pour lui donne l'absolution de le fautes par la grace et puissance qui lui estoit commis de Dieu."

88. Ibid.

89. For a discussion on the spectacle of the public execution of Protestants, see David Nichols, "The Theatre of Martyrdom in the French Reformation," *Past and Present* 121 (1988): 49–73.

90. Procès verbal de l'Execution, U/2505, Le Nain Collection, Registers of the Tournelle, AN.

91. *Vraye histoire*, in *Mémoires de Condé*, vol. 1, 262: "Mes amis, je ne suis point ici comme un larron, ou un meurtrier: mais c'est pour l'Evangile."

92. Ibid.: "Mon Dieu ne m'abandonne point." All of the major narratives cite these exact same last words.

93. Procès verbal de l'Execution, U/2505, Le Nain collection, Registre de la Tournelle, AN.

94. Kelley, *Beginning of Ideology*, 262. Kelley points out that "enough of the leaders were executed to qualify it [the conspiracy and ensuing executions] as a 'massacre' in the eyes of the Huguenots. . . ."

3. The Making of a Martyr

1. See Frank Lestringant, *La cause des martyrs dans "Les Tragiques" d'Agrippa d'Aubigné* (Monte-de-Marsan: Éditions InterUniversitaires, 1991), 13–17, for a useful discussion of the act of martyrdom as inversion.

2. For example, Crespin, Chandieu, and Pierre Viret (to name a few) all cited Tertullian's famous adage, "The blood of the martyrs is the seed of the Church." Chandieu also included portions of Tertullian's *Apology* in his martyrology; see Antoine de la Roche Chandieu, *Histoire des pérsecutions, et martyrs de l'Église de Paris, depuis l'an 1557 jusques au temps du Roy Charles neufviesme* (Lyon, 1563), 17–25. Jean L'Espine also quoted Tertullian in his *Traitte consolatoire et fort utile, contre toutes afflictions qui adviennent ordinairement aux fidèles Chrestiens. Compose nouvellement par I. de Spina Ministre de la Parolle de Dieu: & adresse à un grand seigneur de France* (Lyon, 1565), 14: "qu'il n'y a point de plus bel ordre de Chavlier, ny de plus beaux colliers, que les chaines dont sont attachez les Martyrs de JC, & que pareillement il n'y a point de plus preceiux bracelets que sont les manotes dont on les lie & enserre les mains. . . ." Tertullian's *To the Martyrs* and the *Letter to Scapula* were translated into French and reprinted in 1564. See Tertullian, *Deux petits livres de Florent Tertullian*, ed. Jean Saugrain (Lyon, 1564). Each of these letters made not only a religious statement, but also a political one, contrasting the righteousness of the martyrs' cause against what the state saw as criminal behavior.

3. Jean Crespin, preface to *Histoire des vrays tesmoins de la verité de l'Evangile, qui de leur sang l'ont signée, depuis Jean Hus jusques au temps presente* (Geneva, 1570; reprint, Liège, Centre national de recherches d'histoire religieuse, 1964): "n'ont maintenu autre doctrine que celle des Prophetes & Apostres, ayans puise de la leurs sainctes Confessions et escrits." Interestingly, the marks are clearly spelled out for the first time in this edition, rather than in the earlier editions.

4. Ibid.: "Satan voyant queles vrais serviteurs de Dieu souffrent pour la verité, il a tasche, comme un finge, d'avoir aussi des martyrs d'erreur & mensonge, les mettant en avant aupres des vrais tesmoins de l'Evangile. Ce que nous voyons qu'encore aujourd'hui il prattique par une secte de gens qui sous un titre de la parolle de Dieu souffrans persecution, masquez d'apparence de saincte, abscur-

cissent d'une merveilleuse facon la verité: afin qu'elle ne puisse être discernée d'entre le mensonge." Crespin also stated here that the martyrs not only challenged the doctrines of the Catholics, but also those of the "Servetistes, anabaptistes, Epicuriens, Jesuites, & tant d'Apostats de la verité."

5. Ibid.: "qu'il a jadis donne à tous autres qui ont souffert pour son Nom."

6. There are some differences along gender lines in the way this weakness is represented or discussed. See chapter 4.

7. Crespin, preface to *Histoire des vrays tesmoins*: "la fournaise leur a été plus agreable & ont resonne les louanges de Dieu au milieu des flammes."

8. Chandieu, *Histoire des persécutions*, xxviii.

9. See, for example, L'Espine, *Traitté consolatoire* and Pierre Viret, *Traittez divers pour l'instruction des fidèles qui resident & conversent es lieus & pais esquels il ne leur est permis de vivre en la pureté & liberté de l'Evangile. Revues & augmentez* (Geneva, 1559), especially the epistle and first treatise.

10. Matthew Lelièvre briefly describes many of the sources on Du Bourg, including an evaluation of their overall "reliability" in his "Anne Du Bourg avant son incarcération a la Bastille (1520–10 Juin 1559)," *Bulletin de la Société de l'Histoire du Protestantisme français* 36 (1887): 571–74. His list, however, is somewhat incomplete.

11. Du Bourg's *Confession sur les principaux poincts de la religion Chrestienne. Presentee à la Cour de Parlement de Paris, par Anne du Bourg, conseillier de la ditee Cour: estant pour lors prisonnier pour la defence de la Parolle de Dieu* (n.p., n.d.) was published separately, with the exact same text found in *L'Exemplaire, et forme du procez commis, faict par les commissaires du Roy contre Maistre Anne de Bourg, Conseiller en la Court de Parlement de Paris. Luy estant detenu Prisonnier pour la Religion, Contenant au vray les Interrogations à lui faicts: Et les responses & confession de sa Foy. En laquelle Dieu le veuille maintenir & fortifier* (Envers, 1560), though at the end of the independent work is a narrative entitled "L'Histoire du Martyre." See below.

12. Crespin's account of Du Bourg's martyrdom changes notably in the 1570 edition, incorporating excerpts of the *Oraison*, taken from La Place. See below.

13. Both Chandieu's and Crespin's (1564) incorporated the identical texts of the confession and interrogation. See Lelièvre, "Anne Du Bourg avant son incarcéraction," 572–74. Lelièvre notes that the 1564 version in Crespin was discarded for the 1570 edition by Simon Goulart (who assumed editorship after Crespin's death in 1571) in favor of a transcription of Chandieu's account (I would also add La Place to the mix as well). See below for a brief comparison of the accounts. For the purposes of this chapter, as Goulart's involvement in the changes to the account have never been absolutely proven, I will still consider the 1570 account of Du Bourg to be edited by Crespin.

14. See, for example, *Exhortation aux Princes et Seigneurs du Conseil Prive du Roi* (n.p., 1561), 6–7, which refers to Du Bourg's trial in the former sense. For contemporary histories that cover Du Bourg's case, see Pierre la Place, *Commentaires de l'estat de la religion et république soubs les Rois Henri et François seconds et Charles neufviesme*, in *Choix de chroniques et mémoires sur l'histoire de France*, ed. J. A. C. Buchon (Paris: Desrez, 1836), originally published in 1565; *Recueil des choses memorables* (Strasbourg, 1565); Regnier de la Planche, *Histoire de l'Estat de France, tant de la republique que de la religion, sous le regne de Francois II,* in *Choix de Chroiniques et Mémoires*

sur l'Histoire de France, ed. J. A. C. Buchon (Paris: Desrez, 1836) originally published in 1576; Jacques-Auguste de Thou, *Histoire universelle de Jacques-Auguste de Thou,* vol. 2 (The Hague: Henri Scheurleer, 1740); Agrippa D'Aubigné, *Histoire universelle,* vol. 1 (Geneva: Librarie Droz, 1981), originally published in 1604; Théodore Bèze, *Histoire ecclésiastique,* 2 vols. (Lille: Leleux, 1841–42) originally published in 1580. Bèze's account is a transcription of de la Planche, but was widely read on its own.

15. M. M. Eug. and E. M. Haag, *La France protestante,* vol. 4 (Geneva: Slatkine, 1966), 335.

16. For example, *La Vraye histoire,* explains before its version of the confession "de laquelle confession prinse a l'original, la teneur s'ensuit." 247. Also, Crespin claims, "Nous avons icy mis ladite Confession mot à mot." *Histoire des vrays tesmoins,* 531.

17. One of the more comprehensive studies on the sharing of accounts among Crespin and non-French martyrologists is Brad Gregory, *Salvation at Stake: Christian Martyrdom in Early Modern Europe* (Cambridge, MA: Harvard University Press, 1999).

18. See below for discussion on the *Oraison.*

19. For an in-depth analysis of the different editions, see J.-F. Gilmont, *Jean Crespin, un éditeur réformé du XVIᵉ siècle* (Geneva: Droz, 1981), especially chap. 8.

20. On martyrology as history, see chapter 5.

21. For a more complete analysis of the linkage between Eusebius and Crespin, and a detailed discussion of the establishment of a continuum between the early church and the Reform, see chapter 5.

22. See Leliévre, "Anne Du Bourg avant son incarcèration," 572–74, for a brief discussion of why this transformation occurred.

23. Crespin, *Histoire des vrays tesmoins,* 525: "Ce qu'en la précédente edition n'avoit esté assez distinctement mis, nous l'avons historialement departi en la presente selon l'ordre des temps: tellement qu'apres avoir veu cy dessus les causes & circonstances de l'emprisonnement de M. Anne Du Bourg, il reste la procedure & execution dernier tenue contre lui."

24. Ibid.: "un exemple singulier à toutes personnes constituées en estat de Judicature, pour apprendre de submettre toutes dignitez & honneurs à la Parolle & doctrine de Jesus Christ." This gloss is found in both the 1564 and 1570 editions, though the 1570 edition gloss is augmented. See above.

25. The *Oraison* has been identified as an important, though awkward document by El Kenz and Lelièvre. El Kenz examines the text briefly in terms of Du Bourg's opening the term tyrannicide to the French Reform movement, though in a limited manner (David El Kenz, *Les bûchers du roi: la culture protestante des martyrs [1523–1572]* [Paris: Champ Vallon, 1997], 181–82). Lelièvre was the first modern historian to examine the separately published pamphlet of the *Oraison.* The purpose of his study of the text (arguably the most comprehensive to date) was to rightly attribute authorship to Du Bourg (Matthieu Lelièvre, "Les Derniers jours D'Anne Du Bourg," *Bulletin de la Société de l'Histoire du Protestantisme français* 37 [1888]: 514–23).

26. *La Vraye histoire* in *Mémoires de Condé, servant de'eclaircissement et de preuves à l'histoire de M. De Thou, Contenant ce qui s'est passe de plus memorable en Europe* (Lon-

don, 1743), vol. 1, 223–24, 248: "Je croy qu'a ceste tres-saincte Parole il n'est licite à quelque personne, de quelque estat ou qualite qu'elle puisse estre, adjouster ou diminuer aucune chose en Loi, Edits, ceremonies, ou autrement concernant la Police de la Religion Chrestienne." For a discussion on the term "Police," see Donald Kelley, *Beginning of Ideology: Consciousness and Society in the French Reformation* (Cambridge: Cambridge University Press, 1981), 189. This term refers to the legislation of the preservation of the realm.

27. See especially the Edict of Chateaubriand and Edict of Compeigne.

28. *Vraye histoire*, in *Mémoires de Condé*, vol. 1, 258.

29. Ibid.: "Á iceluy Magistrate toute personne de quelque estat, sexe, ou condition qu'elle soit, doit etre subjette & luy obeir en toutes choses honestes & raisonables, d'autant qu'il represente la personne de Grand Seigneur le vueille diriger en toutes ses voyes, & que nous puissions vivre en toute paix & tranquillité sous iceluy." See also Crespin, *Histoire des vrays tesmoins*, 533.

30. *Vraye histoire*, in *Mémoires de Condé*, vol. 1, 223–24: "le Roy a toute Puissance, meme que Dieu lui a baille le glaive en la main, pour conserver son Eglise en son integrité & pureté. . . . Qu'il faut savoir quels sont les hérétiques & quelle hérésie: & que l'on pourroit punir trop cruellement ceux qui meriteroyent punition légère."

31. Théodore de Bèze, *Traitte de l'Authorite du Magistrat en la Punition des hérétiques, & du moyen d'y proceder, fait en Latin par Théodore Bèze, Contre l'opinion de certains Academiques, qui par leurs escrits soustienent l'impunité de ceux qui sement des erreurs, & les veulent exempter de la sujection des loix. Nouvellement traduit de Latin en Francois par Nicolas Colladon* (Geneva, 1560), 9: "Or pour entrer finalement en propose, la question que nous avons à traitter, consiste en trois points. Le premier, Ascavoir s'il faut punir les hérétiques. Le second, Si ceste punition appartient aussi au Magistrat qui ha l'administration de la justice. Le dernier, Si on les peut memes condamner à mort." This work was originally published as *De haereticis a civili magistratu puniendis* (1554).

32. See John Calvin, *Institutes of the Christian Religion*, ed. John T. McNeill and trans. Ford Lewis Battles, (Philadelphia: Westminster Press, 1977), 4.20. On Calvin and his political thought, see Quentin Skinner, *The Foundations of Modern Political Thought*, vol. 2 (Cambridge: Cambridge University Press, 1978), 189–358; for Calvin's views on resistance in the *Institutes*, see William J. Bouwsma, *John Calvin: A Sixteenth-Century Portrait* (Oxford: Oxford University Press, 1988), chap. 13. The first edition of the *Institutes* was published in 1536.

33. Du Bourg's interrogation in *La Vraye histoire, in Mémoires de Condé*, vol. 1, 238: "Interrogue, quelles oeuvres il a veu de Luther, Calvin, & autre. . . . A dit, qu'il en a leu de Calvin & autres . . . & les achetez de ces porteurs de Livres qui vont & viennent par pays." See also *L'Exemplaire, et Forme du procez.*

34. See Lelièvre, "Les Derniers jours d'Anne Du Bourg," 521–22.

35. La Place did say, however that "Par ceste confession dernière longue, et tel qu'un chascun peult voir ailleurs imprimée avec le procès lui faict tout au long. . . ." (La Place, *L'Estat de la Religion*, 20). His longest citations came from the *Oraison* (or address to the Parlement) with little or no paraphrasing from the sections he cut. Due to the nature of the cuts, they were probably made not for economical reasons, but for their content.

36. *Oraison au Senat de Paris pour la Cause des Chrestiens, à la consolation d'iceux: d'Anne du Bourg Prisonnier pour la parole* (n.p., 1560), 10–11: "Car qui a fait Roy notre Prince, & qui lui a baille auctorité sur tant de peuple: N'a ce pas été le grand Seigneur de tous les Rois: l'auroit il place en un tel lieu pour lui contrevenir, l'exemptant de garder ce qu'il a commande à toutes les nations, au Ciel, & à la terre? Par cela je conclus, que le roy notre Prince est subier, & tous les siens aux Commandements du Souverain Roy: & comment lui meme crime de lèse majesté, s'il determine quelque chose contre la volonté de son Roy, & le notre, Et par ainsi coulpable de mort s'il persiste en une erreur qu'il deveroit condamner."

37. Calvin, *Institutes*, 4.20.8.

38. El Kenz, in his discussion of the *Oraison*, points out the similarities between Du Bourg's stance and those of Calvin and Bèze, though he provides no evidence that Du Bourg ever read either of them. See El Kenz, *Les bûchers du Roi*, 181–82.

39. The two works that discuss the *Oraison*, those by El Kenz and Lelièvre, do not deal in any real depth with other the other cuts. Whereas El Kenz makes no real mention of any of the other cuts made by La Place in his discussion of the *Oraison*, Lelièvre merely mentions one other cut but gives no real analysis beyond that it might have been too vehement for La Place and the martyrologists.

40. *Oraison*, 11–12: "Je conclus aussi ce que vous avez entendu, ou il n'a tenu qu'à vous, que votre dissimulation doit etre accusée de parjure, par laquelle miserablement vous enchantez votre Roi, & abusez le peuple maintenant pour quoi le poure Crestien est-il flamme pour etre si fidèle à Dieu, & à celui qu'il nous a donne pour gouverneur? Je tien qu'il ne faut point en un seul point souller l'honneur de Dieu. Helas cela est-il tant à contre-coeur aux hommes? Je di que je ne contrevien point à ses ordonnances, quant je desire que la Loy de Dieu marche devant, puis qu'il est raisonnable, pourquoi y contrevenez vous?"

41. Ibid., 17–18: "Vous Roys de main tenant pensez vous eschaper la fureur de Dieu, ne portans nomplus de reverence a sa parole? ne pensez vous point que la superbité, l'outrecuidance, & l'ingratitude, des Rois de Babylone, d'Assirie." Lelièvre does note that La Place did find this passage to be too vehement, and in cutting it, continued with his efforts to soften Du Bourg's venom. See Lelièvre, "Les Derniers jours d'Anne Du Bourg," 118–19.

42. Calvin, *Institutes*, 4.20.31.

43. See ibid., 4.20.30.

44. Chandieu describes the *Oraison* as "Du Bourg . . . s'adressant à ses judges . . . beaucoup de belles remonstrances aux uns et auxtres," but includes no excerpts from it. See Chandieu, *Histoire des persecutions*, 424.

45. See for example, François Hotman, *Epistre envoiee au Tigre de la France*, and *Sentence Redoubtable et Arrest Rigoureux du jugement de Dieu, a l'encontre de l'impiete des Tyrans, recueillies tant des sainctes escriptures, comme de toutes autres histoires* (Lyon, 1564). In the *Declaration et Protestation de ceux de la Religion Reformee de la Rochelle sur la prise & capture des armes qu'ils ont fait le neufiseme de Janvier dernier* (n.p., 1568), however, the author stated that "Toute puissance est d'en haut quand ils bataillent & se bandent contre Dieu & son Église, ils ne sont plus vrais Rois mais personnes privées, ausquels il ne faut obeir pour ce regard, comme semblablement en ce cas cessent l'obeissance & repect deus aux pères & mères . . . le sang des innocens en crie encores vengeance à Dieu." The author then softened this statement and

spoke of the king's youth and the bad influences upon him. This pamphlet is an example of the slow transition occurring during the late 1560s. After the St. Bartholomew's Day Massacre of 1572, a shift occurs in the rhetoric of resistance, and calls for tyrannicide and divine justice were aimed at the king himself. For a discussion of the shift in rhetoric see the epilogue, below.

46. Chandieu, *Histoire des pérsecutions*, title page: "Nous sommes livrez à la mort pour toi tous les jours, & sommes estimez comme brebis d'occision." Crespin cites this same passage on his title page of his 1555 edition.

47. The most vivid example of the use of this imagery is Clement Marot and Théodore Bèze, *Les Psaumes de David mis en rime Francoise par Clement Marot & Theodore de Besze. Avec bonnes & sainctes Oraisons nouvellement adjoustees en la fin de chacun Pseume, pour la consolation de l'Eglise, selon la substance du Pseaume* (n.p., 1561). Other examples include *Hymne à Dieu, pour la Delivrance des François de la plus que Egyptienne servitude, en laquelle ils ont été detenus par le passé* (n.p., n.d.).

48. Théodore Bèze, *Du Droit des magistrates* (Geneva, 1574) cited by Donald Kelley, "Martyrs, Myths, and the Massacre: The Background of St. Bartholomew," *American Historical Review* 77 (December 1972), 1340.

49. Kelley, "Martyrs, Myths, and the Massacres," 1340.

50. Chandieu, *Histoire des pérsecutions*, iij: "l'espoir du proffit & contentement que ce vous sera (mes treschers frères) de revoir ici l'image de tout le temps qu'il a pleu à Dieu nous exercer ensemble par tribulations: & puis le desir que j'ai de remettre les poures ignorans, qui nous font tant ennemis, sur l'examen de notre cause, pour les faire penser à leurs injustices & cruautez, & les amener, si possibile est, par ce moyen à quelque composition raisonnable."

51. See, for example, *Juste Complainte des Fidèles de France. Contre leurs adversaires Papistes, & autres. Sur l'affliction & faux crimes, dont on les charge à grand tort* (Avignon, 1560); *Epistre envoyee à la Royne Mere du Roy au commencement du regne de Tres-chrestien Roy François second. En laquelle est sommairement respondu aux calomnies desquelles on a par ci devant chargé malicieusement ceux qui sont profession de l'Evangile* (n.p., 1561); *Advertisement à la Royne Mere du Roy. Touchant les miseres du Royaume au temps present, & de la conspiration des enemis de sa Majeste* (Orleans, 1562); *Remonstrance envoyee au Roy par la noblesse de la Religion reformee du pais & Comte du Maine sur les assasinats, pilleries, saccagements de maisons, seditions, violements de femmes & autres exces horribles commis depuis la publication de l'Edit de pacification dedans ledit Comte* (n.p., 1564); and *Declaration et Protestation de ceux de la Religion Reformee de la Rochelle sur la prise & capture des armes qu'ils ont fait le neufiseme de Janvier dernier* (n.p., 1568).

52. For a useful summary of the parties and motivations involved in the conspiracy, see J. H. M. Salmon, *Society in Crisis: France in the Sixteenth Century* (London: Ernest Benn, 1975), 124–25. For a more in-depth analysis, see Lucien Romier, *La Conjuration d'Amboise. L'Aurore sanglante de la liberté de conscience. Le Règne et la mort de François II.* (Paris: Perrin, 1923); N. M. Sutherland, *The Huguenot Struggle for Recognition* (New Haven: Yale University Press, 1980), chap. 3; Micheline Dupuy, *Pour Dieu et pour le roi: la montée de l'intolérance au XVIᵉ siécle* (Paris: Librairie Académique Perrin, 1984), chap. 14.

53. Salmon, *Society in Crisis*, 125–26. Salmon sees more than a doctrinal appeal to the Reform movement for the lesser nobility: "political disaffection, anti-clericalism, and social malaise" all contributed to their embrace of the movement.

54. El Kenz, *Les bûchers du roi*, 182.

55. In reference to the Conspiracy of Amboise and the St. Bartholomew's Day Massacre, Kelley writes, "Huguenot pamphlets emerged out of a common impulse, a common fund, and were directed at a common goal." Donald Kelley, *François Hotman: A Revolutionary's Ordeal* (Princeton: Princeton University Press, 1971), 234. He argues this in terms of the events that had a significant impact on the Reform faction. To this I would also add the accounts of Du Bourg's martyrdom, and hence the homogeneity of many of the accounts.

56. See Kelley, *Beginning of Ideology*, 255–56, for a discussion of Condé's declaration. The pamphlet literature on Vassy is vast, but two good examples of the propaganda are: *Destruction du saccagement, exerce cruellement par le Duc de Guise & sa cohorte, en la ville de Vassy, le premier jour de Maris 1561* (Caens, 1562), for the Protestant reaction, and Guillaume Morel, *Discours au Vray et en abbrege de ce qui est dernierement advenu a Vassi, y passant Monseigneur le Duc de Guise* (Paris, 1562), for the Catholic response. For the purpose of the essay I have been referring to the Reform in France as a "movement," though many historians point to this event as the moment when a true "cause" and "movement" can be defined. Here they are referring to the Protestants as a political force, rather than as a religious campaign. See Kelley, *Beginning of Ideology*, 255–60, and Sutherland, *The Huguenot Struggle for Recognition*, chaps. 3 and 4.

57. Sutherland, *The Huguenot Struggle for Recognition*, 102–3.

58. Penny Roberts "Martyrs in the French Reformation" in *Martyrs and Martyrologies*, ed. Diana Wood (Oxford: Oxford University Press, 1993), 223. She claims that this shift occurred in hope (on the state's part) to downplay the "martyrly" aspirations of the condemned.

59. See, for example, *Remonstrance envoyee au Roy par la noblesse de la Religion reformee du pais & Comté du Maine sur les assasinats, pilleries, saccagements de maisons, seditions, violements de femmes & autres exces horribles commis depuis la publication de l'Edit de pacification dedans ledit Comté* (n.p., 1564).

60. It is possible to add a third, that is the escape attempt as described in chapter 2. But as Crespin (Chandieu) is the only Protestant source that made any mention of this attempt, and does so only in passing, it is possible that it was not a well-known event; and the brief mention itself alludes only to embarrassment over the event. There is no attempt to defend or explain it, save that he was "mis en une cage en la Bastille" due to "soupçon qu'on avoit qu'il se faisoit entreprise pour delivrer." *Histoire des vrays tesmoins*, 530.

61. See chapter 2.

62. As stated earlier, Crespin's 1570 account is a conglomeration of the other two, though his description of the appeals process is taken directly from Chandieu.

63. La Place, *L'Estat de la Religion*, 20: "aucuns conseillers de ladicte cour de parlement et autres disoyent que toutes ses longeurs n'estoyent que protélations acquises par ledict du Bourg pour gaigner temps, et qu'elles monstroyent bien que le zèle n'estoit tel à Dieu et à la religion qu'il tenoit, qu'il en faisoit semblant."

64. Crespin, *Histoire des vrays tesmoins*, 530.

65. Ibid.: "Que ce n'estoit point qu'il voulust gaigner temps, & prolonger sa vie par subterfuges: mais à fin d'oster toute occasion de penser qu'il se precipitast, & qu'il fust cause de sa mort avant le temps, si'il oublioit quelque chose qui peust servir à sa justification."

66. There is little reason to doubt the description of the letters in Chandieu and Crespin. As pointed out by Leliévre, Chandieu had, as pastor to the Parisian Reform Church, "des relations personnelles avec Du Bourg." See Leliévre, "Anne Du Bourg avant son incarcération a la Bastille," 571. These letters were also described as written to the church, thus in all likelihood, Chandieu held the letters himself.

67. See Chapter 2.

68. Whereas Crespin and Chandieu placed the submission of this confession after the uncompromising one, de la Planche and La Place described the latter as occurring after the ambiguous one, recanting it and setting things right. These specific differences do not contribute greatly to the shaping of the image of Du Bourg.

69. La Place, *L'Estat de la Religion*, 20: "Du Bourg . . . présenté à ladicte cour, portant sa confession entière, par laquelle il déclara qu'il vouloit prendre droict, en révoquant une autre ambiguë et doubteuse, qu'aucuns de ses familiers amis de ladicte cour lui avoyent conseillée pour eschapper."

70. Crespin, *Histoire des vrays tesmoins*, 534. Descriptions of "temporiseurs" or Nicodemites portray them as seductive, attempting to lure the faithful into a comfortable, but damnable position vis-à-vis the persecution. See, for example, Viret, *Traittez divers*, and Jean Saugrain, *Conseilz et Advis de Plusieurs grands & doctes personnages fus la meme matière contenue au precedent Livre du Temporieseur* (Lyon, 1565).

71. See de la Planche, *Histoire de l'Estat de France*, 210.

72. For a description of the letter, see chapter 2.

4. GENDER AND THE RHETORIC OF MARTYRDOM

1. A version of this chapter originally appeared as "Gender and the Rhetoric of Martyrdom in Jean Crespin's *Histoire des vrays tesmoins*," *Sixteenth Century Journal* 35 (Spring 2004): 155–74.

2. Jean Crespin, *Histoire des vrays tesmoins de la verité de l'Evangile, qui de leur sang l'ont signée, depuis Jean Hus jusques au temps presente* (Geneva, 1570; reprint, Liège: Centre national de recherches d'histoire religieuse, 1964), 522.

3. Florimond de Raemond, *L'Histoire de la Naissance, progrez, et decadence de l'Hérésie de ce siècle,* (Arras, 1611), 1283: "les simples femmelettes chercher les tourmens pour faire preuve de leur foi: allant à la mort ne crier que le Christ, le Sauveur, chanter quelque Pseaume: Les jeunes vierges marcher plus gayement au supplice, qu'elles n'eussent fait au lit nuptial . . . brief, mourir en riant, comme eus qui on mangé l'herbe Sardiniene." The "Sardinian herb" is a poisonous plant, possibly *Ranunculus abortivus*, known in English as "crowfoot."

4. Ibid.: "jettoient quelque trouble non seulement en l'ame des simples, mais des plus grans . . . [who] les couvoient de leur manteau."

5. See, for example, Joyce E. Salisbury, *Perpetua's Passion: The Death and Memory of a Young Roman Woman* (New York: Routledge, 1997), 142, on the crowd's reaction to a young woman (Felicity), with milk dripping from her breasts, about to be torn apart by a mad heifer.

6. The literature on Crespin's martyrology, *Histoire des vrays tesmoins*, is quite large, especially that which was produced during the nineteenth century. Some more recent works that focus on his text include: Brad Gregory, *Salvation at Stake: Christian Martyrdom in Early Modern Europe* (Cambridge, MA: Harvard University Press, 1999); David El Kenz, *Les bûchers du roi: la culture protestante des martyrs (1523–1572)* (Paris: Champ Vallon, 1997); Catharine Randall Coats, *(Em)bodying the Word: Textual Resurrections in the Martyrological Narratives of Foxe, Crespin, de Bèze and d'Aubigné* (New York: Peter Lang, 1992); Jean-François Gilmont, *Jean Crespin, Un éditeur réformé du XVIe siècle* (Geneva: Droz, 1981). Crespin's martyrology underwent a number of editions including translations into Latin and parts reproduced in English. All quotations and references to his martyrology in this essay are from the 1570 edition as it was the largest and the last edition edited by Crespin himself (albeit aided by his successor to the project, Simon Goulart).

7. This literature is vast. Some of the more important works, however, are: Phyllis Mack, *Visionary Women: Ecstatic Prophecy in Seventeenth-Century England* (Berkeley: University of California Press, 1989); Carolyn Bynum, *Holy Feast, Holy Fast: The Religious Significance of Food to Medieval Women* (Berkeley: University of California Press, 1987); Sara F. Matthews Grieco, *Ange ou Diablesse: La Représentation de la femme au XVIe siècle* (Paris: Flammarion, 1991), especially chap. 2; Judith Brown, *Immodest Acts: Life of a Lesbian Nun in Renaissance Italy* (Oxford: Oxford University Press, 1986); and Caroline Walker Bynum, Steven Harrell, and Paula Richman, eds., *Gender and Religion: On the Complexity of Symbols* (Boston: Beacon Press, 1986).

8. See, for example, Salisbury, *Perpetua's Passion*; Stuart G. Hall, "Women among the early martyrs," *Studies in Church History* 30 (1993): 1–22; and Francine Cardman, "Acts of the Women Martyrs," in *Women in Early Christianity*, ed. D. M. Scholer (New York: Garland, 1993).

9. Salisbury, *Perpetua's Passion*, 171.

10. Ibid., 172.

11. Ellen Macek, "The Emergence of a Feminine Spirituality in *The Book of Martyrs*," *Sixteenth Century Journal* 19 (Spring 1988): 62–80.

12. This was not only a problem concerning female martyrs of the sixteenth century. Salisbury notes that "One [problem] was the troubling hierarchy that placed martyrs and confessors equal or superior to priests and bishops. This problem was most simply addressed by churchmen taking control of the text itself." *Perpetua's Passion*, 171.

13. On martyrology as a genre, see Hippolyte Delehaye, *The Legends of the Saints*, trans. Donald Attwater, 2nd ed. (New York: Fordham University Press, 1962); *Les passions des martyrs et les genres littéraires*, 2nd ed. (Bruxelles: Society of Bollandists, 1966).

14. Salisbury's study of Perpetua beginning with her arrest through her later representations provides an example of this issue for the late antique/medieval periods. Cf. Salisbury, *Perpetua's Passion*.

15. Raemond, *L'Histoire de la Naissance*, 1256. Raemond also noted that in the early church, it was powerful women of status protected heretics.

16. Ibid.: "Il scait bien que souvent l'homme est un place inaccessible & imprenable par tout autre moyen que celui de la femme."

17. Ibid., 1258.

18. Ibid., 1257: "Cest le propre de la femme de se laisser tromper, dit S. Hierome, & de tromper les autres." "Tu es la porte du diable, dit Tertulian à la femme." He also quoted Origen and John Chrysostome on the weakness of women. Raemond's work is an anti-martyrology directly addressing the Protestant martyrologies and claims to legitimacy. As the martyrologists referred to the church fathers, so would Raemond.

19. On the link between the martyrologies and the church fathers, see chapter 5.

20. Nancy Lyman Roelker, "The Role of Noblewomen in the French Reformation," *Archiv für Reformationsgeschichte* 63 (1972): 168. Roelker's study, groundbreaking at the time and still one of the best surveys, names numerous women of the greater and lesser nobility. Thomas Freeman's work, "'The good ministrye of godlye and vertuouse women': The Elizabethan martyrologists and the female supporters of the Marian martyrs," *Journal of British Studies* 39 (January 2000): 8–33, focuses on another active role women played during the Reform as "sustainers" of imprisoned Protestants. This role is echoed across the Channel during the French Reformation. He rightly points out that this role is given short shrift in the martyrologies of John Foxe and Henry Bull, and the same could be said regarding Crespin's work.

21. Roelker, "The Role of Noblewomen in the French Reformation," 168.

22. Roelker, "The Role of Noblewomen in the French Reformation," 174. On Marguerite and her patronage, see Barbara Stephenson, *The Power and Patronage of Marguerite De Navarre* (Aldershot: Ashgate, 2004).

23. Nancy L. Roelker, "The Appeal of Calvinism to French Noblewomen in the Sixteenth Century," *Journal of Interdisciplinary History* 2 (1972): 402, and "The Role of Noblewomen," 171.

24. Natalie Zemon Davis, "City Women and Religious Change" in *Society and Culture in Early Modern France: Eight Essays by Natalie Zemon Davis* (Stanford: Stanford University Press, 1975), 80.

25. Davis, "City Women and Religious Change," 92.

26. William Monter, *Judging the French Reformation: Heresy Trials by Sixteenth-Century Parlements* (Cambridge, MA: Harvard University Press, 1999), 190–91.

27. The exception to this is iconoclasm. Whether by male or female hands, Crespin for the most part refrained from recounting this destructive behavior in his martyrology.

28. Davis, "City Women and Religious Change," 81.

29. Monter, *Judging the French Reformation*, 192.

30. This does not include a group included in the martyrologies though not individually named: the victims of massacres.

31. Jean Crespin, *Le Livre des Martyrs qui est un recueil de plusieurs Martyrs qui ont endure la mort pour le Nom de nostre Seigneur J-C, depuis jean Hus jusques à ceste année presente M.D.LIIII* (Geneva, 1554), 274–283: "raison des cas & crimes d'héresies & blasphemes exercrables, conventicles privez, & assemblées illicites, schismes & erreurs."

32. Ibid.: See chapter 5 on the *amende honorable.*

33. See, for example, Charmarie Blaisdell, "Calvin's Letters to Women: The Courting of Ladies in High Places," *Sixteenth Century Journal* 13 (1982): 76–84.

34. Pierre Viret, in "Epistre aus Fidèles," *Traittez divers pour l'instruction des fidèles qui resident & conversent es lieus & pais esquels il ne leur est permis de vivre en la pureté & liberté de l'Evangile. Reveus & augmentez* (Geneva, 1559), 88–97, also directly addresses some of the concerns of women and their roles during persecution.

35. Jean Calvin, "Commentary on the First Epistle to the Corinthians," *Calvin's Commentaries on the Epistles of Paul to the Corinthians*, ed. and trans. William Pringle (Grand Rapids, MI: Baker Books, 1979), 354.

36. John Lee Thompson, *John Calvin and the Daughters of Sarah: Women in Regular and Exceptional Roles in the Exegesis of Calvin, his Predecessors, and his Contemporaries* (Geneva: Droz, 1992), 15. Thompson provides an excellent and relatively up-to-date summary of all the approaches to Calvin's views on women.

37. See Jean Calvin, "Commentaries on the First Epistle to Timothy," *Commentaries on the Epistles of Paul to the Galatians and Ephesians*, ed. and trans. William Pringle (Grand Rapids, MI: Baker Books, 1979), 70–71. These were not the only ways, but nevertheless were among the most important.

38. On marriage and marital relations in the Reformation, see Steven Ozment, *When Fathers Ruled: Family Life in Reformation Europe* (Cambridge, MA: Harvard University Press, 1983). For a less rosy view, see Lyndal Roper, *The Holy Household: Women and Morals in Reformation Augsburg* (New York: Clarendon Press, 1989). On Calvin and marriage, see Jane Dempsey Douglass, *Women, Freedom, and Calvin* (Philadelphia: Westminster Press, 1985).

39. Calvin, "Commentary on the First Epistle to Timothy," 71.

40. Ibid., 68.

41. Calvin, "Commentary on the First Epistle to the Corinthians," 358.

42. John Calvin, *Institutes of Christian Religion*, ed. John T. McNeill (Philadelphia: Westminster Press, 1960), 245.

43. Calvin, "Commentary on the First Epistle to Timothy," 70.

44. Calvin, "Commentary on the First Epistle to Timothy," 69. See also Thompson, *Daughters of Sarah*, 17.

45. See Jean Calvin, "Commentary on the Book of Genesis," *Calvin's Commentaries on the Book of Genesis*, ed. and trans. William Pringle (Grand Rapids, MI: Baker Books, 1979), 128.

46. Ibid., 129–30

47. See, for example, Blaisdell, "Calvin's Letters to Women," 76–84.

48. For a similar though less harsh view, see Viret, "Epistre aux Fidèles," *Traittez divers*, 87–96. Viret, in this section, gives direct advice to Calvinist spouses, especially wives, who are married Catholics.

49. Nancy Roelker, "The Appeal of Calvinism to French Noblewomen in the Sixteenth Century," 406. See also Blaisdell, "Calvin's Letters to Women," 67–84.

50. See Thompson, *Daughters of Sarah*, 161–227.

51. Ibid., 277.

52. Ibid., 185.

53. Calvin, "Commentary on the First Espistle to Timothy," 71.

54. Jean Crespin, *Histoire des vrays tesmoins*, epistle: "Vous maris ne faites difficulté de laisser derrière des femmes & enfants; car il y a une eschange de meilleure condition qui vous est preparée. Vous femmes, que l'infirmité de votre sexe ne vous face reculler; il y a des exemples qui vous ouverent le chemin."

55. Monter, *Judging the French Reformation*, 191. For an overall comparison of the trial records to Crespin's martyrology, see ibid., chap. 7.

56. Among the French female martyrs in Crespin, only Philippe de Luns (1557), one of the martyrs emerging from the *affaire de la Rue de Saint-Jacques*, came from a noble family.

57. Elizabeth Eisenstein, *The Printing Press as an Agent of Change: Communications and Cultural Transformations in Early-Modern Europe* (Cambridge: Cambridge University Press, 1979), 243. Though Eisenstein is referring to Foxe's martyrology, this still holds true for Crespin as well. I disagree with Eisenstein's view, that "this kind of vicarious participation by a mass-reading public in a national historic drama has an equivalent in France—but not until the early 19th century," 243.

58. Cf. Stuart G. Hall, "Women among the early martyrs."

59. Crespin, *Histoire des vrays tesmoins*, 42: "surmontant toute fragilité du sexe," It should be noted here that Crespin often copied verbatim accounts from other martyrologies or histories. In the case of Catherine Saube, whose martyrdom incidentally predates Luther, her story was taken from a book Crespin refers to as the "Talamus." The quote above, however, was taken from an introductory section written by Crespin, and not from the bulk of the narrative cited as from the "Talamus." The purpose of this essay is not attribution, but to analyze the representation of the female martyrs to their audience through Crespin's editorial work.

60. Ibid., 96: "de la confession de cette femme tous ces messieurs furent autant estonnez que de voir chose *contre nature*." Emphasis is mine.

61. Ibid., 171: "fut munie de grace & vertu singulière en ce sexe."

62. Ibid., 87: "l'imbecillite de la femme en un courage plus qu'heroique."

63. Though this separation is implied, nonetheless, the rhetoric of martyrdom binds all martyrs together with the living community through the shared experience of suffering. The gendered language mitigates this connection only in terms of "election" by God. See below.

64. Crespin, *Histoire des vrays tesmoins*, 177: "Barbe, m'amie, avise de sauver ta vie; tu es encore jeune femme, si tu nous veux nommer ceux qui vous ont logé, je promets de te delivrer des prisons, remettre en liberté."

65. Ibid., 177: "elle respondit selon la mesure de la foi & connoissance que Dieu lui avoit donnée, de forte qu'elle ne fut divertie aucunement."

66. Ibid., 184: "elle exhortoit les autres à etre constans." The editions differ in this case. While all the editions describe her as a widow, Gillot Vivier is mentioned only after the 1556 edition.

67. Ibid., 171: "elle exhortoit les autres, & principalement son mari à perseverance."

68. Ibid., 179: "Mon Dieu, la belle ceinture que mon époux me baille! Par un Samedi je suis fiancée pour mes premiers noces; mais en ces secondes noces je serai mariée ce Samedi à mon époux Jesus Christ."

69. Ibid., 151: "Adieu Adrian, je m'en vai d'autre noces."

70. Ibid., 483–84. "Elle avoit au par-avant plore son mary, & porte le dueil, habillee de linges blancs a la facon du pays: mais alors elle avoit pose tous ces habillemens de veuage, & reprins le chapperon de velours & autres accoustremens de joie, comme pour recevoir cest heureux triomphe, & etre jointe a son espous Jesus Christ." This account is almost taken verbatim from the martyrology of An-

toine de la Roche Chandieu, *Histoire des Pérsecutions, et Martyrs de l'Eglise de Paris, depuis l'an 1557. jusques au temps du Roy Charles neufviesme* (Lyon, 1563), 79–87.

71. For an analysis of how marital conflict based upon religious difference is handled in the accounts, see the case study of Marguerite le Riche below.

72. Crespin, *Histoire des vrays tesmoins*, 184

73. Barbara Newman, *From Virile Woman to Woman Christ: Studies in Medieval Religion and Literature* (Philadephia: University of Pennsylvania Press, 1995), 81.

74. Ibid.

75. Ibid., 69: "Ma femme & mes enfans me sont si chers, que le Duc de Bavière ne les pourroit acheter de moi pour toute sa chevance: si est-ce que pour l'amour de mon Dieu & Seigneur, je les laisse volontiers."

76. Ibid., 150: "Rien ne le sut divertir, ni les pleurs de sa femme, ni le regard de sa famille qu'on lui mettoit devant."

77. It is difficult to know from where exactly Crespin got his information. In the case of Marguerite le Riche, his account appears to be informed by the version of her death found in Chandieu's *Histoire des Persécutions*, 337–42. Although there are some minor discrepancies between their accounts, the majority of the text appears almost verbatim. As for Étienne Brun, his account is built up through successive editions of Crespin's martyrology, though the sources for the account are unknown. While consisting only of a single short paragraph in the 1555 edition, it is significantly longer and more detailed by the 1570 edition. In the 1555 edition, the account is limited to an arrest, his admonishment to his judges, his exhortation to the crowds, then basic execution. There is no mention of his learning French or Latin, his abjuration, the confrontation by his family, or the problems with his execution which are found in the 1570 edition.

78. Chandieu, *Histoire des Persécutions*, xxix.

79. Crespin, *Histoire des vrays tesmoins*, 522: "de n'aller jamais à la Messe, & plus-tot mourir."

80. Ibid.: "sans rien dissimuler, qu'elle s'estoit absentée de sa maison, & retirée chez ses amis fidèles, pour n'estre contraincte de profaner la Cene de nôtre Seigneur Jesus Christ, à la façon commune des autres: mais bien avoit fait la Cene selon l'ordonnance de Dieu, en l'assemblée des fidèles & chrestiens."

81. Ibid.: "hérétique, pertinax, & obstinée." As the probable source, Chandieu had obviously seen some form of the *arrêt* condemning le Riche. He cites it almost verbatim, and Crespin includes it in his version. See U/2505, Collection Le Nain, AN. Interestingly enough, both leave out the section of the *arrêt* that requires a matron to do a pregnancy examination, to determine if she is carrying a child. According to French law, a woman could not be executed if she was pregnant. Her execution would be delayed until postpartum.

82. Crespin, *Histoire des vrays tesmoins*, 522: "ansi rendit son esprit au Seigneur."

83. Ibid.: "Femmes vertueuses, contemplez ici le courage & zèle de ceste Marguerite vôtre soeur, qui vous est proposée en exemple: & practiquez toutes ses fascheries domestique que vous avez à l'exercice de piété, tant selon le corps que l'esprit. Elle à donné courage à grans & à petits qui d'un même temps estoyent prisonniers."

84. Ibid: "aima mieux mescontenter son Mari que Dieu, auquel elle s'estoit entièrement consacrée . . . elle ne voulut plus longuement être absente de la maison,

mais se delibera de retourner vers celui auquel Dieu l'avoit liée & connjointe, encores qu'elle previst les grans ennui & fascheries qu'elle auroit avec lui."

85. See above.

86. Crespin, *Histoire des vrays tesmoins,* 523: "Elle remonstroit assiduellement aux femmes prisonnières avec elle, & les consoloit. Les Martyrs qui partoyent de la conciergerie pour aller à la mort, passoyent devant sa chambre: & elle n'estoit point descouragée de les voir entre les mains des bourreaux: mais crioit à eux, & les exhortoit de se resjouir, & de porter patientment les opprobres & afflictions de nôtre Seigneur Jesus Christ."

87. Interestingly enough, their interaction is described only in le Riche's account, not in Du Bourg's. The question remains as to whether this was due to a desire to focus on Du Bourg alone without the presence of a strong woman detracting from his significance.

88. While Crespin describes the vehicle for their exchanges, the small window, this description is not included in Chandieu's account.

89. Crespin, *Histoire des vrays tesmoins,* 522: "[elle] servit beaucoup pour le confermer . . . l'incitoit de perseverer constamment, & le consoloit."

90. Ibid.: "Une femme m'a monstre ma leçon, & enseigne comment je me doi porter en ceste vocation-ci: [he said] sentant la force & vertu des admonitions de ceste poure femme."

91. Ibid.: "visage franc & de bonne couleur . . . que de ses graces si grandes, & de la vertu de son Esprit si miraculeuse en ceste femme."

92. Crespin describes how Brun's lands were coveted by a tenant-farmer of the bishop, and in all likelihood Brun's holdings were not insubstantial. See Crespin, *Histoire des vrays tesmoins,* 94.

93. Ibid., 95: "Puis que je suis condamné d'être bruslé, pourquoi me veux-tu assommer?"

94. Ibid.

95. Ibid.: "Il y a en l'exemple de ce Martyr, aucunes choses peculières dignes d'etre notées: assavoir les dons & graces que Dieu donne à gens des champs, sans observer les moyens humains. C'est le premier, apres Jean Cornon, qui est donné pour mirroir aux laboureurs de la terre."

96. Later on in the account, however, we see Brun as an active force in confronting authority, rather than passive (as we see in the account of le Riche). See below.

97. Crespin, *Histoire des vrays tesmoins,* 95: "par le misericorde de Dieu amene à la conoissance de la verité . . . [il] surmonte les astuces & finesses des plus grands du Dauphiné."

98. Ibid.: "Il [Brun] fut circonvenu & induit par tromperies & vaines promesses des supports dudit Evesque d'admettre un formulaire d'abjuration qu'iceux avoyent escrit en Latin en leur stile accoustumé, pour obtenir delivrance."

99. Ibid.: "s'adonnoit avec le labourage à la lecture du nouveau Testament traduit en François: l'un estoit pour la nourriture de sa famille, & l'autre pour l'instruction d'icelle en toute crainte de Dieu."

100. Ibid.: "Moyenant que la pasture de l'âme, qui est la parole de Dieu, ne leur desaille point, je n'ai souci aucun du pain du corps."

5. Nicodemism and the Community

1. Antoine de la Roche Chandieu, *Histoires de Persécutions, et Martyrs de l'Église de Paris, depuis l'An 1557. jusques au temps du Roy Charles neufviesme* (Lyon, 1563), 422. An earlier version of this essay first appeared in *Renaissance et Reformé/Renaissance and Reformation* 27 (Summer/Été 2003).

2. Ibid., vii: "Les uns recognoistront ici leurs frères & compagnons arrachez de leur compagnie, pour être cruellement mis à mort: les femmes y trouveront leurs maris, les pères leurs enfans, & les enfans leurs pères tormentez, & meurtris pour la parolle de Dieu. Les autres y veront le temps de leur emprisonnement, ou bien de leur suite. Les autres y entendront leurs pertes, le ravissement de leurs biens, & la desolation de leurs familles."

3. Théodore de Bèze, "Life of Calvin," in John Calvin, *Tracts and treatises* (Edinburgh, UK: Oliver and Boyd, 1958), 1:lxxxvii. The "holy man" Nicodemus that Bèze referred to is the biblical figure who came to Jesus at night to avoid detection.

4. Not all of the Protestant reformers or writers of the period were consistently or profoundly anti-Nicodemite. And as proven by numerous scholars, there was no organized movement predating the persecution (per Carlo Ginzburg, *Il Nicodemismo* [Turin: G. Einaudi, 1970]) to spread "the message of Nicodemism." See Carlos Eire, "Calvin and Nicodemism: A Reappraisal," *Sixteenth Century Journal* 10 (1979): 45–69; Peter Matheson, "Martyrdom or Mission? A Protestant Debate," *Archiv für Reformationsgeschichte* 80 (1989): 158–65; Perez Zagorin, *Ways of Lying: Dissimulation, Persecution, and Conformity in Early Modern Europe* (Cambridge, MA: Harvard University Press, 1990), 68–70.

5. See, for example, Zagorin, *Ways of Lying*, esp. chap. 4; Matheson, "Martyrdom or Mission?"; Carlos Eire, "Prelude to Sedition? Calvin's Attack on Nicodemism and Religious Compromise," *Archiv für Reformationsgeschichte* 76 (1985): 120–45; and *War Against the Idols: The Reformation of Worship from Erasmus to Calvin* (Cambridge: Cambridge University Press, 1986), esp. chap. 7; Ginzburg, *Il Nicodemismo*; Eugénie Droz, *Chemins de l'Hérésie: Textes et Documents* (Geneva: Slatkine Reprints, 1970), 131–65; Albert Autin, *Un Episode de la vie de Calvin: La Crise du Nicodémisme 1535–1545* (Toulouse: P. Tissot, 1917).

6. See Eire, "Calvinism and Nicodemism," for an analysis of the earlier approaches to Nicodemism.

7. William Bouwsma, *John Calvin: A Sixteenth-Century Portrait* (Oxford: Oxford University Press, 1988), 216.

8. Eire, *War Against the Idols*, 264.

9. Brad Gregory, *Salvation at Stake: Christian Martyrdom in Early Modern Europe* (Cambridge, MA: Harvard University Press, 1999), 154.

10. Jean Crespin, *Histoire des vrays tesmoins de la verité de l'Evangile, qui de leur sang l'ont signée, depuis Jean Hus jusques au temps presente* (Geneva, 1570; reprint, Liége: Centre national de recherches d'histoire religieuse, 1964), 182: "Je di notre captivité, pour ce que vous devez sentir la mienne, & moy la votre. Car tous biens & tous maux font communs entre frères."

11. The literature on the breakdown of community and the clash between Protestants and Catholics within communal bounds is vast. See for example, Denis

Crouzet, *Les Guerriers de Dieu: La Violence au temps des troubles de religion vers 1525–1610*, 2 vols. (Paris: Champ Vallon, 1990); A. N. Galpern, *The Religions of the People in Sixteenth-Century Champagne* (Cambridge, MA: Harvard University Press, 1976); Natalie Zemon Davis, *Society and Culture in Early Modern France* (Stanford: Stanford University Press, 1965); J. H. M. Salmon, *Society in Crisis: France in the Sixteenth Century* (London: Ernest Benn, 1975); Barbara B. Diefendorf, *Beneath the Cross: Catholics and Huguenots in Sixteenth Century Paris* (Oxford: Oxford University Press, 1991); Donald R. Kelley, *Beginning of Ideology: Consciousness and Society in the French Reformation* (Cambridge: Cambridge University Press, 1981); Yves-Marie Bercé, *Fête et révolte: Des mentalités populaires du XVe au XVIIIe siècle* (Paris: Hachette, 1976); David El Kenz, *Les bûchers du roi: la culture protestante des martyrs (1523–1572)* (Paris: Champ Vallon, 1997). For a different interpretation (though of a later period) that examines the continuity of a community regardless of religious difference, see Gregory Hanlon, *Confession and Community in Seventeenth-Century France: Catholic and Protestant Coexistence in Aquitaine* (Philadelphia: University of Pennsylvania Press, 1993). Regarding the role of the Mass, processions, and other Catholic institutions in communal life see, for example, John Bossy, "The Mass as a Social Institution, 1200–1700," *Past and Present* 100 (1983): 29–61.

12. The seminal study on religious conflict and "pollution" is Natalie Zemon Davis's essay, "The Rites of Violence," in *Society and Culture*, especially 157–64. For Calvin's views on pollution, see Eire, *War Against the Idols*, chap. 6. Sin, for all Christians, was pollution; however, during the religious conflicts of the French Reformation, the rhetoric of heresy and anti-idolatry focused particularly on this interpretation.

13. "Edit qui enjoint expressement a tous baillis, senechaux, procureurs, avocats du roi, etc . . . , sous peine de suspension et privation de leurs offices, de rechercher et poursuivre les lutheriens, et de les livrer au jugement des cours souveraines," Fontainebleau, June 1, 1540, no. 305 in François-André Isambert et. al, *Recueil Générale des anciennes lois français depuis l'an 420 jusqu'à la Révolution de 1789*, vol. 14 (Paris, 1822–33): "les seminateurs de cette infection."

14. Gabriel Bounyn, *Harangue au Roi, à la Roine, et aux hommes françois, sur l'entretenement & reconciliation de la Paix, & entree dudict Seg_r en ses villes* (Paris, 1565), 15: "n'endur[e] l'impureté & meschance des coulpables." Also, Claude de Sainctes, *Discours sur les Moyens Anciennement Practiquez par les Princes Catholiques, contre les Sectes* (Paris, 1563).

15. *Signes prodigieux apparuz en Allemaigne comminatifz de l'ire de dieu, sur les ennemys de notre saincte Foy catholique* (Paris, 1565), iij. Larissa Taylor, in her work, *Soldiers of Christ: Preaching in Late Medieval and Reformation Paris* (Oxford: Oxford University Press, 1992), points out how Catholic preachers described the "pollution" of Germany and its environs by the Protestant doctrine (413–14). She specifically cites Guillaume Pepin's sermon "De destruction vici Lutherianorum, i. hereticorum civitatis Ninive." Davis also points out that the presence of heretics in France were blamed for the military loss at the Battle of Saint Quentin. See Davis, citing Jean Crespin, "The Rites of Violence," 167.

16. For some examples of these accusations, see Claude Haton, *Memoires de Claude Haton*, vol. 1 (Paris: M. Felix Bourquelot, 1857), 50–51. Davis points out that Protestants also accused Catholics of polluting, sexual acts. See Davis, "Rites of Violence," 158–59.

17. Antoine de Mouchy, *Responce a quelque apologie que les heretiques ces jours passé ont mis en avant sous ce titre: Apologie ou deffence des bons Chrestiens contre les ennemis de'Eglise Catholique* (Paris, 1558).

18. Jacques-Auguste de Thou, *Histoire universelle de Jacques-Auguste de Thou,* vol. 2 (The Hague: Henri Scheurleer, 1740), 691: "un tres-grand concors de personnes des deux sexes . . . & qu'ensuite les chandelles ayant été eteintes, chacun avoit satisfait ses desirs . . . qu'un d'entre eux avoit eu alors un commerce criminel avec la fille de l'Avocat, & avoit même content sa passion jusqu'a trois fois." De Thou noted that this was obviously a lie, though many believed it.

19. See, for example, in Antoine Fontanon, ed., *Les edicts et ordonnances des roys de France depuis S. Loys iusques à present,* (Paris, 1580): " Edit qui enjoint expressement a tous baillis, senechaux, procureurs, avocats du roi, etc . . . , sous peine de suspension et privation de leurs offices, de rechercher et poursuivre les lutheriens, et de les livrer au jugement des cours souveraines," June 1, 1540, vol. 4, 246–48; "Edit enjoignant aux inquisiteurs de la foi de poursuivre les lutheriens et heretiques comme seitieux, perturbateurs de la paix publique, et conspirateurs contre la surete de l'etat," July 23, 1543, vol. 4, 225–26; "Ordonnance sur l'attribution aux juges d'eglise des *accusations de'heresie* dirigees contre les protestans, et aux juges ordinaires et d'eglise conjointement des causes ou l'heresie et quelque crime public se touvent reunis," November 19, 1549, vol. 4, 249–50. This is just a sample of edicts and ordinances that use this language. For a listing and brief analysis of relevant edicts, see N. M. Sutherland, *The Huguenot Struggle for Survival* (New Haven: Yale University Press, 1980), 333–72.

20. For example, see Martin Luther, "Third Lenten Sermon," in *Luther's Works,* ed. J. Pelikan, vol. 50 (St. Louis: H. T. Lehmann, 1955); Calvin, *Petit Traicte monstrant que c'est que doit faire un homme fidèle congnoissant la vérité de l'Evangile, quand il est entre les Papistes* (1543), in *Ioannis Calvini Opera quae supersunt omnia,* ed. Guilielmus Baum, Eduardus Cunitz, and Eduardus Reuss, vol. 6 (Braunschweig: Schwetschke and Sons, 1867), 542–88, hereafter referred to as *CO*; Calvin, *Quatre sermons de M. Iehan Calvin traictans des matieres for utiles pour nostre temps* (1552), in *CO,* vol. 8, 369–452; Calvin, "On Shunning the Unlawful Rites of the Ungodly and Preserving the Purity of the Christian Religion," in *Calvin's Tracts and Treatises,* ed. Thomas F. Torrance, vol. 3 (London: Oliver and Boyd, 1958), 359–412; Pierre Viret, *Traittez divers pour l'instruction des fidèles qui resident & conversent eslieus & pais esquels il ne leur est permis de vivre en la pureté & liberté de l'Évangile. Revus & augmentez* (Geneva, 1559). The views of the early reformers on idolatry are treated rather comprehensively in Eire, *War Against the Idols,* chap. 3, and on Calvin's views in chap. 6. Calvin however was not the first to address either Nicodemism or intolerance of idolatry. See Eire, "Prelude to Sedition?," 123–25.

21. For a discussion of "pollution" in Calvin, see Bouwsma, *John Calvin,* 36. Not all reformers were of the same mind as Calvin regarding the "pollution" of idolatry. For example, Gérard Roussel, Jacques Lefèvre d'Etaples, and other French Humanist reformers were accused of Nicodemism by Calvin for their attempt to reform the church from within. See Zagorin, *Ways of Lying,* 71, 75.

22. See Calvin, *Excuse de Jehan Calvin, CO,* vol. 6, 611: "Or ce qui me faict insister en ce poinct avec plus grande véhémence, c'est pource que je ne doute pas, que jusque à ceste heure, la plus part n'ait grandement provoqué l'ire de Dieu, en

estimant si peu, et quasi prenant cela pour ieu, de le déshonerer en se meslant avec les idolatres, pour communiquer à leurs superstitions." For other examples, see Jean L'Espine, *Traitté consolatoire et fort utile, contre tous afflictions qui adviennent ordinairement aux fideles Chrestiens* (Lyon, 1565), 7–8.

23. Calvin, "Letter of 1540," in *CO*, vol. 11, 56, cited in Bouwsma, *John Calvin*, 36.

24. Calvin, *Petit traicté*, in *CO*, vol. 6, 557.

25. See, for example, Calvin's letter to Madame de Cany, June 7, 1553, in *CO*, vol. 14, 556–58.

26. See chapter 4 for an detailed analysis of this case.

27. Exile did not ensure freedom from prosecution by the state. Many exiles were tried and executed in effigy, while the state confiscated their goods. See for example, the case of Laurent de Normandie, U/2305, Collection La Nain, AN.

28. See Raymond A. Mentzer, *Heresy Proceedings in Languedoc, 1500–1560*, Transactions of the American Philosophical Society, vol. 74 (Philadelphia, 1984).

29. There are many examples of the addition of a secret condition attached to the death sentences of Protestants stating that "s'il ne persévère [in his blasphemy], sera estranglé avant que sentir le feu." Though this addendum, was not always inserted, the less painful death was often given as an incentive. See for example, the arrets for Jean Boursali (December 17, 1535), and Laurens de Rueil (July 17, 1542) in U/2505, Collection Le Nain, AN.

30. Claude Gauvard, *"De Grace Especial": Crime, état et société à la fin du moyen âge*, vol. 1 (Paris: Publications de la Sorbonne, 1991), 748.

31. Mentzer, *Heresy Proceedings in Languedoc, 1550–1560*, 13–14.

32. See ibid., and Gauvard, *"De Grace Especial,"* vol. 1, 745–48.

33. Crespin, *Histoire des vrays tesmoins*, 494: "au grand regret de tous ceux qui le cognoissoient, & avoient autre esperance de lui."

34. Edict of Châteaubriand, June 27, 1551, in Fontanon, *Les Édicts et ordonnances des rois de France*, IV, 252–57; Edict of Compiègne, July 24, 1557, in Isambert, *Recueil Générale*, vol. 12, 495–97. See also Mentzer, *Heresy Proceedings*, 134–35.

35. One of the most notable examples of the razing of houses was the house on the Rue Saint Jacques where a tragic assembly was held in 1557.

36. U/2305, Collection Le Nain, AN: "condamnes par contumace, pour crime de lèze majesté divine pour d'être soustraits et retirez de la ville de Noyon, et retirez volontairement en la ville de Geneve ville suspecte et receptuelle d'hérésie pour y vivre comme les autres infideles contre les ordonnences et coustumes de notre mere Ste. Eglise et contre les saincts sacremens, commettans par ce moyen volontaire desertion et defection de la foy, d'être trainer sur les clayes, pendus, bruslez en figure, leurs biens confisquez au roy. . . ."

37. Arlette Lebigre, in her work, *La justice du roi: la vie judiciaire dans l'ancienne France* (Paris: Albin Michel, 1988), 136, suggests differently. "Effigier quelqu'un c'est l'atteindre à travers son double, déchaîner contre lui les forces invisibles, porteuses de malheur et de mort."

38. Pierre Imbart de la Tour, *Les origines de la Réforme* vol. 4 (Geneva: Slatkine Reprints, 1978), 98.

39. See below. The martyrs or "prisoners for the cause" also admonished the faithful to attend. See, for example, "Exhortation d'un Evesque de France au trou-

peau de son diocese, qui ha receu la réformation de l'Evangile," (n.p., 1561), in *Ample Discours des acts memorables des Poissy* (n.p., 1561).

40. For example, see Pierre Viret, "Epistre envoyée aux fidèles," *Traittez divers*, 15. This particular passage is quoted by numerous reformers in many different treatises. See also, *Conseilz et Advis de Plusieurs Grands & doctes personnages sus la même matière contenue au précédent Livre du Temporiseur*, ed. Jean Saugrain (Lyon, 1565), especially the contributions by Celius Secundus, Oecolampadius, and Melanchthon.

41. David Nichols, "The Theatre of Martyrdom in the French Reformation," *Past and Present* 121 (1988): 68.

42. Donald R. Kelley, *Beginning of Ideology: Consciousness and Society in the French Reformation* (Cambridge: Cambridge University Press, 1981), 96.

43. Crespin, *Histoire des vrays tesmoins*, aiii: "Entre les marques de la vraye Eglise de Dieu, ceste cy a été l'un des principales, à savoir, qu'elle a de tous temps soustenu les assaux des persécutions."

44. Ibid., 236: "vous pourrez distribuer lesdites lettres aux uns & aux autres, afin qu'il en revienne plus grand fruict à l'Eglise."

45. Ibid., 277: "nous l'avons ici mis pour en faire participan tous fidèles."

46. Ibid., 279: "J'en reciteray aucune chose, estimant que ne le requerez par curiosité: mais seulement pour l'edification de l'Eglise."

47. For a discussion of English martyrs's letter writing and community, see John R. Knott, *Discourses of Martyrdom in English Literature, 1563–1694* (Cambridge: Cambridge University Press, 1993), chap. 3.

48. Jean Crespin, *Recueil de plusieurs personnes qui ont constamment enduré la mort pour le Nom de notre Seigneur JC, depuis Jean Wicleff & Jean Hus jusques a ceste année presente* (Geneva, 1555), iiij: "j'espère qu'il vous servira grandement, selon qu'un chacun de vous aura besoin, ou de consolation ou de confirmation. Car vous avez ici de merveilleux miroirs, & de toutes sortes d'exemples, de tous estats, sexes, ages & nations."

49. El Kenz, *Les bûchers du roi*, 130. See also William Monter, "Les exécutés pour hérésie par arrêt du Parlement de Paris (1523–1560)," *Bulletin de la Société de l'Histoire du Protestantisme français* 142 (1996): 191–224.

50. There are numerous regional studies that examine the actual makeup of the Reformed communities in France. See, for example, Diefendorf, *Beneath the Cross*, chap. 8, on the Parisian community; Judith Pugh Meyer, *Reformation in La Rochelle: Tradition and Change in Early Modern Europe, 1500–1568* (Geneva: Droz, 1996), chaps. 2 and 3; Galpern, *Religions of the People in Sixteenth-Century Champagne*, chaps. 3, 4, and 5.

51. On female martyrs, see chapter 4.

52. El Kenz, *Les bûchers du roi*, 134–35, for a breakdown of percentages.

53. Crespin, *Histoire des vrays tesmoins*, 94: "donne pour miroir aux laboureurs de la terre."

54. Ibid.

55. See Kelley, *Beginning of Ideology*, 143–50, for a description of the universities, especially the University of Paris, and student and faculty activism.

56. Chandieu, *Histoire des Persécutions*, xxix: "Voulez-vous apprendre à renoncer à vous-memes, pourter votre croix, mourir constamment pour l'honneur de Dieu. Voici vos frères en grand nombre, & de toutes sortes, qui on abandonne leurs vies

pour cela & marchent aujourd'hui devant vous, à fin que vous les ensuiviez. . . . Vous lirez ici des simples femmelettes, des poures artisans, des jeunes enfans, armez des forces de l'Espirit de Dieu, avoir surmonté toutes les puisance du monde, & être allez gaiement à la mort."

57. Calvin, "Le second sermon, contenant exortation à souffrir persecution pour suyvre Iesus Christ et son Evangile," in *Quatre Sermons de M. Iehan Calvin* (1552), *CO*, vol. 8, 403: "Nous ne povons alleguer que ce ait esté un petit nombre de gens; car il y a eu pour lors comme une grande armée de Martyrs. Nous ne povons dire que ce ayant esté des Prophetes, lesquels Dieu eust separez du commun peuple; car les femmes et jeunes enfans ont esté de ceste bande."

58. Ludwig Rabe, *Der heiligen aus erwohlten Gottes Zeugen Bekennen und Martyren* (1552); John Foxe, *Acts and Monuments* (1554); Flaccius Illyricus, *Catalogus testium veritatis* (1556); Heinrich Pantaleone, *Martyrum historia* (1563); Adrian Cornelis van Haemstede, *De Gheschiedenisse ende den doodt der vromer Martelaren* (1559). On the national context of these and the French martyrologies, see Gregory, *Salvation at Stake*, 187–96. And on the relationship between the martyrologists, see ibid., 165–71.

59. Donald W. Riddle, *The Martyrs: A Study in Social Control* (Chicago: University of Chicago Press, 1931), 106.

60. John Gillis, ed., *Commemorations: The Politics of National Identity* (Princeton: Princeton University Press, 1994).

61. See, for example, Pierre Nora, *Rethinking France: Les Lieux de Mémoire, Volume I, The State*, trans. Mary Trouille (Chicago: University of Chicago Press, 2001; originally published as *Les Lieux de mémoire* [Paris: Éditions Gallimard, 1984]); Gillis, *Commemorations*; Daniel J. Sherman, *The Construction of Memory in Interwar France* (Chicago: University of Chicago Press, 1999); James Fentress and Chris Wickham, *Social Memory* (New York: Blackwell, 1992).

62. Elizabeth Castelli's excellent *Martyrdom and Memory: Early Christian Culture Making* (New York: Columbia University Press, 2004), chap. 1, provides a helpful analysis of the historiography concerning memory and Christianity.

63. Maurice Halbwachs, *Les cadres sociaux de la mèmoire* (1925; reprint, Paris: Albin Michel, 1994). See also Halbwachs, *The Collective Memory*, trans. Lewis A. Cosner (Chicago: University of Chicago Press, 1992). Halbwach's work has received a mixed reception since its publication in 1925. For example, see Patrick H. Hutton, "Sigmund Freud and Maurice Halbwachs: The Problem of Memory in Historical Psychology," *History Teacher* 27 (February 1994): 145–58; Castelli, "Martyrdom, Mythmaking, and Memory Among the Early Christians," unpublished paper cited with permission, 6; Nathan Wachtel, "Memory and History: An Introduction," *History and Anthropology* 2 (1986): 207–24.

64. As described by Patrick H. Hutton, "The Role of Memory in the Historiography of the French Revolution," *History and Theory* 30 (February 1991): 58.

65. Castelli, *Martyrdom and Memory*, 4.

66. There were instances of Protestants gathering up the ashes or bones of their martyrs. See Gregory, *Salvation at Stake*, 175–76. However, the collection and veneration of relics were denounced by Chandieu, Crespin, and Calvinist reformers in their attacks on Catholic practices regarding martyrs and saints. See below.

67. For an excellent analysis of late medieval Catholic perceptions of martyrdom, see Gregory, *Salvation at Stake*, chap. 2.

68. Crespin, preface to *Histoire des vrays tesmoins*: "il faut aussi remener les actes & faits des Martyrs à leur droit usage." This is taken directly from Chandieu's *Histoire des persecutions*, xxxiij. Sections of Crespin's preface to the 1570 edition were taken verbatim from Chandieu's epistle. This is certainly the case for Crespin's criticisms of the Catholic martyrological accounts.

69. Tertullian, *Deux Petits Livres de Florent Tertullian*, ed. Jean Saugrain (Lyon, 1564), 3–4.

70. Though torture and suffering is described in the martyrological accounts of Crespin and Chandieu, not much detail is given about the pain suffered. Instead, constancy and overcoming pain through God's grace is focused upon. This differs in some respect to Foxe and other Protestant martyrologists, who do give relatively more detail. Crespin does include these accounts, such as Anne Askew, taken verbatim from Foxe.

71. Crespin, preface to *Histoire des vrays tesmoins*.

72. Ibid.

73. Ibid.

74. J.-F. Gilmont, *Jean Crespin: un editieur réformé du XVIe siècle* (Geneva: Droz, 1981), 166.

75. Arthur and Gabrielle Berthoud, *Notes sur le Livre des martyrs de Jean Crespin* (Neuchatel: Université de Neuchatel, 1930), 13–15.

76. For a listing of the editions and other works written or published by Crespin, see Gilmont, *Jean Crespin*, 245–60.

77. The French martyrologists were not only ones inspired by Eusebius. Daniel Woolf in his essay, "The Rhetoric of Martyrdom: Generic Contradiction and Narrative Strategy in John Foxe's *Acts and Monuments*," has an insightful discussion of the influence of Eusebius on Foxe. "The Rhetoric of Martyrdom," in Thomas F. Mayer and D. R. Woolf, eds., *The Rhetorics of Life-Writing in Early Modern Europe: Forms of Biography From Cassandra Fedele to Louis XIV* (Ann Arbor: University of Michigan Press, 1995), 244–46.

78. Ibid., 244–45.

79. For example, see the accounts of Jean Cornon and Marguerite Boulard in Crespin, *Histoire des vrays tesmoins*, 94 and 97–98 respectively.

80. For example, see Chandieu, *Histoire des Persécutions*, xviij–xix, and Crespin, *Histoire des vrays tesmoins*, 58.

81. See Phyllis Mack Crew, *Calvinist Preaching and Iconoclasm in the Netherlands, 1544–1569* (Cambridge: Cambridge University Press, 1978), 113, for an analysis of the continuity of the community of suffering in the Dutch Reform.

82. Chandieu, *Histoire des Persécutions*, vj–vij.

83. Ibid., vj.

84. Heinrich Bullinger, *Deux Sermons de la fin du siècle* (Geneva, 1557), 14: "perpetuelles embuchés, pratiques & tormens."

85. Ibid. There is a connection to the martyrology here as this pamphlet was published by Jean Crespin.

86. Crespin, preface to *Histoire des vrays tesmoins*: "En somme, on ne l'accusoit que de deux crime les plus enormes de tout, assavoir de blaspheme & de sedition.

. . . On les accuse comme seditieux & mutins: faisans des assemblees particulieres, reprenans les vices des gras Prelats de Jerusalem & tout le peuple Judaique. S'il est question des autres, nous y trouverons en effect une meme procedure."

87. *Juste Complainte des Fideles de France. Contre leurs adversaires Papistes, & autres. Sur l'affliction & faux crimes, dont on les charge a grand tort* (Avignon, 1560), 15: "Autant en ont fait ceux de l'Eglise ancienne, comme le tesmoignent les histoires Ecclesiastiques, & les excuses que les Docteurs anciens en ont faites, pource qu'on les chargeoit des memes calomnies, donc on nous á charge jusques á present." The author, continuing this equation, cited Eusebius in a side gloss.

88. Jean Sleidan, *Les Oeuvres de I. SLEIDAN qui concernent les Histoires qu'il a escrites* (Geneva, 1566), 183: "Leur condition est aujourdhui pareille."

89. Chandieu, *Histoire des persecutions,* xviij–xxj.

90. Claude de Sainctes, *Discours sur les Moyens Anciennement Practiquez par les Princes Catholiques, contre les Sectes* (1563, Paris), 3–19.

91. Florimond de Raemond, *L'Histoire de la Naissance, progrez, et decadence de l'heresie de ce siecle* [par feu Florimond de Raemond conseiller du Roy en sa Cour de Parlement de Bourdeaux] (Arras, 1611), 1285.

92. Ibid., 1286.: "Gens malheureus, disoit S. augustin . . . ils vivent comme mechans, meurent comme Heretiques, & sont honnorez comme martyrs."

93. For an analysis of the metaphor of the Christian soldier in the rhetoric of martyrdom in English martyrologies, see Knott, *Discourses of Martyrdom,* 99–101.

94. See, for example, *Declaration et Protestation de ceux de la Religion Reformée de la Rochelle sur la prise & capture des armes qu'ils ont fait le neufiseme de Janvier dernier* (n.p., 1568).

95. See *Prières pour les soldats & prisonniers de l'Eglise reformée* (La Rochelle, 1568).

96. Crespin, preface to *Histoire des vrays tesmoins:* "vaillans champions, qui ont passé par leur combats, & par leur mort surmonte toutes afflictions, sont merveilleusement utiles & necessaires."

97. Tertullian, *To the Martyrs* in *Tertullian: Disciplinary, Moral, and Ascetical Works,* trans. Rudoph Arbesmann, Emily Joseph Daly, and Edwin A. Quain, vol. 3 (New York: Fathers of the Church, 1959), 3.23.

98. Origen, *An Exhortation to Martyrdom* in *Origen: An Exhortation to Martyrdom, Prayer, and Selected Works,* trans. Rowan A. Greer, vol. 1 (Mahwah, NJ: Paulist Press, 1979), 1.41, 21.55.

99. Castelli, *Martyrdom and Memory,* 121. She cites Origen, *Exhortation to Martyrdom,* chap. 18.

100. Crespin, *Histoire des vrays tesmoins,* 183: "Sus donc, mes compagnons de guerre, à l'assaut, courage, soldats, courage, marchez hardiment. Ne les craignez point. ils ne sont pas gens pour nous: car Jesus Christ notre capitaine nous les a tous vaincus. L'esperance donc sa victoire nous servira d'armer notre teste. N'oublions pas notre bouclier, qui est d'avoir une foi vive, puissante & vertueuse, pour repousser les coups de nos ennemis. Gardons que l'espée ne nous eschappe de la main. ce cousteau de sainct Esprit tranchant des deux costez, qui est cest vive parolle de Dieu, laquelle perce & coeurs & ames, & pensées & intentions."

101. Chandieu, *Histoire des Persécutions,* 167: "sous la protection, & deffense duquel nous devons tous batailler, comme vrays champions, & fidèles soldats de notre Capitaine."

102. Jean L'Espine, *Traitté consolatoire*, 15: "Pensons aussi que ce n'est pas grand honneur d'un Chrestien, si quand il part de ce monde, pour retourner au ciel, revoir son père, il ne lui porte son boucher, qui est la foi, & sa lance qui est la parolle, & universallement toutes ses armes rouges, & teintes, tant de son sang, que de celui des ennemis de l'Eglise qu'il n'y a point de plus bel ordre de Chevalier."

103. Calvin, "Le second sermon contenant exhortation à souffrir persecution," *CO*, vol. 8, 397: "il fault qu'un Chrestien, estant mesme en repos, ait tousjours un pied levé pour marcher au combat."

104. For example, see Viret, "De la communication que ceus qui cognoissent la verité de l'Evangile, aux ceremonies des papistes, & principallement a leurs Baptesmes, Mariages, Messes, Funerailles, & Obseques pour les trespassez," *Traittez divers*, 209–11, on the examples of Pierre of Alexandria and Meletius of Thebiade; Calvin, *Petit traicté*, *CO*, vol. 6, 544, on Saint Cyprian and 570, on the Maccabees.

105. While the Edict of Paris (1535), written in the aftermath of the *affair des placards*, imposed harsh penalties upon heretics and those who harbored them, it wasn't until the Edict of Fontainbleau (1540) that the crime of heresy became elevated to high treason against both God and the state. As such, heresy trials became the jurisdiction of the Parlements, rather than solely that of the ecclesiastic courts. Hence, this edict marks the beginning of the official active involvement of the state, rather than acting in an assistant role to the ecclesiastical courts, in prosecuting and hunting down Protestants in France. It is important to note, however, the existence of the Edict of Paris in which the Parlement of Toulouse was granted authority to conduct trials for heresy, though this was only on a local level.

106. In *Petit Traicté*, Calvin differentiates between "dissimulation," which is acceptable, and "simulation," which is not. Dissimulation involves withdrawing from the idolatrous community while not trumpeting one's beliefs down the avenues. Simulation is Nicodemism—attending idolatrous ceremonies and pretending to accept their beliefs while secretly holding the doctrine of the Gospel in one's heart.

107. Although the first of his major French treatises was not published until 1543 (*Petit traicté monstrant que doit faire un homme fidèle*), Calvin did compose at least two others in Latin during the 1530s: "De fugiendis impiorum illicitis sacris" (1536) and "De sacerdotio papale" (1536). The minor work "On Shunning the Unlawful Rites of the Ungodly and Preserving the Purity of the Christian Religion," was also published during the 1530s (1537). Calvin responded to complaints of his unreasonable demands in *Excuse de Jehan Calvin*, a year after the *Petit traicté* (1544). The *Petit traicté* and *Excuse de Jehan Calvin* were then published together in 1545. In the interim period of 1545–1552, Latin editions and other vernacular translations (German, English) of his works were published, thus continuing Calvin's fight against Nicodemism on a more international level. Calvin's next effort to combat Nicodemism in France was the *Quatre Sermons*, published in 1552, and *Reponse à un certain holandois, lequel sous ombre de faire les chrestiens tout spirituels, leur permettent de polluer leurs corps en toutes idolatries* (1562). For the publishing history of these texts, see Droz, *Chemins de l'Hérésie*, 131–77, though she overlooks the *Quatre Sermons* and *Reponse à un certain holandois*.

108. Calvin, *Excuse de Jehan Calvin, CO*, vol. 6, 597. This was, in all likelihood, a reference to the humanist reformers such as Roussel, who would not break with Rome and retained his benefices. Calvin also implied financial motivation for their Nicodemism. Florimond de Raemond noted the antagonism that Calvin developed for Roussel and points to him as the inspiration for some of Calvin's anti-Nicodemite works. See Florimond de Raemond, *L'Histoire de la Naissance, progrez, et decadence de l'hérésie de ce siècle* (Aras, 1611), 1261.

109. Calvin, *Excuse de Jehan Calvin, CO*, vol. 6, 598–99. See Eire, "Prelude to Sedition?," 125.

110. Calvin, *Excuse de Jehan Calvin, CO*, vol. 6, 600–602.

111. Ibid., 595: "Je parle pas icy en general de tous ceux qui sont encor detenuz par leur infirmité, en ceste captivité de Babylonne. . . . Car il y en a a plusiers, qui congoissent en leurs coeurs et confessent de bouche . . . regret, gemissant continuellement à Dieu. . . . Mais je m'adresse seulement à ceux, qui pour se justifier cherchent tous subterfuges qu'il leur est possible." See also Zagorin, *Ways of Lying*, 76. It must be noted that Calvin expressed unease with the use of the term "Nicodemite" as Nicodemus, the biblical character with whom the simulators were associated, who joined Jesus at night, eventually openly confessed his faith (Calvin, *Excuse de Jehan Calvin, CO*, vol. 6, 608).

112. The first of the treatises, originally entitled "Epistre envoyée aux fidèles conversans entre les chrestiens Papistiques, pour leur remonstrer comment ilz se doyvent garder d'estre souillez et polluz par leurs superstitions et idolatries et de deshonorer Jesus Christ par icelles," was published in 1543 and underwent revisions for inclusion in the *Traittez divers*. The second treatise was "De la communication des fidèles qui cognoissent la verité de l'Evangile, aux ceremonies des Papistes, et principalesment à leurs Baptesmes, Mariages, Messes, Funerailles, et Obseques pour les trespassez," which again was revised and enlarged for the larger work. The third treatise of *Traitez divers* was the only original work in the collection. "Admonition et consolation aux fidèles, qui deliberent de sortir d'entre les Papistes pour eviter idolatrie contre les tentations qui leur peuvent advenir, et les dangers ausquelz ils peuvent tomber en leur yssue," the fourth treatise in the work, was originally published independently in 1559. "Remonstrances aux fidèles qui conversent entre les Papistes; et qui ont offices publiques touchant les moyens qu'ils doivent tenir en leur vocation, à l'exemple des anciens serviteurs de Dieu," (1547) made up the fifth treatise, though it too was revised. See Robert Dean Linder, *The Political Ideas of Pierre Viret* (Geneva: Droz, 1964) for an annotated bibliography of Viret's works.

113. Viret, "Epistre envoyée aux fidèles," *Traittez divers*, 19, 20, 22.

114. Ibid., 17.

115. Ibid., 18–19.

116. Zagorin, *Ways of Lying*, 105, cites Viret from the English translation, *An Epistle to the Faithfull, Necessary for All the Children of God; Especially in These Daungerous Dayes* (London, 1582), G4.

117. Eugénie Droz criticizes Calvin's severity and claims that his "reasons are not doctrinal but moral, and, as such, inadequate" (*Chemins de l'Hérésie*, 154–55, 169). Calvin himself pointed out this criticism in the title to his work, *Excuse de Jehan Calvin à Messieurs les Nicodemites sur la complaincte qu'ils font de sa trop grand'rigueur*

(1544), and in the text when he addressed the accusation that he could criticize because he was so far away. See *Excuse de Jehan Calvin, CO*, vol. 6, 606. See also Calvin's letter of September 1540 in which he began to question his strong admonitions, in Herminjard, *Correspondance des Réformateurs*, vol. 6 (Geneva: H. Georg, 1866–97), 304.

118. For a good synopsis of Nicodemite arguments, see Zagorin, *Ways of Lying*, 70, 72–74. On the existence of Nicodemites, see Eire, "Prelude to Sedition," 142–43.

119. See Droz, *Chemins de l'Hérésie*, 173–85.

120. On Calvin's interpretation of community, see Bouwsma, *John Calvin*, 201–2.

121. See ibid., 216. Bouwsma describes how a church was "first of all a community of faith" and a "functioning community" for Calvin, and the significance of communal worship in his thought.

122. Calvin, *Excuse de Jehan Calvin, CO*, vol. 6, 596: "Car je puis protester en verité, devant Dieu et ses anges, que mon intention n'est pas autre, que de procurer, entant qu'en moi est, que nous servions Dieu tous ensemble purement."

123. Calvin, *Petit traicté, CO*, vol. 6, 563: "C'est de ne point donner cause à notre prochain d'estre mal edifié de nous, de ne luy point donner mauvais exemple, de ne rien dire ne faire pour les desbaucher."

124. 85. Viret, "Epistre envoyée aux fidèles," *Traittez divers*, 109: "Car notre confession precedente, & le tesmoignage publique de notre foi, donneroit floire à Dieu, & condamneroit les idolatres, & fortifieroit les fidèles, & osteroit toute occasion de scandale aus bons."

125. Viret, "Epistre envoyée aux fidèles," *Traittez divers*, 7: "un venin tant puant, & tant dangereux, que il soit qu'on se recule de lui, tant qu'il est possible."

126. Ibid.: "il nous pousse encore à induire les autres, à faire le semblable."

127. Calvin, *Excuse de Jehan Calvin, CO*, vol. 6, 598: "induisent les autre par leur exemple à idolatrer."

128. Calvin, *Petit traicté, CO*, vol. 6, 569: "ne scandalizent ilz pas les infirmes, leur donnant mauvais exemple, ou les mettant en doubte et scrupule, qu'ilz ne savent que juger."

129. Calvin, "On Shunning the Unlawful Rites of the Ungodly," 374–75.

130. See also Viret, "De la communication," *Traittez divers*, 38.

131. Calvin, *Excuse de Jehan Calvin, CO*, vol. 6, 612: "Et n'est pas peu de chose de donner mauvais exemple à ses prochains, pour confermer les ignorans en erreur et troubler les infirmes, ou les scandalizer! Mais quand avec tout cela nous adioustons une impudence, et que comme paillardes effrontées, nous nous torchons la bouche, pour dire que nous n'avons rien fait de mal: c'est despiter Dieu apertement, et quasi de propos deliberé le provoquer au combat, et l'armer à faire vengeance contre nous."

132. Calvin, *Petit traicté, CO*, vol. 6, 564: "Finalment ils [Nicodemites] conferment les incredules, et les endurcissent en leurs erreurs."

133. Viret, "De la communication," *Traittez divers*, 38: "Et qui plus est, nous [who might embrace Nicodemism] enflambons la fureur des tyrans, & trahissons nos frères, & sommes cause souventesfois, qu'il sont mis à mort. Car si nous nous declairions d'avantage, ou pour le moins, si nous ne faisions rien pour approuver la fausse religion des idolatres, nous leur serions en confusion, au lieu que nous les

confermons en leur erreur & tyrannie, & les armons de notre authoritie contre nos frères."

134. Calvin, *Petit traicté, CO*, vol. 6, 564: "En nourrissant toute idolatrie par leur feintise, ils sont cause de faire rompre le col aux uns, et de faire blesser griefvement les autres, de faire cheoir les uns, et de faire clocher les autre, ou de s'esgarer hors du droict chemin."

135. Ibid.: "les pays où il y a grande semence de Dieu, demeureoyent desert." This is a reference to Tertullian's oft quoted, "The blood of the martyrs is the seed of the church."

136. See Calvin, *Petit traicté, CO*, vol. 6, 570: "Si nous honnorons ces personnages [the Maccabee martyrs] comme martyrs, et louons leur constance: ne nous convient il pas condamner ce qui se fait au contraire?" See also 573–74.

137. Viret, "Epistre aux Fidèles," *Traittez divers*, 120: "S'ils eussent été autant craint leur peau que nous craignons la notre, la religion chrestienne ne'eust pas été tant augmentée, en si peu de temps."

138. Calvin, *Excuse de Jehan Calvin, CO*, vol. 6, 604.

139. Ibid., 603–4: "N'est-ce pas vouloir transfigurer Jesus Christ, pour l'avoir tel que nostre chair l'appete."

140. Viret, "Epistre aus Fidèles," 15–16: "Et pourtant, qui veut être mon disciple, il faut qu'il renonce soy-meme, & qu'il porte tous les jours sa crois sur ses espaules, & qu'il me suive."

141. Calvin, "Exhortation de souffrir," *Quatre Sermons, CO*, vol. 8, 397: "Ja soit que cela nous semble rude de prime face, si nous debvrions-nous bien contenter de ce mot de sainct Paul, c'est que nous sommes appelez et establis à souffrir: comme s'il disoit que la condition de nostre Chrestienté est telle, en sort qu'il nous fault passer par ce chemin, si nous voulons suyvre Iesus Christ."

142. Ibid., 404: "sainct Paul nous monstre par son exemple que nous avons à nous glorifier aux fletrisseures de Iesus Christ, comme aux marques esquelles Dieu nous recognoist et advoue par siens."

143. See ibid., 403–4; and Viret, "De la communication," *Traittez divers*, 209–11.

144. Viret, "Epistre aux fidèles," *Traittez divers*, 121: "parvenir à ce haut degre, & à cest perfection chrestienne des Martyrs . . . Soyons des disciples secrets avec Nicodeme & avec Joseph d'Arimathie. Et si nous ne manifestons pas clairement, ne faisons point, pour le moins, de deshonneur à Jesus Christ, & ne consentons point avec ses adversaires, en participant à la table des diables."

145. Calvin, *Petit traicté, CO*, vol. 6, 576: "la gloire de Dieu, de laquelle il est ici question, nous doit bien estre plus precieuse que ceste vie caduque et transitoire: qui n'est à dire vray, fors qu'une umbre."

EPILOGUE:
ST. BARTHOLOMEW'S DAY, 1572

1. Conspiracy theories also swirled around "foreign plots" involving Italians and assassinations. See Donald Kelley, "Martyrs, Myths and the Massacre: The Background of St. Bartholomew," *American Historical Review* 77 (December 1972): 1336.

2. The modern spelling of the town is Wassy.

3. Crespin has an account of the "massacres," including a section entitled, "La deliberation & complot des Ecclesiastiques, pour faire executer l'arest de Merindol, & pousuivre la conspiration contre les fidèles." See Jean Crespin, *Histoire des vrays tesmoins de la verité de l'Evangile, qui de leur sang l'ont signée, depuis Jean Hus jusques au temps presente* (Geneva, 1570).

4. The identity of these advisors would range from the Guise and their supporters, to Italians or foreigners in general, to the "minions" of the pope.

5. The polemical literature surrounding the massacres at Mérindole and Vassy is vast, from both a Catholic and Calvinist perspective. On the conspiracy of the Guise to usurp the throne, see, for example, *Brieve remonstrance des estats de France . . . Sur l'ambition, tyrannie, et oppression du tout intolerable des Guyse* (Rouen, 1560) and [François Hotman] *Epistre envoiee au tigre de la France* (Strasbourg, 1560). On Vassy from the Huguenot perspective, see for example, *Advertisement à la Royne Mere du Roy. Touchant les misères du Royaume au temps present, & de la conspiration des enemis de sa Majesté* (Orleans, 1562); *Destruction du saccagement, exerce cruellement par le Duc de Guise & sa cohorte, en la ville de Vassy, le premier jour de Maris 1561* (Caens, 1562); *Le Sommaire des Commentaires de la Religion et Histoire de Notre temps, Contenant les choses memorables advenues en France, sous les Roys Francois ii & Charles ix continunant jusques a present* (Paris, 1567). From a Catholic perspective, see Guillaume Morel, *Discours au Vray et en abbrege de ce qui est dernierement advenu à Vassi, y passant Monseigneur le Duc de Guise* (Paris, 1562).

6. *Prières pour les soldats & prisonniers de l'Eglise reformée* (La Rochelle, 1568): "vouloir faire misericorde a notre Roy, l'illuminer en la cognoissance de ta verite, & ne lui imputer point les tyrannies qui sont commises en ce Royaume sous l'ombre de son nom. Et donne lui sagesse & discretion pour pouvoir recognoistre por ses fidelles serviteurs, ceux qu'on lui persuade, en haine de ton Eglise, etre ses enemis."

7. See [Henri Estienne] *Discours merveilleux de la vie, actions et déportemens de la reine Catherine de Médicis* (n.p. 1575).

8. Barbara Diefendorf, *Beneath the Cross: Catholics and Huguenots in Sixteenth-Century Paris* (Oxford: Oxford University Press, 1991), 100. Diefendorf proves that Charles IX actually ordered a halt to the popular violence, though this was ineffective in the face of popular fury.

9. These numbers are derived from Protestant sources, and, as Donald Kelley states, "in fact posterity has not believed the figures given by contemporary critics." See Kelley, "Martyrs, Myths, and the Massacre," 1339. Robert Kingdon approximates the actual number around ten thousand ("Calvinism and Resistance Theory, 1550–1580," in J. H. Burns and Mark Goldie, eds., *The Cambridge History of Political Thought, 1450–1700* [Cambridge: Cambridge University Press, 1991], 207).

10. The literature on the St. Bartholomew's Day Massacre is, again, vast. As a limited bibliography, see Kelley, "Martyrs, Myths, and the Massacre"; Diefendorf, *Beneath the Cross*; Denis Crouzet, *Les Guerriers de Dieu: La violence au temps des troubles de religion* (Seyssel: Champ Vallon, 1990); N. M. Sutherland, *The massacre of St. Bartholomew and the European conflict, 1559–1572* (London: Macmillan, 1973); Robert Kingdon, *Myths about the Saint Bartholomew's Day Massacres, 1572–1576* (Cambridge, MA.: Harvard University Press, 1988).

11. More specifically, see the *Discours politiques des diverses puissances establies de Dieu au monde* as discussed in detail in Kingdon, *Myths about the Saint Bartholomew's Day Massacres*, chap. 11, though Kingdon questions its practical impact.

12. The work was so controversial that Genevan authorities had refused Bèze permission to publish it in their city. See Kelley, "Martyrs, Myths, and the Massacre: The Background of St. Bartholomew," 1340.

13. For discussion of these texts, see Donald R. Kelley, *Beginning of Ideology: Consciousness and Society in the French Reformation* (Cambridge: Cambridge University Press, 1981), chap. 8; Ralph Giesey, "The Monarchomach triumvirs: Hotman, Beza and Mornay," *Bibliothèque d'Humanisme et Renaissance* 32 (1970): 41–65; Quentin Skinner, *The Foundations of Modern Political Thought*, vol. 2 (Cambridge: Cambridge University Press, 1978); and Kingdon, *Myths about the St. Bartholomew's Day Massacres*.

14. Donald Kelley, *Beginning of Ideology*, 292.

15. Kingdon, *Myths about the St. Bartholomew's Day Massacres*, 5.

Bibliography

MANUSCRIPT SOURCES

Archives Nationales (abbreviated as "AN")
  Collection Le Nain,
    U/2505, Registre de la Tournelle
  U/2305, Table des matières, Tome 60 Hérétiques
Bibliothèque Nationale (abbreviated as "BN")
  Collection Brienne
    MS 205, Procès verbal de la Dégradation d'Anne Du Bourg, Conseiller en la Cour
  Collection Dupuy
  Collection Fontanieu
    MS 298, Chanson Spirituelle d'Anne Du Bourg
Bibliothèque de la Société de l'histoire du protestantisme français
  MS 486, Henri Bordier, *Copie des Extraits fait par le greffier Dongois mort en 1717 des Régistres Criminels du Parlement de Paris, en ce qui se rapporte aux Protestans (1534–1584).*

PRINTED PRIMARY SOURCES

Advertisement à la Royne Mere du Roy. Touchant les misères du Royaume au temps present, & de la conspiration des enemis de sa Majesté. Orleans, 1562. [BN]

Brieve remonstrance des estats de France . . . Sur l'ambition, tyrannie, et oppression du tout intolerable des Guyse. Rouen, 1560. [BN]

Chanson Spirituelle d'Anne Du Bourg, Conseiller du Roy en Parlement: Estant es lieux pour soustenir la parole de Dieu: & pour laquelle il souffrit constamment la mort. Paris, 1560. [BN]

Confession sur les principaux poincts de la religion Chrestienne. presentée à la Cour de Parlement de Paris, Par Anne du Bourg, conseiller de la ditee Cour: estant pour lors prisonnier pour la defence de la Parolle de Dieu. N.p., n.d. [BN]

191

Declaration et Protestation de ceux de la Religion Reformée de la Rochelle sur la prise & capture des armes qu'ils ont fait le neufiseme de Janvier dernier. N.p., 1568.[BN]

Destruction du saccagement, exerce cruellement par le Duc de Guise & sa cohorte, en la ville de Vassy, le premier jour de Mars 1561. Caen, 1562.[BN]

Discours en Forme de Complainte d'un Ministre de la Parole de Dieu, faicte lui estant prisonnier pour l'Evangile. N.p., 1565.[BN]

Epistre envoyee à la Royne Mere du Roy au commencement du regne de Treschrestien Roy François second. En laquelle est sommairement respondu aux calomnies desquelles on à par ci devant chargé malicieusement ceux qui sont profession de l'Evangile. N.p., 1561.[BN]

L'Exemplaire, et Forme du procèz commis, Faict par les commissaires du Roy Contre Maistre Anne du Bourg, Conseiller en la Court de Parlement de Paris. Luy estant detenu Prisonnier pour la Religion, Contenant au vray les Interrogations à lui faicts: Et les responses & confession de sa Foy. Envers, 1560.[BN]

"Exhortation d'un Evesque de France au troupeau de son diocese, qui ha receu la réformation de l'Evangile." In *Ample Discours des acts memorables de Poissy.* N.p., 1561.[BN]

Exhortation et Remonstrance aux Princes du Sang, et Seigneurs du privé conseil du Roy, Pour obvier aux seditions qui occultement semblent menacer les fideles pour le faict de la Religion. N.p., 1561.[BN]

Hymne à Dieu, pour la Delivrance des François de la plus que Egyptienne servitude, en laquelle ils ont été detenus par le passé. N.p., n.d.[BN]

Journal d'un Bourgeois de Paris sous le règne de François Ier. Ed. Ludovic Lalanne. Paris, 1854.[BN]

Juste complainte des fidèles de France, contre leurs adversaires papistes et autres, sur l'affliction et faux crimes dont on les charge à grand tort. Avignon, 1560.[BN]

Oraison au Senat de Paris pour la Cause des Chrestiens, à la consolation d'iceux: d'Anne du Bourg Prisonnier pour la parole. N.p., 1560.[BN]

Prières pour les soldats & prisonniers de l'Eglise reformée. La Rochelle, 1568.[BN]

Remonstrance à tous estats [en faveur sur le huguenotisme ou protestantisme]: Par laquelle est en brief demonstré la foy & innocence des vrays chrestiens: Les abus ausquels font detenus leurs ennemis & persecuteurs. Paris, 1560.[BN]

Remonstrance envoyée au Roy par la noblesse de la Religion reformée du pais & Comté du Maine sur les assasinats, pilleries, saccagements de maisons, seditions, violements de femmes & autres exces horribles commis depuis la publication de l'Edit de pacification dedans ledit Comté. N.p., 1564.[BN]

Remonstrance à la Royne Mere du Roy, par ceux qui sont persecutez pour la parole de Dieu. En laquelle ils rendent raison des principaux articles de la Religion, & qui sont aujourdhui en dispute. N.p., 1661.[BN]

Signes prodigieux apparuz en Allemaigne comminatifz de l'ire de Dieu, sur les ennemys de notre saincte Foy catholique. Paris, 1565.[BN]

Le Sommaire des Commentaires de la Religion et Histoire de Notre temps, Contentant les choses memorables advenues en France, sous les Roys François ii & Charles ix continuant jusques à present. Paris, 1567.[BN]

Traicté de la justice de Dieu, et horrible vengeance contre les meurtres commis par les princes et potentats de la terre. N.p., 1562.[BN]

La vraye histoire, de la fausse procedure contre Anne Du Bourg, Conseiller pour le Roy. Lyon, 1562.[BN]

La vraye histoire, de la fausse procedure contre Anne Du Bourg, Conseiller pour le Roy. N.p., 1561.[BN]

La vraye histoire contenant l'unique jugement & fause procedure faite contre le fidèle serviteur de Dieu Anne du Bourg, Conseiller pour le Roy, en la Cour du Parlement de Paris, & les diverses opinions des Presidens & Conseillers, touchant le fait de la religion Chrestienne. Paris, 1559.[BN]

Augustine of Hippo. *The city of God against the pagans.* Ed. and trans. R. W. Dyson. Cambridge: Cambridge University Press, 1998.

Bèze, Théodore de. *Du Droit des magistrats.* Geneva, 1574.

———. *Histoire Ecclesiastique.* 2 vols. Lille: Leleux, 1841–42.

———. *Traitté de l'Authorité du Magistrat en la Punition des hérétiques, & du moyen d'y proceder, fait en Latin par de Théodore Bèze, Contre l'opinion de certains Academiques, qui par leurs escrits soustienent l'impunité de ceux qui sement des erreurs, & les veulent exempter de la sujection des loix. Nouvellement traduit de Latin en François par Nicolas Colladon.* Geneva, 1560.[BN]

Bouchel, Laurent. *La Bibliothèque ou thrésor du droict François.* Paris, 1615.

Bougler, Pierre. *Explication des articles et chefs du crime de lèze Majesté. Extraicts des anciennes ordonnances de France. Par Maistre Pierre Bougler, Bailly d'Aumalle.* Paris, 1622.[BN]

Bounyn, Gabriel. *Harangue au Roi, à la Roine, et aux hommes françois, sur l'entretenement & reconciliation de la Paix, & entrée dudict Seg_r en ses villes.* Paris, 1565.[BN]

Brulart, L'Abbé. *Journal* in *Mémoires de Condé, servant de'Eclaircissement et de Preuves à l'Histoire de M. De Thou, Contenant ce qui s'est passe de plus memorable en Europe.* Vol. 1. London, 1743.

Bullinger, Henrich. *Deux Sermons de la Fin du siècle.* Geneva, 1557.[BN]

Calvin, Jean. "Commentary on the First Epistle to Timothy." In *Commentaries on the Epistles of Paul to the Galatians and Ephesians.* Ed. and trans. William Pringle. Grand Rapids, MI: Baker Books, 1979.

———. "Commentary on the Book of Genesis." In *Calvin's Commentaries on the Book of Genesis.* Ed. and trans. William Pringle. Grand Rapids, MI: Baker Books, 1979.

———. "Commentary on the First Epistle to the Corinthians." In *Calvin's Commentaries on the Epistles of Paul to the Corinthians.* Ed. and trans. William Pringle. Grand Rapids, MI: Baker Books, 1979.

———. *Excuse de Jehan Calvin à Messieurs les Nicodemites, sur la complaincte qu'ilz font de sa trop grand'rigueur* (1544). In *Ioannis Calvini Opera quae supersunt omnia.* Ed. W. Baum, E. Cunitz, and E. Reuss. Vol. 6. Braunschweig: Schwetschke and Sons, 1867.

———. *Institutes of the Christian Religion.* Ed. John T. McNeill. Trans. Ford Lewis Battles. 2 vols. Philadelphia: Westminster Press, 1977.

———. Letter to Madame de Cany, June 7, 1553. In *Ioannis Calvini Opera quae supersunt omnia.* Ed. W. Baum, E. Cunitz, and E. Reuss. Vol. 14. Braunschweig: Schwetschke and Sons, 1867.

———. *Petit Traicté monstrant que c'est que doit faire un homme fidèle congnoissant la vérité de l'Evangile, quand il est entre les Papistes* (1543). In *Ioannis Calvini Opera quae supersunt omnia.* Ed. W. Baum, E. Cunitz, and E. Reuss. Vol. 6. Braunschweig: Schwetschke and Sons, 1867.

———. *Quatre sermons de M. Iehan Calvin traictans des matières fort utiles pour nostre temps* (1552). In *Ioannis Calvini Opera quae supersunt omnia.* Ed. W. Baum, E. Cunitz, and E. Reuss. Vol. 8. Braunschweig: Schwetschke and Sons, 1867.

Calvin, John. *On Shunning the Unlawful Rites of the Ungodly and Preserving the Purity of the Christian Religion.* In *Calvin's Tracts and Treatises.* Ed. Thomas F. Torrance. Vol. 3. London: Oliver and Boyd, 1958.

Chandieu, Antoine de la Roche. *Histoire des pérsecutions, et martyrs de l'Eglise de Paris, depuis l'an 1557. jusques au temps du Roy Charles neufviesme.* Lyon, 1563.

Condé, Louis, prince de. *Mémoires de Condé, servant de'eclaircissement et de preuves à l'histoire de M. De Thou, contenant ce qui s'est passe de plus memorable en Europe.* Vol. 1. London, 1743.

Correspondance inédite des cinq étudiants martyrs. Geneva, 1854.

Crespin, Jean. *Actes des Martyrs deduits en Sept livres, depuis les temps de Wiclef & de Hus, jusques a present. Contenans un Recueil de vraye histoire Ecclesiastique, de ceux qui ont constamment enduré la mort es derniers temps, pour la verité du Fils de Dieu.* Geneva, 1564.

———. *Histoire des vrays tesmoins de la verité de l'Evangile, qui de leur sang l'ont signée, depuis Jean Hus jusques au temps presente.* Geneva, 1570. Reprint, Liège: Centre national de recherches d'histoire religieuse, 1964.

———. *Le Livre des Martyrs qui est un recueil de plusieurs Martyrs qui ont endure la mort pour le Nom de nostre Seigneur J-C, depuis jean Hus jusques a ceste annee presente M.D.LIIII.* Geneva, 1554.

———. *Recueil de Plusieurs Personnes qui ont constamment enduré la mort pour le Nom de notre Seigneur Jesus christ, depuis Jean Wicleff, & Jean Hus jusques a ceste année present MDLV.* Geneva, 1555.

———. *Troisième partie du Recueil de Plusieurs Personnes qui ont constamment endure la mort pour la vraye doctrine du Fils de Dieu.* Geneva, 1556.

D'Aubigné, Agrippa. *Histoire universelle.* Vol. 1. Geneva: Librarie Droz, 1981.

de Thou, Jacques-Auguste. *Histoire universelle de Jaques-Auguste de Thou.* 11 vols. The Hague: Henri Scheurleer, 1740.

Estienne, Henri. *Discours merveilleux de la vie, actions et déportemens de la reine Catherine de Médicis.* N.p., 1575.

Eusebius. *The History of the Church from Christ to Constantine.* Trans. G. A. Williamson. Minneapolis, MN: Ausburg Publishing House, 1965.

Fontanon, Antoine, ed. *Les edicts et ordonnances des roys de France depuis S. Loys iusques à present.* 4 vols. Paris: 1580.

Foxe, John. *Foxe's Book of Martyrs.* Grand Rapids, MI: Baker Books, 1978.

Haton, Claude. *Mémoires de Claude Haton.* Paris: Imprimerie imperiale, 1857.

Herminjard, A-L., ed. *Correspondance des Réformateurs.* 9 vols. Geneva: H. Georg, 1866–97.

Hotman, François. *Epistre envoiée au Tigre de la France.* N.p., 1560.

————. *Sentence Redoubtable et Arrest Rigoureux du jugement de Dieu, à l'encontre de l'impieté des Tyrans, recueillies tant des sainctes escriptures, comme de toutes autres histoires.* Lyon, 1564.

Isambert, François-André et al., eds. *Recueil Général des anciennes lois français depuis l'an 420 jusqu'à la Révolution de 1789,* 29 vols. Paris, 1822–33.

La Place, Pierre de. *Commentaires de l'estat de la religion et république soubs les Rois Henri et François seconds et Charles neufviesme,* in *Choix de chroniques et mémoires sur l'histoire de France.* Ed. J. A. C. Buchon. Paris: Desrez, 1836.

La Planche, Regnier de. *Histoire de l'Estat de France, tant de la république que de la religion, sous le regne de François II* in *Choix de chroniques et mémoires sur l'histoire de France.* Ed. J. A. C. Buchon. Paris: Desrez, 1836.

L'Espine, Jean. *Traicté, pour oster la Crainte de Mort, et la Faire desirer à l'homme fidèle.* Lyon, 1558.[BN]

————. *Traitté consolatoire et fort utile, contre toutes afflictions qui adviennent ordinairement aux fidèles Chrestiens. Compose nouvellement par I. de Spina Ministre de la Parolle de Dieu: & adressé à un grand seigneur de France.* Lyon, 1565.[BN]

Luther, Martin. "Third Lenten Sermon." In *Luther's Works.* Ed. J. Pelikan. Vol. 50. St. Louis: H. T. Lehmann, 1955.

Marot, Clément, and Théodore de Bèze, *Les Psaumes de David mis en rime Françoise par Clement Marot & Theodore de Besze. Avec bonnes & sainctes Oraisons nouvellement adjoustées en la fin de chacun Psaume, pour la consolation de l'Eglise, selon la substance du Pseaume.* N.p., 1561.

Magnan, L. *Description des Troubles advenus aux Eglises de Provence, avec une eschortation & remonstrance faite aux Papistes dudit pais.* Lyon, 1563.[BN]

Morel, Guillaume. *Discours au Vray et en abbregé de ce qui est dernièrement advenu à Vassi, y passant Monseigneur le Duc de Guise.* Paris, 1562.[BN]

Mouchy, Antoine de. *Responce a quelque apologie que les heretiques ces jours passé ont mis en avant sous ce titre: Apologie ou deffence des bons Chrestiens contre les ennemis de'Eglise Catholique.* Paris, 1558. [BN]

Musculus, Eutichius. *Le Temporiseur en forme de Dialogue.* Lyon, 1561.

Origen. *Exhortation to Martyrdom.* In *Origen: Prayer, Exhortation to Martyrdom.* Ed. and trans. John J. O'Meara. Westminster, MD: The Newman Press, 1954.

Parlement of Paris.

————. *Deux Remonstrances de la cour de Parlement.* N.p., 1561.[BN]

————. *Remonstrances de la cour de Parlement à Paris, l'un sur l'Inquisition pour le fait de la Religion Chrestienne. L'autre touchant la jurisdiction, de ceux que l'on nomme Hérétiques, donne par Edit, aux Evesques & Ecclesiastiques de France.* N.p., 1561.[BN]

Pottier, André, ed. *Revue Retrospective Normande: Documents inedits pour servir à l'histoire de Rouen et de la Normandie.* Rouen, 1842.

Raemond, Florimond de. *L'Histoire de la Naissance, Progrez, et Decadence de l'Hérésie de ce siècle.* Arras, 1616.

Sainctes, Claude de. *Discours sur les Moyens Anciennement Practiquez par les Princes Catholiques, contre les Sectes.* 1563, Paris.[BN]

Saugrain, Jean, ed. *Conseilz et Advis de Plusieurs grands & doctes personnages sus la meme matière contenue au precedent Livre du Temporiseur.* Lyon, 1565.[BN]

Seneca. "On Providence." In *Moral Essays: Volume I.* Trans. John Basore. Loeb Classical Library. 1958.

Sleidan, Jean. *Les Oeuvres de I. Sleidan qui concernent les Histoires qu'il a escrites.* Geneva, 1566.[BN]

Stegmann, André, ed. *Edits des guerres de religion.* Paris, 1979.

Tertullian. *Apology* and *Letter to Scapula.* In *Tertullian: Apologetical Works and Minucius Felix Octavius.* Trans. Rudolph Arbesmann, Emily Joseph Daly, and Edwin A. Quain. New York: Fathers of the Church, 1950.

———. *Deux petits livres de Florent Tertullian.* Ed. Jean Saugrain, Lyon, 1564.[BN]

———. *To the Martyrs* and *Flight in Time of Persecution.* In *Tertullian: Disciplinary, Moral, and Ascetical Works.* Trans. Rudolph Arbesmann, Emily Joseph Daly, and Edwin A. Quain. New York: Fathers of the Church, 1959.

Viret, Pierre. *Traittez divers pour l'instruction des fidèles qui resident & conversent es lieus & pais esquels il ne leur est permis de vivre en la pureté & liberté de l'Evangile. Reveus & augmentez.* Geneva, 1559.[BN]

SECONDARY SOURCES

Allard, Alberic. *L'Histoire de la justice criminelle au seizième siècle.* Gand: H. Hoste, 1868.

Autin, Albert. *Un Épisode de la vie de Calvin: La Crise du Nicodémisme 1535–1545.* Toulouse: P. Tissot, 1917.

Bercé, Yves-Marie. *Fête et révolte: des mentalités populaires du XVe au XVIIIe siècle.* Paris: Hachette, 1976.

Biéler, André. *L'homme et la femme dans la morale Calviniste: La doctrine réformée sur l'amour, le mariage, le célibat, le divorce, l'adultère et la prostitution, considérée dans son cadre historique.* Geneva: Labor et Fides, 1961.

Blaisdell, Charmarie. "Calvin's Letters to Women: The Courting of Laides in High Places." *Sixteenth Century Journal* 13 (1982): 76–84.

Bonnet, J. "Jean Crespin ou le martyrologe réformé." *Bulletin de la Société de l'Histoire du Protestantisme français* 29 (1880): 193–204.

Bossy, John. "The Mass as a Social Institution, 1200–1700." *Past and Present* 100 (1983): 29–61.

Bouwsma, William J. *John Calvin: A Sixteenth-Century Portrait.* Oxford: Oxford University Press, 1988.

Bowersock, Glen. *Martyrdom and Rome.* Cambridge: Cambridge University Press, 1995.

Brown, Judith. *Immodest Acts: Life of a Lesbian Nun in Renaissance Italy.* Oxford: Oxford University Press, 1986.

Brown, Peter. *Augustine of Hippo.* Berkeley: University of California Press, 1967.

Bynum, Carolyn. *Holy Feast, Holy Fast: The Religious Significance of Food to Medieval Women.* Berkeley: University of California Press, 1987.

Bynum, Caroline, Steven Harrell, and Paula Richman, eds. *Gender and Religion: On the Complexity of Symbols.* Boston: Beacon Press, 1986.

Cardman, Francine. "Acts of the Women Martyrs." In *Women in Early Christianity*. Ed. D. M. Scholer. New York: Garland, 1993.

Castelli, Elizabeth. *Martyrdom and Memory: Early Christian Culture Making*. New York: Columbia University Press, 2004.

———."Martyrdom, Mythmaking, and Memory Among the Early Christians." Working paper, Center for Historical Analysis, Rutgers University, New Brunswick, NJ, 1996.

Coats, Catharine Randall. *(Em)bodying the Word: Textual Resurrections in the Martyrological Narratives of Foxe, Crespin, de Bèze and d'Aubigné*. New York: Peter Lang, 1992.

Crew, Phyllis Mack. *Calvinist preaching and Iconoclasm in the Netherlands, 1544–1569*. Cambridge: Cambridge University Press, 1978.

Crouzet, Denis. *Les guerriers de Dieu: la violence au temps des troubles de religion: vers 1525–1610*. 2 vols. Paris: Champ Vallon, 1990.

Davis, Natalie Zemon. *Society and Culture in Early Modern France*. Stanford: Stanford University Press, 1965.

Delehaye, Hippolyte. *The Legends of the Saints*. Trans. Donald Attwater. Second edition. New York: Fordham University Press, 1962.

———. *Les passions des martyrs et les genres littéraires*. Second edition. Bruxelles: Society of Bollandists, 1966.

Diefendorf, Barbara. *Beneath the Cross: Catholics and Huguenots in Sixteenth-Century Paris*. Oxford: Oxford University Press, 1991.

———."Prologue to a Massacre: Popular Unrest in Paris, 1557–1572." *American Historical Review* 90 (December 1985): 1067–91.

Dillon, Anne. *The Construction of Martyrdom in the English Catholic Community, 1535–1603*. Aldershot, UK: Ashgate, 2002.

Douglass, Jane Dempsey. *Women, Freedom, and Calvin*. Philadelphia: Westminster Press, 1985.

Droge, Arthur J., and James D. Tabor. *A Noble Death: Suicide and Martyrdom Among Christians and Jews in Antiquity*. San Francisco: HarperSanFrancisco, 1992.

Droz, Eugénie. *Chemins de l'Hérésie: Textes et Documents*. Geneva: Slatkine Reprints, 1970.

Dupuy, Micheline. *Pour Dieu et pour le roi: La montée de l'intolérance au XVe Siècle*. Paris: Perrin, 1984.

Eire, Carlos. "Calvin and Nicodemism: A Reappraisal." *Sixteenth Century Journal* 10 (1979): 45–69.

———."Prelude to Sedition? Calvin's Attack on Nicodemism and Religious Compromise." *Archiv für Reformationsgeschichte* 76 (1985): 120–45.

———. *War Against the Idols: The Reformation of Worship from Erasmus to Calvin*. Cambridge: Cambridge University Press, 1986.

Eisenstein, Elizabeth. *The Printing Press as an Agent of Change: Communications and Cultural Transformations in Early-Modern Europe*. Cambridge: Cambridge University Press, 1979.

El Kenz, David. *Les bûchers du roi: la culture protestante des martyrs (1523–1572)*. Paris: Champ Vallon, 1997.

Fentress, James, and Chris Wickham. *Social Memory*. New York: Blackwell, 1992.

Fox, Robin Lane. *Pagans and Christians*. New York: Knopf, 1989.

Frazier, Alison Knowles. *Possible Lives: Authors and Saints in Renaissance Italy*. New York: Columbia University Press, 2005.

Freeman, Thomas S., and Sarah Elizabeth Wall. "Racking the Body, Shaping the Text: The Account of Anne Askew in Foxe's *Book of Martyrs*." *Renaissance Quarterly* 54 (Winter 2001): 1165–96.

Frend, W. H. C. *Martyrdom and Persecution in the Early Church: A Study of a Conflict from the Maccabees to Donatists*. New York: Anchor Books, 1967.

———. *The Rise of Christianity*. Philadelphia, PA: Fortress Press, 1984.

Galpern, A. N. *The Religions of the People in Sixteenth-Century Champagne*. Cambridge, MA: Harvard University Press, 1976.

Gauvard, Claude. *De Grace Especial: Crime, État et Société à la fin du Moyen Age*. Vol. 1. Paris: Publications de la Sorbonne, 1991.

Giesey, Ralph E. "The Monarchomach Triumvirs: Hotman, Beza, and Mornay." *Bibliothèque d'humanisme et renaissance* 32 (January 1970): 41–56.

Gillis, John, ed. *Commemorations: The Politics of National Identity*. Princeton: Princeton University Press, 1994.

Gilmont, Jean-François. *Jean Crespin, Un éditeur réformé du XVIᵉ siècle*. Geneva: Droz, 1981.

———. *La Réforme et le livre: L'Europe de l'imprimé (1517–1570)*. Paris: Cerf, 1990.

Ginzburg, Carlo. *Il Nicodemismo*. Turin: G. Einaudi, 1970.

Gordon, Bruce. "The Changing Face of Protestant History and Identity in the Sixteenth Century." In *Protestant History and Identity in Sixteenth-Century Europe: Volume 2, The Later Reformation*. Ed. Bruce Gordon. Aldershot: Scolar Press, 1996.

Gregory, Brad. *Salvation at Stake: Christian Martyrdom in Early Modern Europe*. Cambridge, MA: Harvard University Press, 1999.

Grell, Peter Ole, and Bob Scribner, eds. *Tolerance and Intolerance in the European Reformation*. Cambridge: Cambridge University Press, 1996.

Grieco, Sara F. Matthews. *Ange ou diablesse: la représentation de la femme au XVIe siècle*. Paris: Flammarion, 1991.

Grig, Lucy. *Making of Martyrs in Late Antiquity*. London: Gerald Duckworth, 2004.

Haag, MM. Eug. and EM. *La France Protestante*. Vol. 4. Geneva: Slatkine, 1966.

Halbwachs, Maurice. *Les cadres sociaux de la mèmoire*. 1925; reprint Paris: Albin Michel, 1994.

———. *The Collective Memory*. Trans. Lewis A. Cosner. Chicago: University of Chicago Press, 1992.

Hall, Stuart G. "Women among the Early Martyrs." *Studies in Church History* 30 (1993): 1–22.

Haller, William. *Foxe's Book of Martyrs and the Elect Nation*. London: Jonathan Cape, 1967.

Hanley, Sarah. *The Lit de Justice of the Kings of France: Constitutional Ideology in Legend, Ritual, and Discourse*. Princeton: Princeton University Press, 1983.

Hanlon, Gregory. *Confession and Community in Seventeenth-Century France: Catholic and Protestant Coexistence in Aquitaine.* Philadelphia: University of Pennsylvania Press, 1993.

Hauser, Henri. *Études sur la Réforme Français.* Paris: Alphonse Picard et Fils, 1909.

Higman, Francis. *La Diffusion de la Réforme en France 1520–1565.* Geneva: Labor et Fides, 1992.

Hoffman, J. G. *Le Martyr Evangelique Anne Du Bourg.* Strasbourg, 1841.

Hutton, Patrick H. "The Role of Memory in the Historiography of the French Revolution." *History and Theory* 30 (February 1991): 56–69.

———. "Sigmund Freud and Maurice Halbwachs: The Problem of Memory in Historical Psychology." *History Teacher* 27 (February 1994): 145–58.

Imbart de La Tour, Pierre. *Les Origines de la Réforme.* 4 vols. Geneva: Slatkine Reprints, 1978.

Kelley, Donald R. *Beginning of Ideology: Consciousness and Society in the French Reformation.* Cambridge: Cambridge University Press, 1981.

———. *François Hotman: A Revolutionary's Ordeal.* Princeton: Princeton University Press, 1971.

———. "Martyrs, Myths, and the Massacre: The Background of St. Bartholomew." *American Historical Review* 77 (December 1972): 1323–42.

Kingdon, Robert. "Calvinism and Resistance Theory." In J. H. Burns and Mark Goldie, eds., *The Cambridge History of Political Thought, 1450–1700.* Cambridge: Cambridge University Press, 1991.

———. *Myths about the St. Bartholomew's Day Massacres, 1572–1576.* Cambridge, MA: Harvard University Press, 1988.

Knott, John R. *Discourses of Martyrdom in English Literature, 1563–1694.* Cambridge: Cambridge University Press, 1993.

Kolb, Robert. *For all the Saints: Changing Perceptions of Martyrdom and Sainthood in the Lutheran Reformation.* Macon, GA: Mercer University Press, 1987.

Lebigre, Arlette. *La Justice du roi: la vie judiciaire dans l'ancienne France.* Paris: Albin Michel, 1988.

Lelièvre, Matthieu. "Anne Du Bourg avant son Incarcération à la Bastille." *Bulletin de la Société de l'Histoire du Protestantisme français* 35 (1887): 569–90.

———. "Les Derniers Jours d'Anne Du Bourg." *Bulletin de la Société de l'Histoire du Protestantisme français* 37 (1888): 506–29.

———. "Le Procès et le Supplice d'Anne Du Bourg." *Bulletin de la Société de l'Histoire du Protestantisme français* 36 (1888): 281–95.

Léonard, E.-G. *Histoire générale du protestantisme.* 3 vols. 2nd ed. Paris: P. U. F., 1980.

Lestringant, Frank. *La cause des martyrs dans "Les Tragiques" d'Agrippa d'Aubigné.* Mont-de-Marsan: Editions InterUniversitaires, 1991.

Linder, Robert Dean. *The Political Ideas of Pierre Viret.* Geneva: Droz, 1964.

Macek, Ellen. "The Emergence of a Feminine Spirituality in *The Book of Martyrs.*" *Sixteenth Century Journal* 19 (1988): 62–80.

Mack, Phyllis. *Visionary Women: Ecstatic Prophecy in Seventeenth-Century England.* Berkeley: University of California Press, 1989.

Marshall, Sherrin. "Protestant, Catholic, and Jewish Women in the Early Modern Netherlands." In *Women in Reformation and Counter-Reformation Europe.* Ed. Sherrin Marshall. Bloomington: Indiana University Press, 1989.

Matheson, Peter. "Martyrdom or Mission? A Protestant Debate." *Archiv für Reformationsgeschichte* 80 (1989): 158–65.

Mayer, Thomas F., and D. R. Woolf. "Introduction." In *The Rhetorics of Life-Writing in Early Modern Europe: Forms of Biography from Cassandra Fedele to Louis XIV.* Ed. Thomas F. Mayer and D. R. Woolf. Ann Arbor: University of Michigan Press, 1995.

Mentzer, Raymond. *Heresy Proceedings in Languedoc, 1550–1560.* Transactions of the American Philosophical Society. Vol. 74. Philadelphia, 1984.

Mentzer, Raymond, and Andrew Spicer, eds. *Society and Culture in the Huguenot World, 1559–1685.* Cambridge: Cambridge University Press, 2002.

Meyer, Judith Pugh. *Reformation in La Rochelle: Tradition and Change in Early Modern Europe, 1500–1568.* Geneva: Droz, 1996.

Monter, William. "Les exécutés pour hérésie par arrêt du Parlement de Paris (1523–1560)." *Bulletin de la Société de l'Histoire du Protestantisme français* 142 (1996): 191–224.

———. *Judging the French Reformation Heresy Trials by Sixteenth-Century Parlements.* Cambridge, MA: Harvard University Press, 1999.

Moreau, G. "Contribution à l'histoire du Livre des martyrs." *Bulletin de la Société de l'Histoire du Protestantisme français* 103 (1957): 173–99.

Moriarity, Rachel. "'Playing the Man'–the Courage of Christian Martyrs, Translated and Transposed." In *Gender and Christian Religion.* Ed. R. N. Swanson. Suffolk, UK: Ecclesiastical History Society / Boydell Press, 1998.

Naz, R., ed. *Dictionnaire de droit canonique.* 7 vols. Paris: Librarie Letouzey et Ané, 1957.

Newman, Barbara. *From Virile Woman to Woman Christ: Studies in Medieval Religion and Literature.* Philadelphia: University of Pennsylvania Press, 1995.

Nichols, David. "The Theatre of Martyrdom in the French Reformation." *Past and Present* 121 (1988): 49–73.

Nock, A. D. *Conversion: The Old and the New in Religion from Alexander the Great to Augustine of Hippo.* Oxford: Oxford University Press, 1933.

Nora, Pierre, ed. *Realms of Memory: The Construction of the French Past. Volume II, Traditions.* Trans. Arthur Goldhammer. New York: Columbia University Press, 1997.

Ozment, Steven. *When Fathers Ruled: Family Life in Reformation Europe.* Cambridge, MA: Harvard University Press, 1983.

Paillard, Charles. "Note sur Jean Crespin." *Bulletin de la Société de l'Histoire du Protestantisme français* 27 (1878): 380–84.

Parrow, Kathleen A. *From Defense to Resistance: Justification of Violence during the French Wars of Religion.* Transactions of the American Philosophical Society. Vol. 83. Philadelphia, 1993.

Peterson, Anna L. *Martyrdom and the Politics of Religion: Progressive Catholicism in El Salvador's Civil War.* Albany: SUNY Press, 1997.

Piaget, Arthur and Gabrielle Berthoud. *Notes sur le Livre des Martyrs de Jean Crespin.* Neuchatel: University of Neuchatel, 1930.

Pineaux, Jacques. *La Poésie des Protestants de langue française (1559–1598)*. Paris: Klincksieck, 1971.

Racaut, Luc. "Religious Polemic and Huguenot Self-Perception and Identity, 1554–1619." In *Society and Culture in the Huguenot World 1559–1685*. Ed. Raymond A. Mentzer and Andrew Spicer. Cambridge: Cambridge University Press, 2002.

Richet, Denis. "Aspects socio-culturels des conflicts religieux à Paris dans le seconde moitié du XVIe siècle." *Annales—Economies, Sociétés, Civilisations* 32 (1977): 764–89.

Riddle, Donald W. *The Martyrs: A Study in Social Control*. Chicago: University of Chicago Press, 1931.

Roberts, Penny. "Martyrs in the French Reformation" in *Martyrs and Martyrologies*. Ed. Diana Wood. Oxford: Oxford University Press, 1993.

Roelker, Nancy L. "The Appeal of Calvinism to French Noblewomen in the Sixteenth Century." *Journal of Interdisciplinary Studies* 2 (1972): 391–418.

———. *One King, One Faith: The Parlement of Paris and the Religious Reformations of the Sixteenth Century*. Berkeley: University of California Press, 1996.

———. "The Role of Noblewomen in the French Reformation." *Archiv für Reformationsgeschichte* 63 (1972): 169–95.

Romier, Lucien. *La Conjuration d'Amboise. L'Aurore sanglante de la liberté de conscience. Le Règne et la mort de François II*. Paris: Perrin, 1923.

Roper, Lyndal. *The Holy Household: Women and Morals in Reformation Augsburg*. New York: Clarendon Press, 1989.

Salisbury, Joyce E. *Perpetua's Passion: The Death and Memory of a Young Roman Woman*. New York: Routledge, 1997.

Salmon, J. H. M. *Society in Crisis: France in the Sixteenth Century*. London: Ernest Benn, 1975.

Seeley, David. *The Noble Death: Graeco-Roman Martyrology and Paul's Concept of Salvation*. Sheffield, UK: JSOT Press, 1990.

Sherman, Daniel J. *The Construction of Memory in Interwar France*. Chicago: University of Chicago Press, 1999.

———. "Objects of Memory: History and Narrative in French War Museums." *French Historical Studies* 19 (Spring 1995): 49–74.

Skinner, Quentin. *The Foundations of Modern Political Thought*. Cambridge: Cambridge University Press, 1978.

Sluhovsky, Moshe. "Calvinist Miracles and the Concept of the Miraculous in Sixteenth-Century Huguenot Thought." *Renaissance and Reformation* 19 (1995): 5–25.

Smith, Lacey Baldwin. *Fools, Martyrs, Traitors: The Story of Martyrdom in the Western World*. New York: Knopf, 1997.

Soman, Alfred. *Sorcellerie et Justice Criminelle (16ᵉ–18ᵉ siècles)*. Hampshire, UK: Variorum, 1992.

Spierenburg, Pieter. *The Spectacle of Suffering: Executions and the Evolution of Repression: From a Preindustrial Metropolis to the European Experience*. Cambridge: Cambridge University Press, 1984.

Stephenson, Barbara. *The Power and Patronage of Marguerite De Navarre.* Aldershot, UK: Ashgate, 2004.

Sutherland, N. M. *The Huguenot Struggle for Recognition.* New Haven: Yale University Press, 1980.

———. *The Massacre of St. Bartholomew and the European conflict, 1559–1572,* London: Macmillan, 1973.

Taillandier, M. A. *Memoire sur les Régistres du Parlement de Paris pendant le règne de Henri II.* Paris, 1842.

Taylor, Larissa. *Soldiers of Christ: Preaching in Late Medieval and Reformation Paris.* Oxford: Oxford University Press, 1992.

Thompson, John Lee. *John Calvin and the Daughters of Sarah: Women in Regular and Exceptional Roles in the Exegesis of Calvin, his Predecessors, and his Contemporaries.* Geneva: Droz, 1992.

Tinsley, Barbara Sher. *History and Polemics in the French Reformation: Florimond de Raemond, Defender of the Church.* Selinsgrove, PA: Susquehanna University Press, 1992.

Verheyden, Alphonse. *Le Martyrologe Protestant des Pays-Bas du Sud au XVIe siècle.* Brussels: Editions de la Librairie des éclaireurs unionistes, 1960.

Viénot, John. *Histoire de la Réforme Française.* Paris: Fischbacher, 1926.

Wachtel, Nathan. "Memory and History: An Introduction." *History and Anthropology* 2 (1986): 207–24.

Watson, David. "Jean Crespin and the Writing of History in the French Reformation." In *Protestant History and Identity in Sixteenth-Century Europe: Volume 2, The Later Reformation.* Ed. Bruce Gordon. Aldershot, UK: Scolar Press, 1996.

Weiner, Eugene and Anita. *The Martyr's Conviction: A Sociological Analysis.* Atlanta, GA: Scholars Press, 1990.

Weiss, Nathanaël. *La Chambre Ardente. Étude sur la liberté de conscience en France sous François Ier et Henri II (1540–1550).* Geneva: Slatkine Reprints, 1970.

Woolf, D. R., ed. *A Global Encyclopedia of Historical Writing.* 2 vols. New York: Garland, 1998.

———. "The Rhetoric of Martyrdom: Generic Contradiction and Narrative Strategy in John Foxe's *Acts and Monuments.*" In *The Rhetorics of Life-Writing in Early Modern Europe: Forms of Biography from Cassandra Fedele to Louis XIV.* Ed. Thomas F. Mayer and D. R. Woolf. Ann Arbor: University of Michigan Press, 1995.

Zagorin, Perez. *Ways of Lying: Dissimulation, Persecution, and Conformity in Early Modern Europe.* Cambridge, MA: Harvard University Press, 1990.

Index